STUDY GUIDE

to accompany

Macroeconomics

4th EDITION

Paul Wonnacott
University of Maryland

Ronald Wonnacott
The University of Western Ontario

JOHN WILEY & SONS
New York   Chichester   Brisbane   Toronto   Singapore

ISBN 0-471-51950-2
Printed in the United States of America

10 9 8 7 6 5 4 3 2

Preface

This *Study Guide* is designed to be used with the introductory economic textbook, *Economics*, by Paul Wonnacott and Ronald Wonnacott. This *Study Guide* makes no attempt to be self-contained; it is a supplement to, not a substitute for, the textbook.

Each chapter is designed for you to read and work through after reading the corresponding chapter in the text. Each chapter of this *Study Guide* contains seven sections:

- **Learning Objectives.** This section lists the things that you should know after you have studied the chapter in the text and in the study guide. The purpose of this section is twofold. First, it provides a direction and focus as you study the chapter. Second, it provides a checklist to test your understanding after you have completed the chapter.

- **Major Purpose.** This section sets out the basic ideas that will be developed in the chapter.

- **Highlights of Chapter.** This section contains a summary of the important points in the chapter. Its main purpose is to reinforce the textbook by adding illustrative examples and going over the main points from a somewhat different perspective. To a student learning a subject for the first time, everything may seem equally important. This section helps identify the most important ideas in the chapter.

- **Important Terms: Match the columns.** This section lists the important concepts in the chapter, along with a definition or explanation of each. Your task is to match each term with its definition or explanation. Before

looking in the right-hand column, you should try to remember the definition first.

- **True-false questions.**

- **Multiple choice questions.**

- **Exercises.**

The last three sections are designed to help you learn by doing, and to provide a check on your understanding of the chapter. (They may also help you with your exams directly. The questions in the study guide are included in the computerized testbank available to teachers who are making up exams. If teachers wish, they can use questions taken directly from the study guide.)

After going over these three sections, you should check the answers at the end of the chapter in the study guide. Note that each answer refers you to the page in the textbook which covers the point addressed in the question. If you get the wrong answer, you should reread the relevant page in the text. (Note: we have tried to exercise great care in checking the answers, but cannot absolutely guarantee that every answer is correct. We have found and corrected two wrong answers in the proofs; it is conceivable that we have missed a few.)

About half the chapters include a *crossword puzzle* that includes some of the key terms in the text. We hope that you will find them entertaining, and that they will act as a final check on your understanding of the concepts in the chapter. The completed crossword puzzles are reproduced at the end of this study guide.

We would like to thank Ron Blue for the care and imagination with which he has designed and produced this *Study Guide*.

Paul Wonnacott
Ronald Wonnacott

Contents

Preface

Contents

STUDY GUIDE

to accompany

Macroeconomics

4th EDITION

BASIC ECONOMIC CONCEPTS

CHAPTER 1

ECONOMIC PROBLEMS AND ECONOMIC GOALS

LEARNING OBJECTIVES

After you have studied this chapter in the textbook and study guide, you should be able to

✔ List five major economic goals

✔ Describe, in broad terms, what has happened to U.S. unemployment, inflation, growth, and the distribution of income in recent decades

✔ Distinguish the views of Adam Smith and J. M. Keynes with respect to the proper role of the government

✔ Define terms such as inflation, deflation, recession, and efficiency

✔ Distinguish between *allocative efficiency* and *technological efficiency*

✔ Describe briefly how changes in relative prices may contribute to allocative efficiency

✔ Explain why it is harder to identify the problems created by inflation than those created by unemployment

✔ Explain the distinction between equity and equality

✔ Explain how some goals may be *complementary*, while others are in *conflict*

If you have studied the appendix to Chapter 1 in the textbook, you should also be able to

✔ Describe some of the ways in which people may be misled by graphs

✔ Explain the advantage of using a ratio (or logarithmic) scale

✔ Explain the difference between a nominal and a real measure

MAJOR PURPOSE

The major purpose of this chapter is to provide a broad overview of *economic developments* and *economic objectives*, as a background for the more detailed topics of the following chapters. Five major economic objectives are discussed:

- high employment,

- a stable average level of prices,

- efficiency,

- equity, and

- growth.

You should gain some understanding of the problems which have arisen in the U.S. economy, and why it is not always easy to solve these problems. In particular, it may be difficult to deal with problems when the government has a number of goals, some of which are *in conflict*. That is, solving one problem may make others more difficult to solve. For example, inflation generally gets worse as the unemployment rate falls.

HIGHLIGHTS OF CHAPTER

Economics is one of the social sciences — it involves the systematic study of human behavior. The aspect of behavior which interests economists is how people earn a living, and the problems which may make it difficult for them to do so. In the words of Alfred Marshall, economics is the study of people "in the ordinary business of life."

The objective of *economic theory* is to discover and explain the basic principles and laws that govern economic life. Economic theory helps us to understand questions such as: Why are some prices higher than others? Why does the average level of prices rise? Why are some people richer than others? What causes large-scale unemployment?

Economic policy addresses such questions as: How can the government reduce inflation? How can it reduce the unemployment rate? What steps can individuals take to increase their incomes, or reduce the risks of unemployment? How does a business increase its profits?

Economic theory and economic policy go hand-in-hand. Just as a physician needs to know how the human body works in order to heal patients, so the economic policymaker needs to understand economic theory in order to prescribe economic policies that will be successful. Scientific studies of how things work are often inspired by a policy motive — to do something about problems. Thus, scientists strive to unlock the mysteries of the human cell in order to find out why cancer occurs, and ultimately to be able to cure cancer. Similarly, studies of how the economy works are often motivated by the desire to solve economic problems, such as recession and large-scale unemployment.

ECONOMIC POLICY

Perhaps the most hotly contested issue in all of economics is the question of how much the government should intervene in the economy. Many of those in government are motivated by the desire to promote the public welfare. After all, the policies that they promote will be their monument in history. But well-meaning policymakers do not always adopt policies that work in practice. Furthermore, the government may be used to benefit individuals or groups at the expense of the public as a whole.

Adam Smith attacked many governmental interventions in the economy as being contrary to the public interest. Even though tariffs benefited the protected sectors of the economy, they inflicted higher costs on consumers, and acted as a drag on efficiency. Smith conceived of the private economy as a self-regulating mechanism. By pursuing their own interests, individuals would regularly contribute to the common good. There was no need for extensive government interference to ensure that things would come out all right.

A century and a half later, J. M. Keynes was skeptical of Smith's message of laissez faire. Things were not coming out all right. The economy was in a deep depression, with many people out of work. It was the responsibility of the government, said Keynes, to do something about this tragic situation. He recommended government spending on roads and other public works as a way to provide jobs.

ECONOMIC GOALS

Full employment is one of the major economic objectives. Four others are also described in this chapter:

- a stable average level of prices,
- efficiency,
- an equitable distribution of income, and
- economic growth.

Other goals might be added to this list, for example, economic freedom, economic security, and the control of pollution.

The first two goals—full employment and stable prices—come under the heading of maintaining a stable *equilibrium* in the economy. There has in fact been considerable instability in the U.S. economy. The most notable disturbance occurred during the Great Depression of the 1930s, when output and employment dropped sharply, and remained at very low levels for a full decade. During World War II, there was an effort to produced as many munitions as possible. Unemployment ceased to be a significant problem, but prices began to rise substantially. Since the end of World War II in 1945, we have avoided severe disturbances comparable to those from 1929 to 1945. However, there have been periodic recessions, with rising unemployment. Inflation was severe during the late 1940s and the 1970s. During the decade of the 1970s, the average level of prices doubled.

Of the major economic problems, unemployment is perhaps the most obvious. When employment declines, we have less output to enjoy. We not only forego the output which might have been produced, but we also must face the demoralization that comes with unemployment.

The problems with inflation are less obvious. When people buy goods, they obviously dislike higher and higher prices. But there are two sides to every transaction—the buyer's side, and the seller's. With widespread inflation, not only do the prices of what we buy increase. Wage rates also go up, as well as the prices of what we sell. It is not so clear whether individuals are net gainers or net losers.

However, there are certain segments of the population who do lose. Those who have pensions set in money terms lose: As prices rise, their pensions buy less. (However, some pensions, including the Social Security pensions paid by the government, are increased to compensate for inflation.) Those who own government bonds or other interest-bearing securities lose. Through the years, they receive payments whose value becomes smaller and smaller as prices rise. On the other hand, people who have borrowed can benefit: They repay their loans in money whose value has declined.

Inflation generates a feeling that the economic system is unfair. There are arbitrary redistributions of income and wealth, such as the gains to debtors and losses to bond owners. Inflation can also make it more difficult to make wise and well-informed decisions. *Prices* provide an important source of information to the business executive and consumer. During periods of rapid inflation, when all prices are rising at a brisk pace, the message carried by prices may be obscured. It becomes more difficult to make good decisions.

If inflation accelerates to very high rates—such as 1,000% per year—it becomes known as *hyperinflation*. Money is losing its value so rapidly that people may refuse to accept it. Because money is practically useless, sellers may feel compelled to barter their products for other goods. Such barter transactions are very cumbersome and time-consuming.

Most inflations do not accelerate into hyperinflation. Hyperinflation is relatively rare, except for losers during wartime or early postwar periods. There are, however, a few cases where countries have very rapid rates of inflation even though they have not been defeated in a war—for example, present-day Brazil.

There are two important types of efficiency. *Technological efficiency* means getting the most output from a given set of inputs (labor, machinery, raw materials). *Allocative efficiency* occurs when the economy is producing the best combination of outputs, using the lowest-cost combination of inputs. Allocative efficiency means producing the goods and services which the consuming public wants most. It is possible for an economic system to produce "white elephants" in a technologically efficient manner. But this system would not be producing what people want; it would not be allocatively efficient. Similarly, if everyone were a lawyer, and nobody a doctor, there would be allocative inefficiency—even if everyone were a superb lawyer.

Equity means *fairness*, and that raises the question of what fairness means. There can be obvious disagreements. Those with low incomes are likely to argue that a more equal distribution of income would be fairer. Those with higher incomes often argue that their high incomes are the result of hard work; it is fair for them to be paid more because they have worked harder.

Many people would, however, agree that the government should take some steps to help those who are poverty-stricken, for example, by taxing the rich to provide services for the needy. The question arises, however, as to how far this process should be taken. Clearly, if the government confiscated all incomes above the average, and gave the revenues to low income people, then it would severely interfere with the incentive to work hard. (This would also greatly increase the incentive to cheat on taxes!) Even less drastic steps to redistribute income can decrease incentives, and thus decrease the size of the national "pie." The size of the pie depends in part on how it is cut up.

Economic growth is often advocated for its own sake. In a growing economy, we enjoy more goods and services. Furthermore, growth may make it easier to meet other goals, such as reducing poverty. However, we should not simply assume that the more growth, the better. Growth comes at a cost. Most obviously, if we produce more machinery and equipment to help us grow, then we will give up the current consumer goods that might have been produced instead of the machinery and equipment.

COMPLEMENTARY AND CONFLICTING GOALS

Some goals—such as a high level of employment and an elimination of poverty—are *complementary*. Progress on the one contributes to progress on the other. If jobs are provided for people, they are less likely to be poor.

Other goals are *in conflict*. If people buy more goods and services, they will help to increase the number of jobs. But they will also make it easier for sellers to raise their prices. Thus, if the government takes steps to encourage spending, it may help ease one problem (unemployment) while making another worse (inflation). In such circumstances, good policies may be particularly difficult to develop.

IMPORTANT TERMS: MATCH THE COLUMNS

Match the term in the first column with the corresponding explanation in the second column.

n	1.	Laissez faire
c	2.	Great Depression
l	3.	Labor force
j	4.	Population
h	5.	Recession
e	6.	Duty
k	7.	J. M. Keynes
a	8.	Adam Smith
m	9.	Inflation
g	10.	Deflation
o	11.	Allocative efficiency
i	12.	Technical efficiency
b	13.	Complementary goals
f	14.	Conflicting goals
d	15.	This can help promote allocative efficiency

a. Put forward the idea of the "hidden hand."
b. Pursuing one helps in attainment of other
c. When large-scale unemployment existed
d. A change in relative prices
e. A tax on an import
f. Pursuing one makes other more difficult to attain
g. A decrease in the average level of prices
h. A broad decline in production, involving many sectors of the economy
i. Avoiding sloppy management and wasted motion
j. Total number of people in a country
k. Put forward the idea that government should spend for public works when necessary to get economy out of depression, and restore full employment
l. Sum of those employed and those unemployed
m. An increase in the average level of prices
n. Leave the economy alone
o. Producing the best combination of outputs, using the lowest-cost combination of inputs

TRUE-FALSE

T   F   1.   Adam Smith argued that the government should build public works whenever needed to reduce the rate of inflation.

T   F   2.   By definition, a depression occurs whenever the output of the nation falls.

T   F   3.   During the great depression of the 1930s, the unemployment rate rose above 15% of the labor force.

T   F   4.   The Employment Act of 1946 required the government to provide a job for anyone who wanted one but could not find employment from a corporation.

T   F   5.   Since 1970, recessions have been much less severe than those of the 1950s and 1960s.   *1982. 10.6%*

T   F   6.   A recession is a decline in total output, employment, and income, and is marked by a widespread contraction in *many* industries.

T   F   7.   Changes in the average level of inflation make an important contribution, since they are the key to improvements in allocative efficiency.   *relative (prices)*

T   F   8.   The percentage of the population living in poverty has declined slowly but consistently since 1960.

T   F   9.   Over the past three decades, there has been a consistent trend in the United States: the rich have gotten richer, and the poor have gotten poorer.

T   F   10.   Inflation is caused by a decline in purchases by consumers.

MULTIPLE CHOICE

1. Since 1900, output per capita in the United States:

    a. has approximately doubled, while the length of the work week has declined
    b. has grown approximately sixfold, while the length of the work week has declined
    c. has approximately doubled, while the length of the work week has remained stable
    d. has grown approximately sixfold, while the length of the work week has remained stable
    e. has remained stable, while the length of the work week has declined sharply; all the gains have come in the form of more leisure

2. Between 1960 and 1987, which country grew most rapidly:

    a. France
    b. Italy
    c. Japan
    d. United States
    e. West Germany

3. By the phrase, "invisible hand," Adam Smith was expressing the idea that

    a. there are no economic conflicts among nations
    b. there would be no economic conflicts among nations, if countries would eliminate tariffs
    c. there are no conflicts between what is good for an individual, and what is good for society as a whole
    d. by pursuing their own individual interests, people frequently promote the interests of society
    e. business executives have a natural interest in keeping prices down, and preventing inflation

4. Suppose that the U.S. government is considering increasing the tariffs on imported steel. Which organizations in the United States are **most likely** to **oppose** such an increase?

    a. steelworkers union and autoworkers union
    b. General Motors and Caterpillar
    c. steelworkers union and the U.S. Treasury
    d. U.S. Steel and the U.S. Treasury
    e. U.S. Steel and General Motors

5. In his *General Theory*, Keynes' principal concern was with the goal of:

   a. stable prices
   b. low unemployment
   c. allocative efficiency
   d. technological efficiency
   e. an equitable distribution of income

6. Unemployment is likely to be highest during

   a. war
   b. peacetime prosperity
   c. rapid growth
   d. recession
   e. depression

7. Between 1929 and 1933, during the early part of the Great Depression, total output in the United States:

   a. declined about 30%
   b. declined about 20%
   c. declined about 10%
   d. declined about 5%
   e. remained approximately stable; the Depression represented an interruption of growth, not an actual decline in output

8. Which of the following is counted as being unemployed:

   a. someone who has just retired at age 65
   b. a full-time student not looking for a job
   c. someone who has recently graduated from college, and is looking for his or her first full-time job
   d. convicts in prisons
   e. all of the above

9. A moderate rate of inflation (of, say, 4% per annum)

   a. creates no problems in the economy
   b. hurts people living on fixed money incomes
   c. hurts people who have borrowed money
   d. occurs whenever money wages rise more rapidly than prices
   e. is likely to be caused by war

10. The key role in promoting allocative efficiency is played by changes in

    a. the average level of prices
    b. the rate of inflation
    c. the rate of growth

    d. relative prices
    e. the distribution of income

11. Economists distinguish changes in the **average** level of prices and changes in **relative** prices. Changes in the average level of prices are generally considered

    a. undesirable, while changes in relative prices can perform a useful function in promoting efficiency
    b. undesirable, but changes in relative prices are even more undesirable, since they hurt some people while helping others
    c. undesirable, but changes in relative prices are neither good nor bad; they just happen
    d. desirable, but the government should attempt to prevent changes in relative prices
    e. desirable, but changes in relative prices are even more desirable, and the government should take steps to increase changes in relative prices

12. Suppose that every factory worker were in the job best suited for him or her, and they were working as productively as possible, but were producing cars that nobody wanted to buy. This would be an example of

    a. Technical inefficiency and allocative inefficiency
    b. Technical efficiency and allocative inefficiency
    c. Technical inefficiency and allocative efficiency
    d. Technical efficiency and allocative efficiency
    e. Technical efficiency and allocative efficiency, but slow growth

13. During the past two decades, the prices of computers have fallen, while the price of oil has risen. As a result, manufacturers and other businesses have used more computers, and have conserved on energy. This switch toward more computers and less energy is an illustration of:

    a. allocative efficiency
    b. technological efficiency
    c. the effects of inflation
    d. a less equal distribution of income
    e. a more equal distribution of income

14. Which is the best example of **technological** inefficiency

    a. producing too many cars, and not enough housing
    b. slow growth
    c. inflation
    d. inequality of incomes
    e. sloppy management

15. **Equity** in the distribution of income means:

    a. equality
    b. fairness
    c. more for everyone, as a result of growth
    d. more for those who can't work
    e. more for those who work hard

16. Suppose that the incomes of all families are perfectly equal. Then the poorest 10% of the families will get what share of total income

    a. 5%
    b. 10%
    c. approximately 15%
    d. 20%
    e. 25%

17. Which of the following pairs is the clearest example of conflicting goals:

    a. less unemployment and less inflation
    b. less unemployment and less poverty
    c. less unemployment and more growth
    d. less unemployment and more efficiency
    e. more efficiency and less poverty

18. If, during the coming six months, there is a boom in the purchases of machinery by businesses, then we would be most likely to observe

    a. an increase in the rate of inflation, and a decline in the rate of unemployment
    b. a decrease in the rate of inflation, and a decline in the rate of unemployment
    c. an increase in the rate of inflation, and an increase in the rate of unemployment
    d. a decrease in the rate of inflation, and an increase in the rate of unemployment
    e. a decrease in inflation, growth, and unemployment

19. Economists study

    a. inflation
    b. unemployment
    c. efficiency
    d. poverty
    e. all of the above

(Appendix)

20. A reason for using a logarithmic or ratio scale on the vertical axis of a chart is that this

    a. makes it easier to start measuring from zero
    b. allows readers to quickly see when the rate of increase was most rapid
    c. avoids the necessity of choosing an arbitrary beginning year
    d. shows when profits were at a maximum
    e. shows when profits were at a minimum

EXERCISES

1. In the following passage, choose the correct word or phrase in the brackets.

   Economic history is a story of both progress and problems. Some evidence of progress shows up in Figure 1-1 in the textbook. Here we see that output per person has increased by approximately (100%, 200%, 500%) since 1900, and about (25%, 75%, 150%) since 1960. If we were to look at total output of the economy—rather than at output **per person**— we would find that total output has increased by (an even greater percentage than output per person, a somewhat smaller percentage).

   The right-hand panel of Figure 1-1 shows another source of gain. Not only have we produced more, but we have done so with a shorter workweek. The decline in the workweek occurred mainly in the period from (1900 to 1950, 1950 to 1989). Notice also the very sharp drop between 1925 and 1935.

   This decrease was the result of (a much more rapidly improving economy which allowed more leisure, the depression which reduced the demand for output, a loss of the work ethic).

   Successes and problems also show up in Figure 1-3 in the textbook. The (upward trend in output, downward trend in unemployment, both) since 1950 show(s) how things have improved. One of the problems is shown by the vertical shaded bars, which mark periods of (recession, depression, inflation, poverty). During such periods, (the unemployment rate increases, output declines, both).

   Figure 1-4 shows the average level of prices. A rise in this curve is an indication of inflation. The more rapid is inflation, the steeper is the curve. We see that inflation was very rapid between (1950 and 1960, 1960 and 1970, 1970 and 1980).

Finally, Figure 1-5 shows the percentage of the population living in poverty; a decline in the percentage is a sign of success. Observe that, at the beginning of the period shown, the incidence of poverty declined, from about (15%, 22%, 30%) in 1960 to about (5%, 8%, 11%) when it reached its low point in the 1970s. Largely as a result of the deep recession of the early 1980s, the percentage living in poverty increased to about (15%, 22%, 30%) by 1983.

2. In Figure 1-3 in the textbook, how many recessions have there been since 1946? This is an average of one every _____ years.

How long was the longest period between recessions? The shortest? Does this suggest that expansions die more or less regularly, as a result of old age?

The length of each recession is shown by the width of the colored vertical bars. Which two recessions were longest?

Did these two long recessions come after relatively long expansions, or relatively short ones? Does this suggest that a long expansion is most likely to end in a long recession?

ANSWERS

(Note: page numbers after answers to Multiple Choice and True-False questions provide references to passage on which the question is based.)

Important Terms:	1 n, 2 c, 3 l, 4 j, 5 h, 6 e, 7 k, 8 a, 9 m, 10 g, 11 o, 12 i, 13 b, 14 f, 15 d
True-False:	1 F (p. 5)
	2 F (p. 7)
	3 T (p. 8)
	4 F (p. 8)
	5 F (p. 8)
	6 T (p. 9)
	7 F (p. 11)
	8 F (p. 12)
	9 F (p. 12)
	10 F (p. 13)
Multiple Choice:	1 b (p. 3)
	2 c (p. 3)
	3 d (p. 5)
	4 b (p. 5)
	5 b (p. 6)
	6 e (p. 7)
	7 a (p. 7)
	8 c (p. 7)
	9 b (p. 10)
	10 d (p. 10)
	11 a (p. 10)
	12 b (pp. 10-11)
	13 a (p. 11)
	14 e (p. 11)

Exercises:

1. 500%, 75%, an even greater percentage than output per person, 1900 to 1950, the depression which reduced the demand for output, upward trend in output, recession, both, 1970 and 1980, 22%, 11%, 15%.

2. 8, 5.5, approximately 8 years (1961-69) although the expansion late 1982 may eventually prove to be longer, about one year (1981-1982), they do not seem to die of old age (there is no apparent tendency for a recession to come regularly after an expansion of four or five years), 1973-75 and 1981-1982, the first came after three years of expansion (1970-1973) while the second came after one year (1980-1981), no — severe recessions seem as likely after sort expansions as after long ones (again suggesting that recessionary forces do not build up in a steady or consistent way).

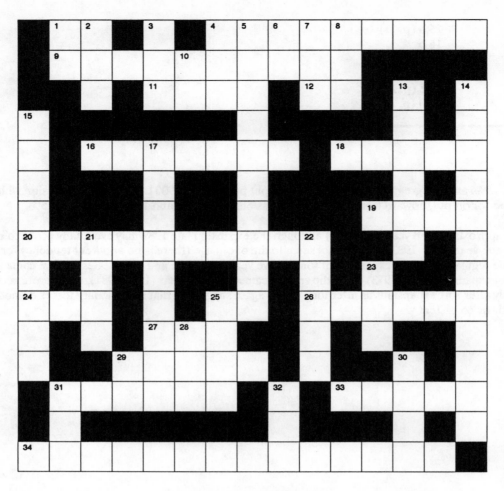

Across

1. college degree
4. his *Wealth of Nations* was an early classic (2 words)
9. getting the most from efforts
11. shedder of light
12. preposition
16, 18. keeping government to a minimum
19. assist
20. the _____ countries, also known as the third world
24. this company helps you to talk to your friends at home
25. above
26. fairness
27. charged particle
29. during hyperinflation, this becomes practically worthless
31. advocated government spending to restore full employment
33. represents workers
34. losers in war often suffer this

Note to students: answers to crossword puzzles are at the end of the Study Guide.

Down

1. exist
2. labor organization
3. be ill
4. objective
5. the economic disease of the 1930s
6. indef. article
7. provider of long-distance telephone services
8. artificial (abbrev.)
10. a business degree
13. important source of information
14. an economic problem
15. international institution lending to developing nations
17. rise in average level of prices
21. needed when looking for a job
22. large, powerful
23. early economist (see inside cover of text)
25. individuals
28. number
29. 1st person, possessive
30. holds corn or missiles
31. he wrote the words to "The Star-spangled Banner"
32. its price skyrocketed in 1970s

APPENDIX

This appendix provides additional information and practice for those who have already studied the appendix to Chapter 1 in the textbook.

Graphs

During rainy spells, sales of lawn furniture decline. A simple version of the relationship between weather and the sales of lawn furniture is illustrated in Figure 1.1 below.

The two measures used in this graph—sales of furniture and rainfall—are examples of **variables**. A variable is something that can change, or vary, from time to time or from place to place. For example, the amount of rain in April is generally different from the amount in July.

The statement that the sales of lawn furniture decline during rainy weather means that there is a relationship between the two variables in Figure 1.1. In particular, it means that when rainfall increases, sales decline. This idea can be illustrated in the figure.

The two *axes*, marked with numbers, meet at the **origin** 0. The *vertical axis* shows the quantity of lawn furniture sold. The *horizontal axis* shows the amount of rainfall. The relationship between the two variables is

Figure 1.1

Sales of lawn furniture (in thousands of dollars)

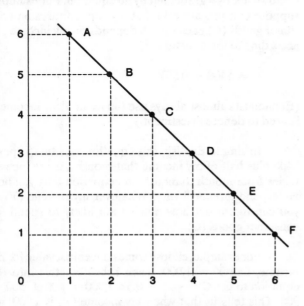

Amount of rainfall (inches per month)

depicted by the line marked with the letters *A* through *F*. For example, point *A* shows that when the rainfall is one inch per month (measured along the horizontal axis), there are $6,000 worth of sales of lawn furniture (measured up the vertical axis). Likewise, at point *B*, 2 inches of rainfall result in sales of $5,000. In this way, each time you read a point on the line you get one bit of information. These "bits" are shown in Table 1.1.

Table 1.1

Point	A	B	C	D	E	F
Rainfall	1	2	3	4	5	6
Sales	6	5	4	3	2	1

Thus, the rule for reading the graph is as follows. If you want to find out how much furniture will be sold when there is some particular amount of rain (say, 3 inches), go along the horizontal axis to 3 units. Then go directly up to the line. This shows sales of $4,000 worth of furniture when the rainfall is 3 inches. Question 1 at the end of this appendix provides an exercise in reading graphs.

Slope

Figure 1.1 shows not only that rainfall and sales are related. It shows the direction of that relationship. Specifically, when rainfall increases, sales decrease. In other words, sales are **negatively** or **inversely** related to rainfall. This negative relationship means that the line in Figure 1.1 slopes downward to the right. As you move to the right (as rainfall increases), the height of the line decreases (sales decrease). For example, by comparing points *A* and *B*, we see that when rainfall increases from 1 to 2 inches, sales decrease from $6,000 to $5,000.

A **positive** or **direct** relationship is illustrated in Figure 1.2; both variables change in the same direction. When snowfall increases, sales of skis increase, too. This means that as we move to the right (more snow), the line slopes upward (more sales of skis).

A graph such as Figure 1.2 shows not only the *direction* of the relationship between the two variables; it also shows the *strength*. For example, it shows that when snow increases by 1 inch (from 2 to 3 inches), 2,000 more skis are sold. The *strength* of the relationship is shown by the **slope** of the line. The slope of the line is defined as the

Figure 1.2

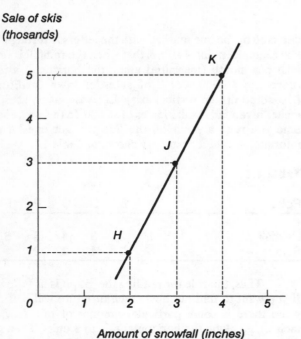

Sale of skis
(thosands)

Amount of snowfall (inches)

Figure 1.3

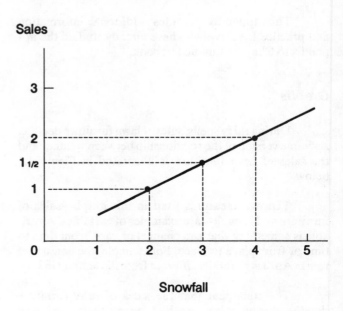

Sales

Snowfall

amount by which the height of the line changes when you go one more unit to the right on the horizontal axis. In Figure 1.2, the slope is 2; a 1 unit increase in snow causes a 2 unit increase in the sales of skis. Alternatively, the slope of a line between two points (such as *H* and *K* in Figure 1.2) is defined as the *rise* (that is, the vertical change of 4 units) *divided by the run* (the horizontal change of 2 units). Again, we see that the slope of the line is 2 (that is, 4 divided by 2).

Observe that ski sales respond much more strongly to snow in Figure 1.2 than in Figure 1.3. In Figure 1.3, the much weaker response is illustrated by the relatively flat curve; when snowfall increases by 1 unit, ski sales increase only a half unit; the slope is only 1/2.

Back in Figure 1.1, an increase in one variable (rain) caused a decrease in the other variable (sales of lawn furniture). The line slopes downward; that is, the slope is negative. (For example, between points *A* and *C*, the rise is -2 while the run is 2; thus the slope is -1.) A negative slope thus means that the two variables are negatively or inversely related.

In summary, the slope of the line shows two ideas — the direction and strength of the relationship between two variables. The *direction* of the relationship depends on whether the line slopes up or down — that is, whether the slope is positive or negative. The *strength* of

the relationship depends on the steepness of the line. Questions 3 and 4 at the end of this appendix deal with the concept of slope.

Linear Equations

Sometimes the relationship between two variables is shown not by a graph, but by an equation. For example, suppose that you are told that my expenditures on consumer goods (C) each month depends on my income (Y) according to the equation:

$$C = \$400 + 0.50Y$$

(Economists almost always use the letter Y for income. I is used to denote investment.)

In simple English, this equation says that I spend $400 plus half of my income that month. As my income varies from month to month, the equation tells you how my expenditures will vary. Whatever my income (Y) is, you can figure out how much I am likely to spend for consumer goods (C).

For example, choose some convenient value for my income, like $Y = 1,000$. Then substitute this into the equation to get $C = 400 + 0.5 \times 1,000 = 400 + 500 = 900$. This tells us that when my income (Y) is 1,000, my expenditures on consumer goods (C) is 900. Now choose any other convenient value, like Y = 1,100. Substituting this into the equation indicates that when my income is 1,100, my expenditures on consumer goods is C = 400 + 0.5 x 1,100 = 950. Each time you choose a value of Y and make this substitution you thus get one bit of information. These two bits are shown in Table 1.2. As an exercise, fill in the rest of the table.

Figure 1.4 shows this relationship in a graph. The slope of the line is 0.5. This is because every time my income increases by $100 (shown as a move of one unit along the horizontal axis), I spend another $50 (shown as a rise of 0.5 of a unit). In contrast, the equation C = 400 + 0.75Y represents the behavior of individuals who spend $400 plus three quarters of their income. In this case, the slope of the line would be 0.75, because every increase of $100 in income would cause an increase of $75 in consumption.

In general, any equation of the sort C = a + bY represents a line with a slope equal to b. Such an equation

is a **linear** equation. For example, the linear equation illustrated in Figure 1.4 has a = 400 and b = 0.5.

The number b (in this example, 0.5) is known as the **coefficient** of the variable Y. It indicates the slope of the line. The number a (400) shows how high the line is where it meets the vertical axis (point A). Thus, a is often called the **vertical intercept** of this equation. For example, the vertical intercept in Figure 1.4 is 400; this corresponds to the equation where a = 400.

At this time, you should do questions 5 and 6, which deal with linear equations.

Curves

So far we have drawn only straight lines. A straight line is easy to use because it has a *constant* slope. For example, in Figure 1.1, the slope of the line is the same between A and B as it is between any other two points on the line.

However, sometimes a relationship is described better by a curve, like the one in Figure 1.5 which illustrates how a student's final grade depends on how many hours he or she spends studying during the average week. A curve does not have a constant slope; as you move to the right on this curve, it gets flatter. For example, the first hour of studying causes an increase in the grade by 30 points—from 20 to 50. However, the second hour makes it rise by only 20 more (to 70), and the third hour causes an increase by only 5 more points. Each move to the right by 1 hour per week causes a smaller increase in the grade. In this example, it would obviously be impossible for the relationship to continue in a straight line in the way it began . The first hour caused an increase of 30 points. Four hours obviously couldn't cause an increase of 120 points, for the simple reason that the exam has a maximum grade of 100 points.

In this curve, as before, the slope is still identified as the amount by which the height of the curve changes as you go one more unit to the right along the horizontal axis. But in this case, the slope changes as you go to the right. For the first hour, it is 30; for the second, 20; then 5, and so on.

$$\frac{9-x}{10} = \frac{5-x}{3} \qquad 7x = 23 \quad x = \frac{23}{7}$$

$$27 - 3x = 50 - 10x$$

Figure 1.4

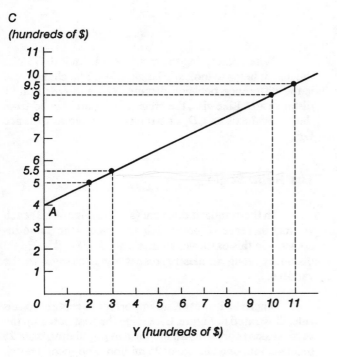

C
(hundreds of $)

Y (hundreds of $)

Table 1.2											
Y	100	200	300	400	500	600	700	800	900	1000	1100
C										900	950

Figure 1.5

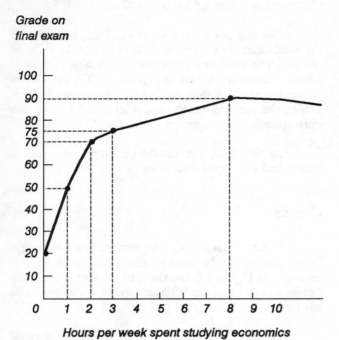

Grade on final exam

Hours per week spent studying economics

Figure 1.6

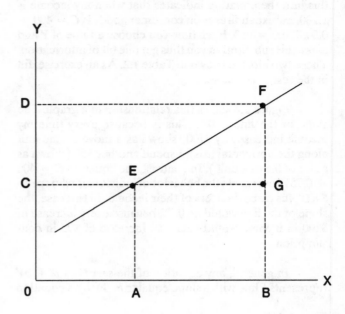

The decreasing slope in Figure 1.5 indicates that as the student spends more and more time studying, each additional hour may raise the grade, *but not by as much as the previous hour*. The first hour raises the grade by 30 points, the next by only 20. This is an example of diminishing returns; the payoff (in terms of a higher grade) diminishes as a person studies more and more.

Notice that, according to Figure 1.5, the curve reaches its maximum. No matter how much time the student spends studying, he or she can't get more than 90. Indeed, after 8 hours, the student gets tired and stale. Any more time with the books will be counterproductive. The slope of the curve becomes negative; each additional hour results in a lower grade.

Other Graphs

Sometimes, in presenting a general argument, we don't bother to put numbers on the axes. For example, the linear relationship in Figure 1.6 shows no numbers (except for the 0 at the origin). Without numbers, we can't tell exactly how strong the relationship is between the variables X and Y. But the graph still provides important information—that the relationship is linear, with a constant direction and slope. In this diagram, we can put in letters as points of reference. Point E represents OA units of X, and its height is measured as OC units of Y.

When describing the movement from E to F along the line, it helps to look at triangle EFG. The change in X is the difference between distance OB and OA; that is, distance AB. Likewise, the change in Y can be read from the vertical axis as CD, or from the triangle as distance GF.

The Ratio Scale

In the standard diagram (such as Figure 1.2) each vertical increase of one notch represents the same increase—in this example, an increase of 1,000 skis. Equal distances along an axis represent equal changes in the variable.

There is, however, an important exception to this rule, illustrated in Figure 1.7. Going the first notch up the vertical axis represents an increase in population from 25 to 50 million, or a change of 25 million. The second notch represents an increase of 50 million—from 50 to 100 people. Here, each notch represents a constant *percentage* change—specifically an increase of 100% in population. Such a diagram, where equal moves along an axis measure equal *percentage* changes, is known as a **ratio scale** or **logarithmic scale**.

In economics, a ratio scale is used most frequently along the vertical axis, with time shown on the horizontal axis (as in Figure 1.7). Such a diagram is used when we're interested in the percentage rate of growth of something—for example, the percentage rate of growth of population or the percentage increase in prices. When such a curve becomes steeper, the percentage rate of increase in population or prices is becoming greater. We can identify the period when the rate of growth was the most rapid. It is the period when the curve is the steepest.

QUESTIONS

1. Point *A* in Figure 1.8 has a height of _____ and lies distance _____ to the right of the origin. Thus, it indicates that when there is a light rainfall of _____ centimeters during rush hour, _____ thousand workers will arrive to work on time. If rain is heavier, at 6 cm., only _____ thousand workers will be on time. With a very heavy rain of 10 cm., _____ thousand workers will be on time.

Figure 1.7

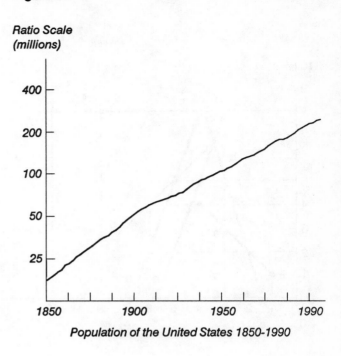

Ratio Scale (millions)

Population of the United States 1850-1990

Figure 1.8

Number of Workers on Time (thousands)

Rainfall during rush hour (centimeters)

2. From Figure 1.2 fill in Table 1.3

Table 1.3

Amount of snow	2	3	4
Sales of skis			

3. There are six different lines in Figure 1.9. In Table 1.4, fill in the slope of each line.

Table 1.4

Line	a	b	c	d	e	f
Slope						

Figure 1.9

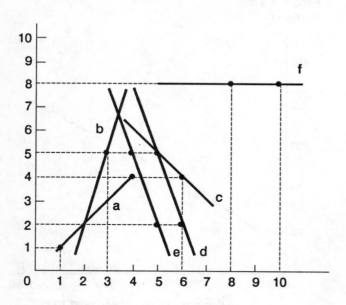

Figure 1.10

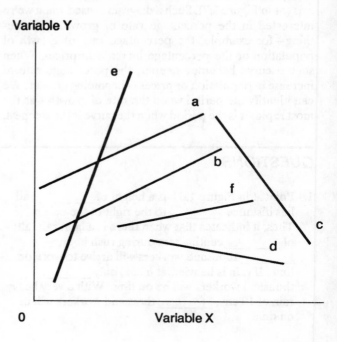

4. Which of the lines in Figure 1.10 show a positive relationship between variables *X* and *Y*?_____.
When *X* increases by 1 unit, which of these lines shows the greatest increase in *Y*? _____. When *X* increases by 1 unit, which of these lines shows the greatest decrease in *Y*? _____.

5. Consider two variables, *X* and *Y*, that are related according to the linear equation $Y = 8 - 2X$. From this equation, fill in Table 1.5.

Figure 1.11

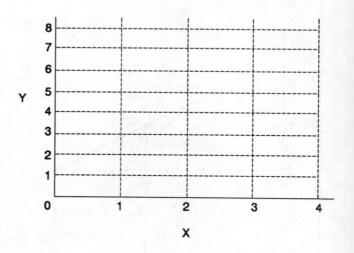

Table 1.5

X		0	1	2	3	4
Y						

Draw the line representing this equation in Figure 1.11.

The slope of this line is _____.

The vertical intercept is _____.

6. The following linear equations show how one variable, Y, depends on another variable, X.

   (a) $Y = 90 + 10X$
   (b) $Y = 50 + 15X$
   (c) $Y = 80 - 5X$
   (d) $Y = 3X$
   (e) $Y = -10 + 5X$
   (f) $Y = 50$

   Line _____ has the largest vertical intercept and line _____ has the largest slope.

   When X increases by 1 unit, which line shows the largest increase in Y? _____.

   When $X = 0$, the highest line is _____.

   Which equations show a positive relationship between X and Y? _____.

   Which a negative relationship? _____.

   What is the slope of (f)? _____.

   Which line has a vertical intercept of zero? _____.

   Which line passes through the origin? _____.

ANSWERS

Table 1.2, completed:											
Y	100	200	300	400	500	600	700	800	900	1000	1100
C	450	500	550	600	650	700	750	800	850	900	950

1. 8, 2, 2, 8, 6, 4

2. **Table 1.3 completed:**

Amount of snow	2	3	4
Sales of skis	1	3	5

3. **Table 1.4 completed:**

Line	a	b	c	d	e	f
Slope	1	3	-1	-3	-3	0

4. $(a, b, e, f), e, c$

5. **Table 1.5, completed:**

X	0	1	2	3	4
Y	8	6	4	2	0

   -2, 8

6. $a, b, b, a, (a, b, d, e), c, 0, d, d.$

CHAPTER 2

SCARCITY AND CHOICE
The Economic Problem

LEARNING OBJECTIVES

After you have studied this chapter in the textbook and study guide, you should be able to

✔ Understand why the combination of limited resources and unlimited wants requires us to *make choices*

✔ Define the three major *factors of production* P26-27

✔ Explain the *difference* between *real capital* and *financial capital*, and explain why economists focus on real rather than financial capital when studying the productive capacity of the economy

✔ Explain the functions of the *entrepreneur*

✔ Explain the concept of *opportunity cost*, and explain how it is related to the production possibilities curve (PPC)

✔ Explain why the PPC slopes downward to the right 反比例关系

✔ Explain why the PPC usually bows outward from the origin 机会成本递增

✔ Explain a circumstance in which the PPC might be a straight line, instead of bowing outward
constant of opportunity cost

✔ Explain why production occurs within the PPC if there is large-scale unemployment

✔ Explain the difference between a high-growth and a low-growth policy, using a PPC with capital goods on one axis and consumer goods on the other (Figure 2-5 in the textbook)

✔ Explain why it is impossible to develop a theory without simplifying

MAJOR PURPOSE

The major purpose of this chapter is to introduce the concept of *scarcity*. Because of limited resources, we cannot have all the goods and services that we want. We must therefore *make choices*, picking some items and foregoing others. This idea—that we face scarcity and therefore have to make choices—is at the center of economics. A standard definition of economics is "the study of the allocation of scarce resources to satisfy alternative, competing human wants."

The ideas of scarcity and choice are illustrated by the *production possibilities curve*. This illustrates the idea of scarcity because we are limited to a point on (or within) the curve; we cannot go outside the curve with our present resources and technological capabilities. The curve also illustrates the need to make *choices*. When we pick one point on the production possibilities curve, we pass over all the other points, and forego the goods which we might have had if we had picked some other point.

This chapter applies the production possiblities curve to illustrate the *choice between consumer goods now and consumer goods in the future*. We can forego some consumer goods now and use the resources to produce capital equipment instead. The additional capital will help us to produce even more consumer goods in the future.

Finally, this chapter provides an introduction to *economic theory*. Economic theory *must* be a *simplification* of the real world. If we strove for a complete theory which took into account all the complexities of our world, we would get bogged down in a swamp of detail. When we simplify, we should keep in mind a central question: Does our theory include the most important relationships in the economy, or *have we left out something of critical importance*?

HIGHLIGHTS OF CHAPTER

Scarcity is one of the most important concepts in economics. Scarcity requires us to *make choices*; we cannot have everything we want. Why? The answer is that our resources are limited, while our wants are not.

When we make choices, we pick some goods and services, and forego others. If we pick a college education, for example, we may have to put off buying a car for several years. The *opportunity cost* of our education is the car and other goods and services which we forego to pay tuition, room, and board. Similarly, for the society as a whole, opportunity cost is an important concept. For example, when we decide to produce more weapons, we forego the consumer goods and services we might have produced instead. Individuals, corporations, and governments are continuously making choices among the options open to them.

The ideas of scarcity, the need to make choices, and opportunity cost are summarized by the *production possibilities curve* (PPC). The PPC shows the options from which a *choice* is made. The fact that we are limited by the PPC, and cannot pick a point outside it with our present resources and technology, illustrates the idea of *scarcity*. The *slope* of the PPC shows how much of one good we must forego when we choose more of another. In other words, the slope shows the *opportunity cost* of choosing more of a specific good.

The PPC has two important properties. First, it slopes downward to the right. This means that, if we decide to produce more of one good, we give up some of the other. The idea that there is an opportunity cost when we produce more of one good is illustrated by the downward slope of the PPC curve.

The second feature of the typical PPC curve is that it is *bowed out*—that is, it is *concave* to the origin. This is so because resources are *specialized*. If we decide to produce more and more wheat, we will use land which is less and less suited to the production of wheat, even though it was very good for producing cotton. For each additional unit of wheat, we will have to give up more cotton. Thus, the outward bend in the PPC illustrates the idea of *increasing opportunity cost*.

Under certain circumstances, however, the PPC need not bow outward. It is possible that two goods might require the same set of resources in their production. For example, radios and telephones might take the same combination of resources in their production—the same combination of copper, plastic, silicon, labor, etc.—in which case the PPC would be a *straight line*. In this particular case, the *opportunity cost of radios would be constant* in terms of the telephones foregone. (The opportunity cost of both radios and telephones might nevertheless still increase, in terms of the food or clothing foregone. In other words, the PPC would be a straight line if we put radios and telephones on the two axes, but would bow out if we put radios on one axis and food on the other.)

It is worth emphasizing that a downward slope and an outward bow are two *different* features. A PPC can slope downward without bowing outward—as in the example of radios and telephones. A downward slope means that the opportunity cost is *positive*. An outward bow means that the opportunity cost *increases* as more of a good is produced.

One of the important choices facing the society is the choice between consumer goods and capital goods. If we produce only a little capital, we will be able to enjoy a large quantity of consumer goods now. But, with little investment, we will have slow growth. In other words there is a *tradeoff between a high current level of consumption and high growth*. This tradeoff or choice is illustrated when we draw a PPC curve with consumer goods on one axis and capital goods on the other. For example, Figure 2-5 in the textbook illustrates the difference between a high-growth and a low-growth strategy. A high-growth strategy requires that a sizable fraction of our resources be committed to investment in plant and equipment (capital goods). But this makes possible a rapid growth—that is, a rapid outward movement of the PPC.

This chapter provides a brief introduction to economic theory. When we develop economic theories, we *must* simplify. The world is much too complex to describe in all its detail. The objective of theory is to strip away the nonessential complications in order to see the important relationships within the economy. Theory should not be dismissed because it fails to account for everything, just as a road map should not be discarded as useless just because it doesn't show everything. But, because of simplifications, theory must be used carefully. Just as last week's weather map is useless for planning a trip in a car, so the theory which helps to explain one aspect of the economy may be inappropriate or useless for explaining others.

Finally, this chapter explains the distinction between *positive* and *normative* economics. Positive or descriptive economics is aimed at explaining what has been happening and why. Normative economics deals with policies; it deals with the way things *ought* to be.

IMPORTANT TERMS: MATCH THE COLUMNS

Match the first column with the corresponding phrase in the second column.

g	1. Economic resources	a.	Outward bow of PPC
d	2. Financial capital	b.	Choices open to society
j	3. Real capital	c.	Specialized resources
h	4. Increase in real capital	d.	Stocks and bonds
f	5. Entrepreneur	e.	Straight-line PPC
b	6. PPC	f.	Organizer of production
i	7. Opportunity cost	g.	Basic inputs used in the production of goods and services
a	8. Increasing opportunity cost	h.	Investment
e	9. Constant opportunity cost	i.	Alternative foregone
c	10. Cause of outward bow of PPC	j.	Machinery, equipment, and buildings

TRUE-FALSE

T   F   1.   Resources are said to be scarce because they are incapable of producing all the goods and services that people want; therefore, choices must be made.

T   F   2.   Wants were *unlimited* during the early days of the study of economics in the eighteenth and nineteenth centuries. But they are no longer unlimited in the affluent countries of North America and Western Europe.

T   F   3.   Suppose that a production possibilities curve meets the clothing axis at 5 units of clothing, and at 20 units of food. This illustrates that the society can have a total of 5 units of clothing plus 20 units of food, but no more.

T   F   4.   The production possibilities curve bends outward because resources are not uniform in quality; some are better at producing one good than the other.

T   F   5.   Just as it is possible to select a combination of goods inside the PPC, so it is possible to choose a combination of goods that lies outside the PPC.

T   F   6.   An increase in the quantity of labor causes the production possibilities curve to move outward from the origin.

T   F   7.   Suppose that two countries, A and B, were identical in 1979. Suppose that, between 1979 and 1989, the economy of A grew at 4% per annum, while B grew at 3% per annum. Then, from that fact, we may conclude that economy A was allocatively more efficient than B during the 1979-1989 period.

T   F   8.   *Positive* economics is the study of how policymakers can achieve desirable (that is, *positive*) social goals.

MULTIPLE CHOICE

1. Economists often speak of wants being *unlimited* because:

   a. the cost of living has increased; it costs more to meet our basic needs now than it did twenty years ago
   b. more people live in the cities now than in an earlier age, and it is more expensive to live in cities than on the farm
   c. even though our incomes have risen, we still want *more*; we do not believe all our wants are satisfied
   d. resources such as oil have become scarcer because we have been using them up
   e. as people's incomes have risen, they have decided to take more leisure, and work fewer hours

2. By real capital, economists mean:

   a. real estate, particularly land
   b. plant and equipment
   c. the real value of bonds, adjusted for inflation
   d. the real value of common stock, adjusted for inflation
   e. both (c) and (d)

3. The production possibilities curve has one major purpose: to illustrate the need to:

   a. stop inflation
   b. cut taxes
   c. cut government spending
   d. make choices
   e. stop pollution

4. The textbook has a picture of a production possibilities curve (PPC), joining six points.

   a. All six points are equally desirable, since they all represent full employment
   b. All six points are equally desirable, since they all are consistent with zero inflation
   c. All six points are equally desirable, since they all provide for some growth
   d. All six points are possible, but the PPC curve doesn't give enough information to tell which point is best
   e. Only one of the six points is presently achievable; the others can be achieved only if the economy grows

5. An **outward bow** in the production possibilities curve illustrates what concept:

   a. scarcity
   b. unlimited wants
   c. increasing opportunity cost
   d. unemployment
   e. inflation

6. The opportunity cost of a good is measured by:

   a. the slope of the PPC
   b. how far the PPC is from the origin
   c. the slope of a line from the origin out the the PPC
   d. how far the economy is operating within the PPC
   e. how fast the PPC is shifting outward

7. Suppose the production possibilities curve is a straight line if goods X and Y are put on the axis. Then we know that:

   a. X and Y are really the same good
   b. the problem of scarcity has been solved
   c. we can have all the X and Y we want without incurring an opportunity cost, even though the general problem of scarcity has not been solved
   d. the opportunity cost of X is zero, in terms of Y foregone
   e. the opportunity cost of X is constant, in terms of Y foregone

8. We speak of a production possibilities curve as a *frontier* because:

   a. we can produce within it or on it, but not beyond it with presently available resources and technology
   b. it reflects the concept of scarcity, and goods were particularly scarce for U.S. settlers on the

western frontier in the 19th century
   c. it is no longer relevant, now that the U.S. frontier has been tamed and we have an affluent society
   d. unemployment problems provide the frontier for economic research
   e. differences among resources provide the frontier for economic research

9. Suppose that the society has only one objective, to maximize growth. Then, the best choice among the five points shown on Figure 2.1 is:

   a. A
   b. B
   c. C
   d. D
   e. E

Figure 2.1

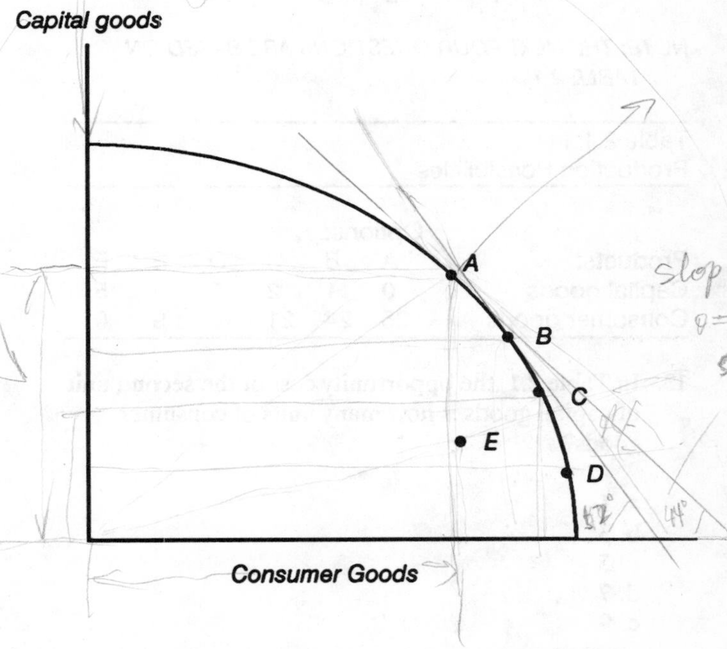

Capital goods

Consumer Goods

10. In Figure 2.1, a growth of the economy can be illustrated by:

   a. a move from point A to B
   b. a move from point B to A
   c. a move from point A to E
   d. a move from point D to E
   e. an outward shift of the production possibilities curve

11. In Figure 2.1, suppose that the economy is originally at point E. Then there will be:

   a. rapid growth
   b. no capital formation
   c. more capital formation than at points A, B, or C
   d. a high rate of unemployment
   e. rapid inflation

12. The production possibilities curve generally bends outward because:

   a. sensible people want to divide their purchases; they want to choose some food and some clothing
   b. there are economies of large-scale production
   c. most people have a comparative advantage in the production of at least one good
   d. there is much less unemployment now than during the Great Depression of the 1930s
   e. resources are not uniform in quality; some are better for producing one good than the other

NOTE: THE NEXT FOUR QUESTIONS ARE BASED ON TABLE 2.1

Table 2.1
Production Possibilities

	Options:					
Products:	A	B	C	D	E	F
Capital goods	0	1	2	3	4	5
Consumer goods	25	24	21	16	9	0

13. In Table 2.1, the opportunity cost of the second unit of capital goods is how many units of consumer goods?

   a. 1
   b. 3
   c. 5
   d. 7
   e. 9

14. Given the options in Table 2.1, a total output of 5 units of capital goods and 25 units of consumer goods:

   a. is unattainable at present
   b. represents a situation of large-scale unemployment
   c. can be achieved only if the economy achieves technological efficiency

   d. can be achieved only if the economy achieves allocative efficiency
   e. can be achieved only if the economy achieves both allocative and technological efficiency

15. Given the options in Table 2.1, a total output of 2 units of capital goods and 10 units of consumer goods:

   a. is unattainable at present
   b. represents a situation of large-scale unemployment
   c. can be achieved only if the economy achieves technological efficiency
   d. can be achieved only if the economy achieves allocative efficiency
   e. can be achieved only if the economy achieves both allocative and technological efficiency

16. The choice of option C rather than B:

   a. represents a mistake, since only 23 total units are produced (that is, 2 + 21) rather than 25 (that is, 1 + 24)
   b. represents a mistake, since consumers have fewer goods
   c. means that there will be more unemployment
   d. represents a choice of more growth
   e. represents a choice of less growth

17. The production possibilities curve shifts outward, away from the origin:

   a. if the number of workers increases
   b. if the skill of workers increase
   c. if there is more capital
   d. if technology improves
   e. if any of the above happens

18. Oil now being pumped in a pipeline is an example of:

   a. the land resource, because oil comes out of the ground
   b. real capital, because it has been produced in the past and will be used in the production of other goods
   c. financial capital, because it is valuable and is worth money
   d. financial capital, because it can be used as collateral for bank loans
   e. financial capital, because it was costly to pump out of the ground

EXERCISES

1. Consider the following production possibilities table:

Table 2.2

	Options:							
	A	B	C	D	E	F	G	H
Consumer goods	0	1	2	3	4	5	6	7
Capital goods	23	22	20	17	13	9	5	0
Opportunity cost of consumer goods		1	2	3	4	4	4	5

a) Complete the third line, showing the opportunity cost of each additional unit of consumer goods.

b) Draw the PPC on Figure 2.2.

c) What is unusual about this curve?

d) In the range between points *A* and *D*, the PPC (bows outward, bows inward, is a straight line). This shows that opportunity cost is (increasing, decreasing, constant) in this range. However, between points *D* and *G*, the curve (bows outward, bows inward, is a straight line). This shows that opportunity cost is (increasing, decreasing, constant) in this range.

2. Consider a hypothetical economy with a labor force of 10,000 workers, each of whom can be put to work building either houses or roads. Each worker is available for 2,000 hours per year. Thus, there are 20 million labor hours available during the year to produce houses and roads. Table 2.3 shows how many labor hours it takes to build various quantities of houses. For example, in order to build 18,000 houses, 15 million labor hours are needed. Likewise, Table 2.4 indicates how many labor hours are needed to build various amounts of roadway. In Figure 2.3, only one point, *A*, on the PPC has been plotted. It shows that if no houses are built, the 20 million labor hours can be used to produce 1,000 miles of road. Using the data in Tables 2.3 and 2.4, plot four other points, and draw a PPC to connect them.

Figure 2.2

Table 2-3

Millions of labor hours	Thousands of houses
20	20
15	18
10	14
5	8
0	0

Table 2-4

Millions of labor hours	Hundreds of miles of road
20	10
15	9
10	7
5	4
0	0

Figure 2.3

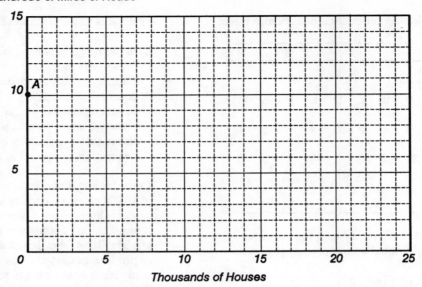

Thousands of Houses

ANSWERS

Matching columns: **1 g, 2 d, 3 j, 4 h, 5 f, 6 b, 7 i, 8 a, 9 e, 10 c**

True-False:
1 T (p. 26)
2 F (p. 26)
3 F (p. 28)
4 T (p. 29)
5 F (p. 29)
6 T (p. 30)
7 F (p. 31)
8 F (p. 33)

Multiple Choice:
1 c (p. 26)
2 b (p. 26)
3 d (p. 27)
4 d (p. 28)
5 c (pp. 28-29)
6 a (pp. 28-29)
7 e (p. 29)
8 a (p. 29)
9 a (p. 32)
10 e (p. 32)
11 d (p. 29)
12 e (p. 29)
13 b (p. 29)

Exercises

1.   a)   3, 4, 4, 4, 5.

     c)   over part of its range, it is a straight line (between *D* and *G*).

     d)   bows outward, increasing, is a straight line, constant.

2.   Four other points are:

	B	C	D	E
Hundreds of miles	9	7	4	0
Thousands of houses	8	14	18	20

SPECIALIZATION, EXCHANGE, AND MONEY

LEARNING OBJECTIVES

After you have studied this chapter in the textbook and study guide, you should be able to

✔ Explain why specialization and exchange go hand in hand *P36*

✔ Explain why barter is inferior to exchange with money *P37*

✔ Explain why people may nevertheless revert to barter in some circumstances

✔ Give an example of Gresham's law

✔ Explain the two major reasons why there can be gains from specialization and exchange

✔ Explain the difference between absolute advantage and comparative advantage

✔ Explain why a country may have an absolute advantage in a product without having a comparative advantage in that product

MAJOR PURPOSE

In this chapter, we study specialization, exchange, and money. People specialize and engage in exchange because there are gains from doing so. By specializing, people can achieve higher standards of living. There are *two major sources* of gain from specialization:

- *comparative advantage*, and
- *economies of scale*.

These two phenomena are the forces that motivate specialization and exchange; that is, they are the *twin engines that drive commerce*.

Money, on the other hand, *is the oil* which makes the machinery of commerce run smoothly, with a minimum of friction. Without money, people would engage in cumbersome barter. But, if some money helps to make the system work smoothly, we should not conclude that more money would make it work even better. Just as too much oil can gum up an engine, so too much money can

Chapter 3   Specialization, Exchange, and Money

31

cause difficulty. Specifically, it causes inflation. The Federal Reserve (the central bank of the United States) acts as the chief mechanic. Its task is to create the right amount of "oil" [money]—neither too much, nor too little. The operations of the Federal Reserve will be considered in detail in Chapter 12.

HIGHLIGHTS OF CHAPTER

One reason for economic progress has been an increase in *specialization*. Individuals, cities, and countries are now more specialized than they were a hundred years ago. When production is specialized, people engage in exchange, selling the products they produce to buy the wide variety of goods and services that they want to consume. We live in a highly interdependent economy, in which each of us depends on the specialized production of others.

Specialization and exchange would be very cumbersome without money. It is easy to imagine the difficulties that would arise if we tried to do without money and engaged in barter exchange instead. Barter requires a *coincidence of wants*—people engaging in exchange must each be able to provide a good or service that the other wants. Furthermore, for barter to work, there must be some rough equivalence in the value of the two goods or services to be exchanged. To buy toothpaste, a farmer would scarcely offer a cow in exchange. However, with money, such problems of indivisibility do not arise. The farmer may sell the cow for $1,000 and spend just a bit of the money to buy toothpaste, using the rest for a wide variety of other purchases. Money provides people with *general purchasing power;* money can be used to buy any of the wide variety of goods and services on the market. Those wishing to make exchanges no longer have to search for unlikely coincidences (such as the ill-clad farmer looking for someone who not only has clothes to exchange, but who also wants to get beef in return).

Because it is so useful for those who wish to engage in exchange, money is used even in rudimentary societies with little or no government. The prisoner-of-war camp provides an example of such a simple society. However, governments have gotten deeply involved in the monetary system. Every country uses paper money printed by the central bank or treasury.

One reason for the government to be involved in the monetary system is that the government can provide a *uniform* currency. In the United States, for example, every $1 bill (Federal Reserve Note) is worth the same as every other dollar bill. This uniformity of the money stock is very convenient. When selling something for $1, we only

have to find out if the buyer has a $1 bill. Except for the rare cases where counterfeiting is suspected, we do not need to ask the much more complicated question of whether the dollar bill is inferior to some other dollar bill.

In passing, we might note that the United States has not always had a uniform currency. In the 19th century, privately-owned banks issued currency. The value of this currency depended on the soundness of the bank that issued it. Thus, sellers did have to worry about the value of the dollar bills they accepted. Similar problems have arisen throughout history. For example, when gold coins were in use, their value could depend on the amount of gold they contained. Before the development of modern methods of producing coins with hard edges, such coins were sometimes *clipped*. That is, people chipped off bits before spending them. As a result, not every coin was worth the same as every other coin of the same denomination. People had to examine the physical condition of the coins they were accepting.

In addition to providing a uniform currency, the Federal Reserve has the responsibility of providing an appropriate quantity of money. If too many dollar bills are created, there will be "too much money chasing too few goods." Inflation will result; the dollar will decline in value. On the other hand, if the quantity of money is allowed to decline sharply, spending will decline. Sellers will have a very difficult time finding buyers. Sales will fall, unemployment will rise, and prices will be under downward pressure. The authorities do not always perform their monetary duties well. In some countries—for example, Brazil—prices are galloping ahead by more than 100% per year. This reduces the convenience of money. If prices are rising rapidly, sellers feel under pressure to spend their money as soon as possible, before its value declines significantly.

With the proper quantity of money, the monetary system can work very smoothly, making transactions very convenient. But this is all that money does—it makes exchange convenient. It is not the reason why exchange is desirable in the first place.

There are two reasons why specialization and exchange can yield benefits. The first is *comparative advantage*. The notion of comparative advantage is illustrated in the textbook by the example of the gardener and the lawyer. The lawyer has an absolute advantage in both the law and gardening; she can do both quicker than the gardener. It follows that the gardener has an absolute disadvantage in both the law and gardening—he is slower at both. However, the gardener has a comparative advantage in gardening, while the lawyer has a comparative advantage in the law. Comparative advantage provides the basis for *mutually beneficial* trade. *Both* the gardener and the lawyer can gain from specialization and exchange. (Details are provided in Box 3-3.)

Two points should be emphasized.

- Absolute advantage is not necessary for gain; the gardener can gain by specializing in gardening, even though he is not the best gardener.

- A person (or a nation) cannot have a comparative disadvantage in everything.

In the simple case of two people and two activities (law and gardening), if one person has a comparative advantage in one activity, the other person *must* have the comparative advantage in the other activity.

Economies of scale provide the second major reason why there are gains from specialization and exchange. Economies of scale exist if an increase of $x\%$ in all inputs (labor, machinery, land, steel, etc.) leads to an increase of more than $x\%$ in output. Economies of scale are the major reason why big firms have an advantage in many industries, such as automobiles and main-frame computers. Economies of scale are the major reason why costs per unit of output often decline as more is produced. For example, a car company can produce 100,000 cars at a much lower cost per car than if it produces 1,000 cars. Clearly, if a person tried to put together a car in the back yard or in a small shop, it would be very expensive. There are gains when car production is left to the specialists.

IMPORTANT TERMS

Match the first column with the corresponding phrase in the second column.

d	1.	Barter
i	2.	Required by barter
f	3.	General purchasing power
a	4.	A function of money
j	5.	Inflation
k	6.	Cause of inflation
h	7.	Absolute advantage
c	8.	Comparative advantage
e	9.	Economies of scale
g	10.	Example of economies of scale
b	11.	Gresham's law

a. Acting as medium of exchange
b. Bad money drives out good
c. Reason the lawyer gains by practicing law
d. Exchange of one good or service for another
e. Reason costs per unit fall as more is produced
f. Money
g. Adam Smith's pin factory
h. Good can be produced with fewest resources
i. Coincidence of wants
j. Fall in value of money
k. Too much money chasing too few goods

TRUE-FALSE

T (F) 1. One reason that barter is inconvenient is that many commodities cannot easily be divided into smaller parts.

T (F) 2. Monetary systems develop only when there is a strong national government, since strong national governments are required to provide money with value.

these were not used for money.

(T) F 3. Suppose that, in the prisoner-of-war camp with its "cigarette money," the value of cigarettes rises compared to the value of other items (such as beef, etc.). Such an increase is known as inflation.

(T) (F) 4. Comparative advantage is the reason why wheat is grown in Nebraska, and not in the city of Chicago.

T (F) 5. If everyone had the exactly the same talents and training, and exactly the same quantity of capital, then economies of scale would not exist.

T (F) 6. In the absence of a government, money is valuable only if it is useful. Therefore, cigarette money would be used exclusively in transactions between smokers in the prisoner-of-war camp.

T (F) 7. Economies of scale are the primary reason why coffee is grown in Brazil rather than New England.

(T) F 8. Even if everyone has the same abilities, specialization may be beneficial if there are economies of scale.

MULTIPLE CHOICE

1. One of the problems with barter is that it requires a *coincidence of wants*. This means that:

   a. everybody must want money
   b. everybody must want the same good
   c. at least two people must want the same good
   d. everybody must want my good, before I am able to exchange it
   e. for there to be an exchange between individuals A and B, individual A must want what B has, while B must want what A has

2. When a monetary system first replaces barter, it becomes possible for the first time to distinguish between:

   a. a good and a service
   b. the buyer and the seller
   c. private entrepreneurs and the government
   d. owners of capital and workers
   e. all of the above

3. Money is said to represent *general purchasing power* because:

   a. it can be used to buy any of the goods and services offered for sale

   b. the government guarantees its value
   c. the government is committed to accept money in payment of taxes
   d. Gresham's law no longer is valid
   e. Gresham's law applies to other goods, but not money

4. When we draw a diagram showing the circular flow of payments between households and businesses, the two major markets we show are:

   a. goods and services
   b. capital and labor
   c. capital and land
   d. consumer goods and economic resources
   e. products made by private entrepreneurs, and those provided by the government

5. In the present-day United States, what would an economist consider to be the *medium of exchange*?

   a. Supermarkets
   b. Corner drug stores
   c. The Sears, Roebuck catalogue
   d. Real estate brokers
   e. Dollar bills

6. When the best-tasting cigarettes started to disappear from circulation in the prisoner-of-war camp, this was an example of:

   a. economies of scale
   b. absolute advantage
   c. comparative advantage
   d. inflation
   e. Gresham's law

7. In the prisoner-of-war camp, in which cigarettes acted as money, suppose that the quantity of cigarettes coming into the camp remained constant, while the quantity of all other goods decreased. Then the most probable result would be:

   a. a rise in the value of cigarettes, measured in terms of other items
   b. a fall in the prices of other goods, measured in terms of cigarettes
   c. inflation
   d. deflation
   e. bad money driving out good money

8. Suppose that a building supervisor can lay bricks more rapidly and better than a bricklayer. Then, considering only these two individuals, we may conclude that:

   a. the bricklayer has an absolute advantage in bricklaying
   b. the supervisor has an absolute advantage in bricklaying
   c. the bricklayer has a comparative advantage in bricklaying
   d. the supervisor has a comparative advantage in bricklaying
   e. we can't tell which of the above is true without knowing how much brick cost, compared to the wage for bricklayers

9. The theory of comparative advantage was put forward by:

   a. Adam Smith
   b. John Maynard Keynes
   c. David Ricardo
   d. David Hume
   e. Karl Marx

10. Suppose that there are only two countries, A and B, and only two goods, food and clothing. If country A has a comparative advantage in the production of food, B is most likely to have a comparative advantage in:

    a. food also
    b. clothing
    c. both food and clothing
    d. neither food nor clothing
    e. we don't have enough information to decide

11. Suppose 10 workers with 1 machine can produce 100 TV sets in a month, while 20 workers with 2 machines can produce 250 TV sets in a month. This is an example of:

    a. technological efficiency
    b. allocative efficiency
    c. economies of scale
    d. comparative advantage
    e. absolute advantage

12. Suppose that (1) there are economies of scale in the production of each good, and (2) land and labor have specialized capabilities—for example, land and the climate give Brazil a comparative advantage in coffee. Then the gains from specialization will probably be:

    a. larger than if either (1) or (2) had existed alone
    b. small, since (1) and (2) tend to offset each other
    c. negative, since the combination of (1) and (2) create confusion
    d. about the same as with (1) alone, since (2) doesn't make much difference
    e. about the same as with (2) alone, since (1) doesn't make much difference

13. When tariffs among countries are reduced, this generally leads to gains from:

    a. economies of scale
    b. wider use of money rather than barter
    c. comparative advantage
    d. (a) and (b)
    e. (a) and (c)

EXERCISES

1. This exercise illustrates the idea of comparative advantage. Assume the following. A doctor working on home repairs can fix a leaky faucet in 10 minutes. A plumber takes 15 minutes. Then the (doctor, plumber) has an absolute advantage in plumbing. The doctor's time is worth $80 per hour in the practice of medicine. The plumber is paid $20 per hour.

   Suppose the doctor's house has six leaky faucets. If he fixes them himself, it will take _____ minutes. Thus, to fix the faucets, the doctor will use $_____ worth of his time. If the plumber is hired to fix the faucets, he will take _____ minutes, which is (longer, shorter) than the doctor would take.

   The cost in this case is $_____, which is (more, less) by $_____ than if the doctor fixed the faucets himself. The (doctor, plumber) has a comparative advantage in plumbing.

2. Table 3.1 shows how many cars can be produced in a country with various amounts of inputs. Each unit of input represents a specific quantity of labor and capital. Table 3.2 provides similar information for TV sets. Table 3.1, by itself, illustrates the idea of (comparative advantage, absolute advantage, economies of scale, none of these). Table 3.2, by itself, illustrates the idea of (comparative advantage, absolute advantage, economies of scale, none of these). Suppose that the economy has 5 units of inputs to be devoted to cars and TV sets. Plot the PPC for these 5 units of input in Figure 3.1. How is the shape of the PPC different from the PPCs in Chapter 2? _____

   The opportunity cost of producing cars (increases, decreases, remains constant) as more are produced.

Table 3.1 Production of cars

Number of Cars (millions)	Units of input
1	1
3	2
6	3
12	4
20	5

Table 3.2 Production of TV sets

Number of TV Sets (millions)	Units of input
20	1
40	2
60	3
80	4
100	5

Figure 3.1

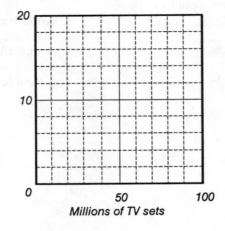

Millions of cars

Millions of TV sets

ESSAY QUESTIONS

1. The textbook explains why comparative advantage can mean that there are benefits from specialization and exchange. But it does not explain why specific people or nations might have a comparative advantage. How would you explain Iowa's comparative advantage over New England in producing corn? Why does Pennsylvania have a comparative advantage over most of the other states in the production of steel? Why does Taiwan have a comparative advantage in the production of transistor radios and TV sets?

2. Why do you think that most economists are usually in favor of reducing tariffs and other barriers to international trade? Why might anyone oppose the reduction of tariffs? The president has generally been more strongly in favor of freer trade than have individual members of the House of Representatives. How might this be explained?

3. There are disadvantages associated with specialization, as well as advantages. What are they?

ANSWERS

Matching columns: 1 d, 2 i, 3 f, 4 a, 5 j, 6 k, 7 h, 8 c, 9 e, 10 g, 11 b

True-False:
1 T (p. 37)
2 F (p. 39)
3 F (p. 40)
4 T (p. 41)
5 F (p. 42)
6 F (p. 40)
7 F (p. 41)
8 T (p. 43)

Multiple Choice:
1 e (p. 37)
2 b (p. 37)
3 a (p. 37)
4 d (p. 39)
5 e (p. 39)
6 e (p. 40)
7 c (p. 40)
8 b (p. 41)
9 c (p. 41)
10 b (p. 41)
11 c (p. 43)
12 a (pp. 41-43)
13 e (p. 43)

Exercises

1. doctor,
60,
$80,
90,
longer,
$30,
less,

$50,
plumber.

2.   economies of scale,
none of these,
it bows inward,
decreases.

Figure 3.1, completed

Millions of cars

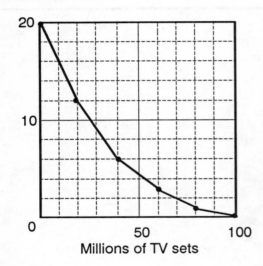

Millions of TV sets

Across

1, 4, 5. reason why there are gains from specialization
8. it's mightier than the sword
9. covering of spun silk
11. Princeton; also, capital of Bahamas
12. top of the cake
14. in a light spirit; jauntily
16. *really* bad
17. his 300-year old law worked in the Prisoner-of-war camp
19. factor of production, which has itself been produced
22. attribute of money (2 words)
24. for beneficial trade, this type of advantage is good enough
25. required for barter (3 words)

Down

1. if people specialize, this becomes necessary
2. oil for the wheels of commerce
3. a way of increasing living standards
4. above
5. because of this, not all our wants can be met
6. this advantage is desirable, but not necessary for specialization
7. if all incomes are _____, top 10% of population get 10% of total income
10. production possibilities _____
13. a type of economics
15. doctors' organization (abbrev.)
18. sharp (Lat.)
20. what someone does in an economy with no money
21. item produced for exchange
23. all

CHAPTER 4

DEMAND AND SUPPLY:
The Market Mechanism

LEARNING OBJECTIVES

After you have studied this chapter in the textbook and study guide, you should be able to

✔ Explain why the demand curve slopes downward to the right P 49

✔ Explain why the supply curve slopes upward to the right P 50

✔ Explain why a price that begins away from equilibrium will move to equilibrium P 51

✔ List and explain three things that can shift the demand curve and four that can shift the supply curve P 53   P 55

✔ Give one example each of a pair of goods that are *(1)* substitutes in use *(2)* complements in use *(3)* substitutes in production, and *(4)* complements in production. In each case, you should be able to explain why the pair fits into the category.

✔ Explain the distinction between product markets and markets for factors of production

✔ Explain how the factor markets can help answer the question, *For whom?*

✔ Explain how changes in factor markets can affect what happens in a product market, and vice versa

✔ Explain the main strengths and main shortcomings of the market mechanism as a way of answering the questions, *What? How?* and *For whom?*

MAJOR PURPOSE

This chapter is one of the most important in the book. It introduces the concepts of *demand* and *supply*, which help us to understand what is happening in the market for a specific product. The demand curve illustrates how buyers respond to various possible prices:

At lower prices, they buy more. On the other hand, sellers react negatively to low prices: They offer less for sale. This response of sellers is illustrated by the supply curve.

When drawing a demand or supply curve, we isolate the effect of *price alone* on the behavior of buyers and sellers. Of course, many other things besides price can affect their behavior. When we draw a demand or supply curve and look at the effect of price alone, we make the *ceteris paribus* assumption — that all these other things do not change. In cases where they do in fact change, we are no longer on a single demand or supply curve; the demand or supply curve *shifts*.

Other important concepts introduced in this chapter are:

- the concept of *equilibrium*,
- *surplus* and *shortage*, and
- *substitutes* and *complementary goods*.

HIGHLIGHTS OF CHAPTER

In every economy, some mechanism is needed to decide three major questions: *What* will be produced? *How* will it be produced? And *for whom* will it be produced? There are two major ways of answering these questions:

- through the market — that is, through voluntary exchanges between buyers and sellers, and
- through governmental decision-making.

(Other ways are sometimes used — for example, in a family or in a monastery. But we are not primarily interested in these alternatives.)

All nations have some reliance on markets and some reliance on governmental decision-making. However, there are substantial differences among nations. In the United States, the market is the most important mechanism, although the government does play a significant role in modifying the outcome of the market. In the U.S.S.R., government plays a much more central role, although there is some reliance on markets.

The central feature of a market is *price*. Different prices for different goods provide *incentives* for producers to make some goods rather than others, and incentives for consumers to purchase cheap goods rather than expensive ones. *Prices* also provide *signals* and *information* to buyers and sellers. For example, the willingness of buyers to pay a high price acts as a signal to producers, showing that people are eager to obtain the product.

To study how buyers respond to different prices, we use a *demand curve* or *demand schedule*. This curve or schedule shows the quantity of a specific good that buyers would be willing and able to purchase at various different prices. The demand curve slopes downward to the right, illustrating that people are more eager to buy at lower prices. A major reason is that, at a lower price, people have an incentive to *switch* away from other products and buy the product whose price is lower instead.

On the other side of the market, the supply curve shows how much sellers would be willing to offer at various prices. It slopes upward to the right, because sellers will be increasingly eager to sell as the price rises. Again, the willingness to *switch* is an important reason for the slope. If the price of a good is higher, firms have an incentive to drop other products, and make more of this good instead.

What happens in the market depends on both demand and supply. To find the *equilibrium* price and quantity, we put the demand and supply curves together, to find where they intersect. At this price, the quantity offered by sellers is equal to the quantity which buyers want to purchase. There is no unfulfilled demand to pull prices up, nor any excess offers to pull prices down.

When the price is not at its equilibrium, there are pressures for it to change. If the price is below its equilibrium, for example, there are eager buyers who are unable to find the good for sale. In other words, there is a *shortage*. Producers notice this and conclude that they can sell at a higher price. The price rises to its equilibrium level. On the other and, if the price is initially above its equilibrium, there is a *surplus*. Eager sellers are unable to find buyers. They are willing to sell at a lower price. The price falls to its equilibrium.

When we draw a demand or supply curve, we are looking at the way in which buyers and sellers respond to price, and to price *alone*. In practice, of course, buyers and sellers are influenced by many other things than the price of the good — for example, buyers generally purchase more when their incomes rise, and sellers are less willing to sell when the costs of their inputs rise. But these other things are held constant when a single demand or supply curve is drawn. This is the important assumption of *ceteris paribus*, that other things do not change. If they do change, the demand or supply curve *shifts*. For example, an increase in income generally causes a rightward shift in the whole demand curve. However, in the case of inferior goods, the demand curve shifts left; when people can afford better alternatives, they do so.

If the demand curve shifts to the right while the supply curve remains stable, then both price and quantity will increase. On the other hand, if the supply curve shifts to the right while the demand curve remains stable, then quantity will increase but price will fall. In brief, *a change in demand makes price and quantity change in the same direction, whereas a change in supply markets price and quantity move in opposite directions*. In practice, of course, many things can happen at once; often the demand and supply curves both shift. In this case, it becomes more difficult to predict what will happen.

Supply and demand theory is often used to study the market for a single good. However, there are strong connections among markets. When a price changes in one market, it can change conditions in other markets. For example, an increase in the price of gasoline in the 1970s caused a decline in the demand for large cars. This is an example of *complementary goods*—large cars and gasoline are used *together*. When the price of gasoline increases, the demand for large cars shifts left.

Whereas gasoline and cars are complements, some other products—such as bus tickets and train tickets—are *substitutes*. A person wanting to travel to the next city can go either by train or by bus. The higher is the train fare, the more people will use busses instead. Thus, a higher price of train tickets causes the demand for bus tickets to shift to the right.

Goods may also be substitutes or complements in production. Substitutes in production are goods which use the same inputs; the inputs can be used to produce either the one good or the other. For example, land can be used to produce either wheat or corn. If there is a crop failure abroad and the United States exports much more wheat, the price of wheat will be bid up. Farmers will be encouraged to switch out of the production of corn and produce additional wheat instead. The supply curve for corn will shift to the left.

On the other hand, complements are produced together. For example, wheat and straw are produced together. If the price of wheat is bid up, more wheat will be produced. In the process, more straw will be produced as a by-product. The supply curve of straw will shift to the right.

The question of *what* will be produced is decided primarily in the product market. To throw light on the other two questions—*how?* and *for whom?*—we look first at the markets for inputs. For example, the market for labor helps to answer these two questions. If the demand for labor is high compared to its supply, then wage rates will be high. Thus, wage rates are much higher in the United States than in India because there are fewer workers for each unit of land and capital in the United States. As a result of the high wage, producers in the United States have an incentive to use only a little labor, and substitute capital instead. In an Indian factory, in contrast, many more things are done by hand because of the low wage rate. The wage rate not only helps to determine how things are produced, but it also helps to determine who gets the product. Because wage rates are high in the United States, the American worker can buy and consume many more products than the Indian worker.

Observe that high wage rates affect what the worker can buy; with high wages, workers are more likely to buy TV sets and homes. This means that wages—determined in the factor markets in the lower box in Figure 4-8 in the textbook—have an impact on the demand for TV sets, homes, and other products in the upper box. Thus, there are important connections among markets.

Finally, this chapter summarizes the strengths and weaknesses of the market as a mechanism for answering the three central questions—What, How, and For Whom? The strong points of the market are that:

- it encourages producers to make what consumers want,

- it provides people with an incentive to acquire useful skills,

- it encourages consumers to conserve scarce goods,

- it encourages producers to conserve scarce resources,

- it provides a high degree of economic freedom, and

- it provides buyers and sellers with information on market conditions, including local conditions.

The market mechanism is also subject to major criticisms:

- some people may be left in desperate poverty,

- markets don't work in the case of public goods such as defense and the police,

- monopolies and oligopolies may have the power to keep production down and keep prices up,

- the market does not provide a strong incentive for producers to limit pollution and other negative side-effects,

- a market economy may be unstable (although government policies will not necessarily increase stability), and

- producers may simply be satisfying a want that they have created in the first place through advertising.

To evaluate the market, it is important to compare it with the alternatives which exist in fact, not with some ideal, unattainable system. The textbook outlines a few of the problems which can arise when the government sets prices—in particular, the problem of black markets and shortages. A number of countries that have interfered very heavily in economic activity—such as the Soviet Union—have run into severe problems, including shortages.

IMPORTANT TERMS

Match the first column with the corresponding phrase in the second column.

_d_	1. Capitalism	a. All the producers of a single good
_h_	2. Monopoly	b. If price of A rises, demand for B increases
_l_	3. Oligopoly	c. Surplus
_i_	4. Perfect competition	d. Free enterprise
_a_	5. Industry	e. Demand for this declines as income rises
_k_	6. Firm	f. Nothing else changes
_c_	7. Excess supply	g. Goods used together
_j_	8. Excess demand	h. Market with only one seller
_e_	9. Inferior good	i. Where every buyer and seller is a price taker
_g_	10. Complementary goods	j. Shortage
_b_	11. Substitutes	k. A single business organization, such as General Motors
_f_	12. *Ceteris paribus*	l. Market dominated by a few sellers

TRUE-FALSE

T   F   1.   Perfect competition exists only when the government fixes the price, so that no single buyer or seller is able to influence the price of the good.

T   F   2.   Perfect competition will not exist in a market if there is only one seller, or if there is only one buyer.

T   F   3.   In a perfectly competitive industry, every buyer and seller takes the quantity as given, and is left with only a pricing decision.

T   F   4.   Even if there are many buyers, imperfect competition can exist in a market.

T   F   5.   Even if there are many sellers, imperfect competition can exist in a market.

T   F   6.   In a capitalist economy, most of the capital equipment is owned by the government.

T   F   7.   A surplus drives the price down; a shortage drives the price up.

T   F   8.   If the price of wheat increases, the supply curve of straw will probably shift to the right.

T   F   9.   The demand curve for Pepsi Cola will probably shift to the right if the price of Coke rises.

T   F   10.   If the price of paper increases, the supply curve of books will probably shift to the right.

T   F   11.   If demand increases while supply decreases, the price will increase.

T   F   12.   If the demand curve shifts to the right, the result will be an increase in the quantity sold and an increase in the market price.

T   F   13.   If both the demand and supply curves for a product shift to the right, we can expect the quantity sold to increase, but we cannot be sure whether the price will rise or fall.

T   F   14.   One essential characteristic of a free enterprise economy is that the government make it easier to enter businesses freely by subsidizing new businesses.

T   F   15.   Factor markets are different from the markets for most goods, in that goods markets are generally perfectly competitive, while the markets for factors are usually monopolized.

MULTIPLE CHOICE

1. Economists sometimes speak of a *free* market. By *free*, they mean:

    a. prices are low
    b. people do not have to pay admission to the marketplace
    c. transactions take place with little or no government interference
    d. the government is not a buyer or seller in the market
    e. there is perfect competition in that market

2. The U.S. government uses four major ways to influence What will be produced, How, and For Whom. It uses every one of the following except one. Which one does not belong on this list?

    a. Spending
    b. Taxes
    c. Regulation
    d. Comprehensive central planning
    e. Public enterprises

3. What is the most important characteristic of perfect competition?

   a. Each seller has at least one powerful competitor to worry about
   b. There is at least one powerful, efficient producer who acts to keep prices down
   c. Every buyer can go to at least three or four sellers to see who has the lowest price
   d. Every buyer and seller is a price taker; none has any power to set price
   e. There must be many buyers, and at least three or four sellers

4. A market with one seller and a few buyers is an example of:

   a. monopoly
   b. oligopoly
   c. perfect competition
   d. technological inefficiency
   e. a black market

5. It is most accurate to speak of General Motors as:

   a. a plant
   b. a firm
   c. an industry
   d. a monopoly
   e. a perfect competitor

6. A surplus of wheat exists when:

   a. wheat production is lower than last year
   b. wheat production is higher than last year
   c. wheat production exceeds the production of all other grains combined
   d. the quantity of wheat demanded exceeds the quantity supplied
   e. the quantity of wheat supplied exceeds the quantity demanded

7. Suppose that a surplus exists in a market. Then we may conclude that:

   a. the price is below the equilibrium
   b. the price is above the equilibrium
   c. the government has imposed a price ceiling
   d. the quantity demanded has decreased
   e. the quantity supplied has increased

8. When we draw the demand curve for a product, we assume that:

   a. there are many sellers
   b. there are only a few sellers
   c. all *supply shifters* are held constant
   d. all *demand shifters* are held constant
   e. both (c) and (d)

9. When incomes increase, the demand curve for an individual good:

   a. usually shifts down
   b. always shifts down
   c. usually shifts to the right
   d. always shifts to the right
   e. doesn't move, since only price affects demand

10. Suppose that we know that an increase in the price of good A will cause a rightward shift in the demand curve for good B. Then we may conclude that:

    a. producers of A and B use the same set of inputs
    b. consumers of A and B have the same levels of income
    c. consumers of A and B have different incomes
    d. A and B are complementary goods
    e. A and B are substitutes

11. Tennis rackets and tennis balls are:

    a. substitutes
    b. complementary goods
    c. inferior goods
    d. independent goods
    e. monopolistic goods

12. Apples and textbooks are:

    a. substitutes
    b. complementary goods
    c. inferior goods
    d. independent goods
    e. monopolistic goods

13. Which illustrate best the idea of substitutes in production?

    a. Copper and aluminum
    b. Wheat and rye 里麦
    c. Wheat and bananas
    d. Beef and leather
    e. Cream and sugar

14. Peanuts and tobacco can be grown on similar land. Therefore, they are:

   a. substitutes in production
   b. joint products
   c. inferior goods
   d. normal goods
   e. an oligopoly

15. Suppose that the demand for beef increases. This is most likely to cause:

   a. a rightward shift in the supply curve for beef
   b. a leftward shift in the supply curve for beef
   c. a fall in the price of beef
   d. a fall in the price of leather
   e. an upward shift in the demand for leather

16. In a typical market,

   a. an increase in demand, with no change in supply, will result in a fall in price
   b. an increase in demand, with no change in supply, will result in a decrease in quantity
   c. an increase in demand, with no change in supply, will result in an increase in both price and quantity
   d. an increase in supply, with no change in demand, will result in a decrease in quantity
   e. an increase in supply, with no change in demand, will result in an increase in price

17. Suppose that, between year 1 and year 2, the demand curve and the supply curve for wheat both shift to the right. From this information, we may conclude that, in year 2:

   a. the quantity of wheat sold will be larger, while the price will be higher
   b. the quantity of wheat sold will be larger, while the price will be lower
   c. the quantity of wheat sold will be larger, while we

   do not have enough information to tell if the price will be higher or lower
   d. the quantity of wheat sold will be smaller, while we do not have enough information to tell if the price will be higher or lower
   e. we do not have enough information to tell what will happen to either the price or the quantity

18. Incomes are determined primarily in the markets for:

   a. goods
   b. services
   c. factors of production
   d. machinery
   e. parts

19. The advantages of the market mechanism (as contrasted to government controls) as a way of deciding What? How? and For whom?) include:

   a. prices provide incentives for producers to make what the public wants
   b. prices provide incentives for producers to conserve scarce resources
   c. prices provide incentives for consumers to conserve scarce goods
   d. high wages in skilled occupations act as an incentive for workers to undertake training
   e. all of the above

20. A black market is most likely to exist when:

   a. the government controls the price of a good
   b. the supply of a good is controlled by a monopolist
   c. the supply of a good is controlled by two or three producers
   d. the government imposes an excise tax on a good
   e. the government urges producers to produce more to promote the general welfare of the public

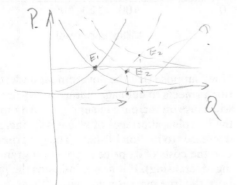

EXERCISES

1. Using the demand schedule in the first two columns of the table below, plot the demand and supply curves in Figure 4.1. Label the axes, and mark in appropriate numbers on each axis. Then fill in the last column of the table.

    a. The equilibrium quantity is _____.

    b. The equilibrium price is _____.

    c. At the equilibrium price, what is the surplus or shortage shown in the last column? _____. Does this confirm that this price is an equilibrium?

    d. Now suppose that the government sets a price of 60. At this price, there will be a (surplus, shortage) of _____.

Figure 4.1

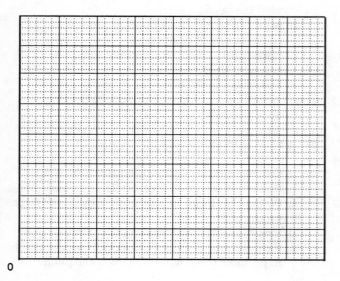

0

Price of Hamburgers	Quantity Demanded	Quantity Supplied	Surplus (+) or Shortage (−)
	(thousands per week)		
$1.40	200	700	
$1.20	240	600	
$1.00	300	500	
$0.80	400	400	
$0.60	600	300	
$0.50	800	250	

2. Figure 4.2 illustrates some of the issues that arise when the government undertakes price supports (for example, in agriculture). D shows the demand curve, and S_1 the supply curve. Initially, the equilibrium quantity is _____ million bushels, and the price is _____. Now suppose that the government passes a rule that says that wheat cannot be sold at a price less than P_3. The result of this law will be a (surplus, shortage) amounting to _____ million bushels.

If all the government does is set a high price, not all wheat farmers will be better off. Those who are better off will be those who (cut back production, sell their wheat at the high price). On the other hand, some will be worse off, specifically those who (are unable to sell their wheat at the high price, sell their wheat at a low price). To ensure that wheat farmers are better off, the government can (buy the surplus wheat, reduce the price to P_1).

Figure 4-2

Price

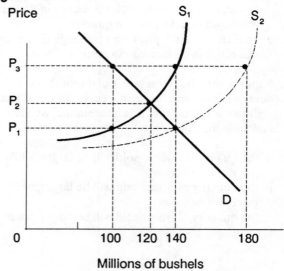

Millions of bushels

Now, suppose that the government undertakes irrigation projects to help agriculture in dry areas. This will cause an increase in supply from S_1 to S_2, and the (surplus, shortage) of wheat will (increase, decrease) to million bushels. The government will find the costs of its price support program (increasing, decreasing). If it now eliminates the price support, the free market price will settle at _____.

3. Suppose that supply is given by the equation:

$$Q = -30 + 4P$$

This supply is plotted in Figure 4.3 in the following way. First, choose some convenient value for P, such as 10. Put this value into the equation to get $Q = -30 + 40 = 10$. This means that when $P = 10$, $Q = 10$, so that point A is on the supply curve. Then, choose another value of P, say $P = 15$. Substituting this into the equation, we find that the corresponding $Q = $ _____. This is plotted as point B. The supply relationship is a straight line; there are no squared terms or other reasons for supply to bend. Thus, with the two points A and B, we can draw the straight-line supply S_1.

Figure 4-3

Price

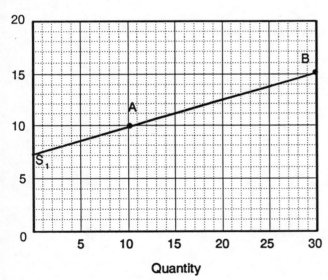

a. Suppose that demand is also a straight line:

$$Q = 20 - P$$

Then, if $P = 15$, $Q = $ _____, and if $P = 5$, $Q = $ _____. Plot demand in Figure 4-3 and label it D_1. On this figure, we see that the equilibrium price is _____ and the equilibrium quantity _____. Confirm these figures by solving the two equations algebraically, to find P and Q.

b. Suppose now that income increases and demand consequently increases, with 15 more units being demanded at each price. Thus, the new demand is

$$Q = 35 - P$$

To plot this new demand, we find two points. For example, if $P = 15$, $Q = $ _____, and if $P = 5$, $Q = $ _____. Plot the new equilibrium demand, labelling it D_2. At the new equilibrium, $P = $ _____ and $Q = $ _____. Again, confirm these numbers by solving the demand and supply equations. The price has (increased, decreased), and the quantity has (increased, decreased) as a result of this increase in demand.

c. Now, suppose we are back with the original demand, D_1, but that supply is now:

$$Q = -10 + 2P$$

If $P = 10$, $Q = $ _____, and if $P = 15$, $Q = $ _____. Plot this new supply and label it S_2. With supply S_2 and demand D_1, the equilibrium price is _____, while quantity is _____. Again, confirm these numbers by solving the demand and supply equations.

d. Finally, suppose that demand shifts from D_1 to D_2, while supply remains at S_2. At the new equilibrium $P = $ _____ and $Q = $ _____. When the demand curve shifted this time, why is it that the price rose more, and the quantity less, than in part (b)?

Answer:_____.

ESSAY QUESTIONS

1. A demand or supply curve applies to a specific time and a specific location. For example, the market for milk in Washington, D.C., is not the same thing as the market for milk in Baltimore. Would you expect the price of milk in these two cities to be similar? Precisely the same? Explain.

2. Suppose that, as a result of an increase in the population of Washington, there were an increase in the demand for milk in that city. If you were an all-powerful social planner, you would probably want to persuade people in Baltimore to give up some of their milk in order to provide for the higher number of people in Washington. What sort of rationing

scheme might you devise to accomplish this goal? How would you know how much to allocate to each family? How large a staff do you think you would need?

Suppose, alternatively, that you allowed market forces to work freely. What would happen to the price of milk in Washington? What would happen to the quantity? How would the changing conditions in Washington affect the supply curve for milk in Baltimore? What would happen to the price of milk in Baltimore? To the quantity? Draw demand and supply curves for Washington and Baltimore to illustrate what is happening. Would your intentions as a social planner be carried out by the market instead? Which policy—rationing or the market—works more efficiently? Are there any disadvantages to the more efficient system?

3. The prices printed on a restaurant menu apply whether the restaurant is crowded or half empty on any particular evening. If you ran a restaurant,

   a. would you charge higher prices on Friday and Saturday evenings, when the restaurant is crowded, than on other evenings?

   b. would you charge higher prices during the evening than for an identical meal at lunch? Why or why not? (Or, under what circumstances might you?)

   c. Does McDonalds behave in the way you have suggested? How do you explain that?

ANSWERS

Matching columns: 1 d, 2 h, 3 l, 4 i, 5 a, 6 k, 7 c, 8 j, 9 e, 10 g, 11 b, 12 f

True-False:
1 F (p. 48)
2 T (p. 48)
3 F (p. 48)
4 T (p. 48)
5 T (p. 48)
6 F (p. 47)
7 T (p. 51)
8 T (p. 55)
9 T (p. 53)
10 F (p. 55)
11 T (p. 54)
12 T (p. 55)
13 T
14 F (p. 47)
15 F

Multiple Choice:
1 c (p. 46)
2 d (p. 47)
3 d (p. 48)
4 a (p. 48)
5 b (p. 49)
6 e (p. 51)
7 b (p. 51)
8 d (p. 52)
9 c (p. 53)
10 e (p. 53)
11 b (p. 53)
12 d (p. 53)
13 b (p. 55)
14 a (p. 55)

Exercises

1 a. 400,
   b. $0.80,
   c. zero, yes,
   d. shortage, 300.

2. 120, P_2, surplus, 40, sell their wheat at the high price, are unable to sell their wheat at the high price, buy the surplus wheat, surplus, increase, 80, increasing, P_1.

3. 30,
   a. 5, 15, 10, 10,
   b. 20, 30, 13, 22, increased, increased,
   c. 10, 20, 10, 10,
   d. 15, 20, because S_2 is steeper than S_1.

Figure 4.1 Completed

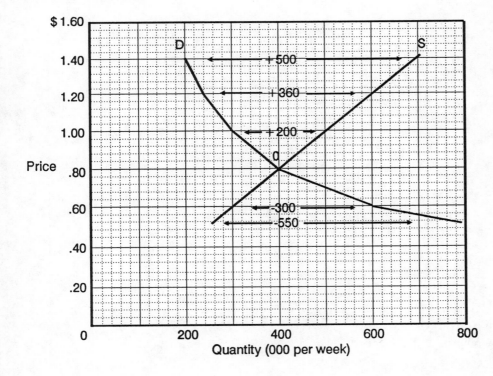

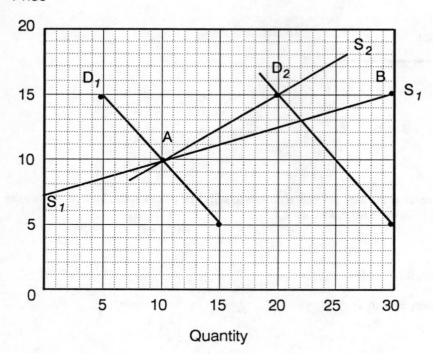

Price

Quantity

CHAPTER 5

THE ECONOMIC ROLE OF THE GOVERNMENT

LEARNING OBJECTIVES

After you have studied this chapter in the textbook and study guide, you should be able to

✔ Describe the four ways in which the government affects the economy *P65*

✔ Explain the difference between government spending for goods and services, and transfer payments *P66-67*

✔ Explain the difference between a progressive and a regressive tax, and give an example of each *P69*

✔ Describe the (five) major reasons for government intervention in the economy *P76*

✔ Explain the objectives that should be kept in mind when designing a tax system *4 points P72-73*

✔ Explain the difference between the *benefit principle* and the *ability to pay principle* *P72-74*

✔ Explain why the U.S. tax system is less progressive than we might guess by looking at the income tax schedule

---

MAJOR PURPOSE

The major objective of this chapter is to explain how the government affects the economy. It does so in four ways: spending, taxation, regulation, and the operation of public enterprises. In the United States, public enterprises are much less important than in other countries, and the other three are the principal ways in which the government affects the economy.

There are a number of reasons for government intervention in the economy.

• The government provides *public goods* — that is, goods that cannot be provided by the private sector because everyone can enjoy them, regardless of who pays for them. An example is police protection; we all gain the benefits from an orderly society, whether we pay taxes or not.

• The government can control or discourage externalities, such as pollution. Free markets don't work very well in polluting industries, since they provide no incentive to keep pollution down.

- The government provides merit goods — such as education — that it considers particularly important for the society.

- The government provides programs to help the poor.

- Another important objective of the government is to promote stability.

HIGHLIGHTS OF CHAPTER

The government affects the economy in four major ways:

- spending,

- taxation,

- regulation, and

- public enterprises.

There are some public enterprises in the United States — for example, the Tennessee Valley Authority and the Post Office. However, public enterprise is much less important in the United States than in many other countries, as we saw in Chapter 4. This chapter therefore concentrates on the first three points.

SPENDING

In dollar terms, government spending has risen very rapidly in the United States, from $100 billion per year in 1955 to $1,640 billion by 1988. However, if we look at the size of the government relative to the economy, we get a much less spectacular picture. Indeed, government *purchases of goods and services* have remained approximately stable as a percentage of GNP in the past three decades; increases at the state and local levels have been offset by decreases at the federal level. Nevertheless, if transfer payments are included, government spending has been going up as a percentage of GNP. In other words, the increase in the size of the government reflects mainly the increase in transfer payments, of which social security is the most important program.

TAXES

The primary purpose of taxes is to raise the revenues to finance government spending programs. Per-

sonal income taxes and social security taxes are by far the largest revenue raisers — by a wide margin. Social security tax revenues have grown very rapidly, doubling between 1980 and 1988, and further increases are scheduled for the coming years. These large increases have been necessary to finance the large increases in pensions and other benefits under the social security system.

On most income — up to a maximum of $48,000 in 1989 — the social security tax is *proportional*; it is a flat 15¢ on each $1 in income. However, no tax is collected on incomes over the $48,000 maximum, which means that the social security tax is somewhat *regressive*. That is, it is a smaller percentage of an income of $80,000 than of an income of $40,000. Nevertheless, the overall social security system is *progressive*, because the benefits to lower income people are greater, compared to the taxes they have paid, than the benefits of higher income people.

Income tax rates are generally *progressive* — the tax rate on high incomes is generally larger than the tax rate on low incomes. However, the overall tax system is less progressive that the tax rates suggest, both because of the existence of regressive taxes such as social security, and because of "loopholes" — various tax deductions or tax credits. The term "loophole" implies that the deduction or credit is undesirable, and there is considerable debate over what is desirable and what is not. One item sometimes put on the list of loopholes — the provision that homeowners can deduct the interest on their mortgages from their taxable incomes — has such overwhelming political support that it is rarely questioned. (President Carter once hinted that the interest rate deduction might be eliminated, but there was such a storm of protest that he quickly dropped the idea.)

The Tax Reform Act of 1986 closed a number of loopholes, while it also reduced tax rates. The Act was intended to be *revenue neutral* — the increases in tax revenues from the closing of loopholes were designed to compensate for the lower tax rates. By lowering tax rates and plugging loopholes, the government hoped to make the economy more efficient. People now have a greater incentive to engage in productive activities, and less incentive to hunt for loopholes (both because they are harder to find, and because the gains — in terms of taxes saved — are smaller once they are found).

Other than raising revenues, there are a number of other objectives that should be considered in designing a tax code.

- One objective is *equity*, or fairness. As we suggested in Chapter 1, there is some controversy over just what is fair. Nevertheless, discussions of fairness usually begin with one of two approaches to taxation:

° *Ability to pay*. According to this idea, taxes should be imposed according to income or wealth; people with high incomes should pay more because they are better able to do so. The progressive income tax is one application of this principle. (The inheritance tax is another.)

° *Benefit principle*. According to this idea, taxes should depend on who benefits most from government programs. Those who benefit most should pay the most.

• *Simplicity* is an important objective in the tax system. Discussions of tax reform in recent years have often centered around the criticism that the income tax has become hopelessly complicated. Unfortunately, the Tax Reform Act of 1986 made a complex tax system even more complicated. Even some ex-commissioners of the Internal Revenue Service find the income tax too complicated for them to make out their own forms; they get professional help.

• *Neutrality*. As a starting point, most economists believe that the tax system should be designed to disturb market forces as little as possible. It should not capriciously introduce incentives for people to change their behavior in order to avoid taxes.

• *Meeting social objectives*. Nevertheless, in some cases it may be desirable to encourage people to change their behavior. For example, in order to encourage people to give to charities, the government allows people to deduct their contributions to charities from their taxable income. Taxes may also be used to discourage businesses from polluting the air or water.

REGULATION

More direct means are available for encouraging some behavior, and discouraging other activities. For example, there are regulations limiting the amount of pollutants that factories are allowed to discharge into the air and water. In the early days of regulation about a hundred years ago, the government took steps to discourage monopolistic behavior by the so-called "robber barons" of the time. Other regulations are aimed at protecting the safety of workers and discouraging discrimination.

Government regulations are generally aimed at reducing major problems. Nevertheless, regulation has been a source of controversy. There are two major problems with regulation:

• regulatory agencies may require major reporting efforts from business, and sometimes generate expensive red tape of little value; and

• regulatory agencies sometimes come under the control of the industry they are supposedly regulating.

The government may be the means for an industry gaining oligopolistic or monopolistic power.

REASONS FOR GOVERNMENT ACTIVITY

The government becomes involved in the economy for many reasons. Here are the five most important:

• Governments often provide goods and services which the private sector would otherwise fail to provide or would provide only with difficulty and at a high cost. Roads are one example. If the roads within a city were run by private entrepreneurs, motorists would have to stop frequently to pay tolls. National defense is unlikely to be organized and paid for privately. There is a problem of *free riders* — people who let others pay because they will reap the benefits even if they don't contribute. If people benefit whether they pay or not, we have an example of a *public good*.

• The government may intervene when *side effects* prevent people from making socially desirable decisions. For example, vaccinations protect not only the individuals who are vaccinated; they also protect the public from communicable diseases. Smallpox has been eradicated by the combined action of governments and international organizations.

Benefits that go to people other than those who are vaccinated (or their doctors) are known as an *external benefits*. There also can be *external costs*, such as the cost to people downwind from a polluting factory. Just as the government encourages activities with external benefits — such as vaccinations — so it may discourage those with external costs.

- The government may provide *merit* goods or services, such as education, that it considers very desirable from a social viewpoint.

- The government has programs to *help the poor;* for example, food stamps and welfare programs.

- The government may increase or decrease its expenditures in order to *promote economic stability*. For example, during a period of high unemployment, it may undertake public projects in order to provide jobs.

There have been substantial changes in attitudes toward government activity. Between 1930 and 1960, there was a strong upward trend in government activity. One reason was to protect people from the insecurities that were particularly obvious during the depression.

During the 1980s, there has been a movement to reduce the role of government in some countries, such as Britain. The government has sold — or *privatized* — much of the housing and some of the businesses that it owned.

IMPORTANT TERMS

Match the first column with the corresponding phrase in the second column.

_____ 1. Transfer payment
_____ 2. Progressive tax
_____ 3. Proportional tax
_____ 4. Average tax rate
_____ 5. Marginal tax rate
_____ 6. Deficit
_____ 7. Privatization
_____ 8. Externality
_____ 9. Public good
_____10. Neutral tax

a. Tax paid divided by income
b. One that takes the same percentage of high and low incomes
c. Sale of government-owned businesses
d. One that takes a higher percentage of high incomes
e. People get the benefit of this, regardless of who pays
f. Expenditure by government, for which government receives no good or service in return
g. Tax which leaves market forces undisturbed
h. Side effect of production or consumption
i. Excess of expenditures over revenues
j. Percentage of additional income paid in tax

TRUE-FALSE

T   F   1.   Payments to the unemployed are a form of transfer payment.

T   F   2.   If we include all levels of government (federal, state, and local), then government spending on goods and services is more, as a fraction of national product, than it was even at the height of World War II in 1943-44.

T   F   3.   Since 1960, transfer expenditures by the federal government have risen, both as a fraction of total federal government expenditures and as a fraction of national product.

T   F   4.   Defense expenditures have risen consistently as a percentage of national product since the beginning of the conflict in Vietnam.

T   F   5.   A tax is progressive if high-income people pay a larger percentage of their income than low-income people.

T　F　6.　Suppose that a state imposes a tax of 5% of all income. Because it "hits the poor as hard as the rich," such a tax is regressive.

T　F　7.　Suppose that a state imposes a sales tax of 5%. Because high-income people buy more than low-income people, they will pay more sales tax. Therefore, such a tax is progressive.

T　F　8.　According to the benefit principle of taxation, government expenditures should be undertaken whenever they benefit the public.

T　F　9.　According to the ability to pay principle of taxation, only those who have enough income that they are able to save should be required to pay taxes.

T　F　10.　The term "merit good" is used in describing a feature of the British economy. Specifically, a "merit good" is one which the upper class consumes more heavily than the lower classes.

MULTIPLE CHOICE

1.　Which of the following is the best example of government expenditure for goods or services

  a. salaries of judges
  b. social security pensions paid to the elderly
  c. welfare payments
  d. unemployment compensation
  e. the progressive income tax

2.　The two largest categories of expenditure for the federal government are:

  a. interest and education
  b. education and social security
  c. defense and interest
  d. defense and social security
  e. defense and education

3.　Social security plus medicare expenditures together are equal to approximately what percent of GNP?

  a. 1%
  b. 5%
  c. 12%
  d. 18%
  e. 25%

4.　As a percentage of GNP, defense expenditures:

  a. have grown rapidly since 1960
  b. have grown slowly and steadily since 1960
  c. have declined slowly and steadily since 1960
  d. decreased between 1960 and 1979, but rose between 1979 and 1983
  e. fell rapidly from 1979 to 1989

5.　More than two thirds of federal government expenditures are made up of three large categories. Those three categories are:

  a. defense, education, and social security
  b. defense, education, and agriculture
  c. defense, social security, and agriculture
  d. social security, agriculture, and interest on the national debt
  e. social security, defense, and interest on the national debt

6.　Of the following, which provides the largest source of revenue for the federal government?

  a. sales taxes
  b. corporate income taxes
  c. personal income taxes
  d. customs duties
  e. excise taxes on cigarettes and alcohol

THE NEXT TWO QUESTIONS ARE BASED ON TABLE 5.1

Table 5.1
Income taxes
(hypothetical)

Income	Tax
$10,000	$1,000
$20,000	$3,000
$30,000	$5,000

7. For a person with an income of $20,000, the **average** tax rate in Table 5.1 is:

   a. 10%
   b. 15%
   c. 20%
   d. 30%
   e. we don't have enough information to tell

8. For a person with an income of $20,000, the **marginal** tax rate in Table 5.1 is:

   a. 10%
   b. 15%
   c. 20%
   d. 30%
   e. 50%

9. If a tax takes $1,000 from someone with an income of $10,000, and $2,000 from someone with an income of $50,000, that tax is:

   a. neutral
   b. progressive
   c. regressive
   d. proportional
   e. marginal

10. The social security tax is:

    a. neutral
    b. marginal
    c. mildly progressive
    d. highly progressive
    e. regressive

11. Last year, the government's debt increased by the amount of last year's

    a. tax revenues - expenditures
    b. interest payments
    c. transfer payments
    d. surplus
    e. deficit

12. During the past decade, the federal government has

    a. run a surplus every year
    b. run a surplus most years, but not every one
    c. had about the same number of surpluses as deficits
    d. run a deficit most years, but not every one
    e. run a deficit every year

13. In his successful campaign for the presidency in 1988, Mr. Bush unequivocally promised:

    a. no new taxes
    b. an increase in defense spending, over that advocated by President Reagan
    c. a comprehensive national health insurance program by 1990
    d. a most favored nation trade treaty with the Soviet Union by 1990
    e. all of the above

14. According to the "neutrality" principle of taxation,

    a. income taxes should be progressive
    b. taxes should be imposed only on goods about which people are neutral (that is, neither very enthusiastic nor very negative)
    c. taxes should be imposed on tobacco and alcoholic beverages
    d. taxes should be designed to disturb market forces as little as possible
    e. the government should rely on the corporate profits tax, not the personal income tax

15. The Tax Reform Act of 1986 was designed to help achieve the objectives of greater:

    a. fairness and simplicity
    b. fairness and neutrality
    c. simplicity and neutrality
    d. simplicity, neutrality, and revenue
    e. fairness, simplicity, neutrality, and revenue

16. The agency of the federal government that requires corporations to disclose information about their financial positions is the:

    a. FTC
    b. EPA
    c. EEOC
    d. FAA
    e. SEC

17. A public good:

    a. creates no positive externalities
    b. creates no negative externalities
    c. cannot be produced by a private corporation
    d. can be enjoyed by all, even those who do not pay for it
    e. must be provided by the federal government if it is to be provided at all

18. Which of the following is the best example of a negative economic externality:

   a. an increase in the international price of oil
   b. an increase in the international price of grain
   c. air pollution created by a steel mill
   d. the rise in the price of steel when the government requires steel mills to reduce pollution
   e. vaccinations

19. Which of the following is designed specifically to be **non**-neutral:

   a. a proportional income tax
   b. a general sales tax of 5%
   c. a tax on polluting activities

   d. all of the above
   e. none of the above

20. The presence of externalities means that

   a. a tax system that seems to be progressive will in fact be regressive
   b. a tax system that seems to be regressive will in fact be progressive
   c. the market system will generally not work as well as it would in the absence of externalities
   d. the rich will generally get richer, and the poor poorer
   e. the federal government will find it much more difficult to balance its budget

EXERCISES

1. The table below shows two different taxes—tax A and tax B. For each of these taxes, fill in the column showing the average tax rate at various incomes, and the marginal tax rate. Also note on the last line whether the tax is proportional, regressive, or progressive.

2. Suppose that a family with an income of $35,000 pays $5,000 in interest on its mortgage, and is allowed to deduct that $5,000 from its taxable income. As a result, taxable income falls from $35,000 to $30,000. This would mean a reduction of $ _750_ in tax payable under Tax A, and a reduction of $ _1500_ under Tax B. Thus, the higher is the marginal tax rate, the (greater, less) is the tax saving from a deduction.

Income		TAX A Average Rate	TAX A Marginal Rate		TAX B Average Rate	TAX B Marginal Rate
$10,000	$1,500	15 %		$1,500	15 %	
			15 %			20 %
$20,000	3,000	15 %		3,500	17.5 %	
			15 %			25 %
$30,000	4,500	15 %		6,000	20 %	
			15 %			30 %
$40,000	6,000	15 %		9,000	22.5 %	
Type of tax:		proportional			progressive	

ESSAY QUESTIONS

1. During the past 15 years, there has been a controversy over the appropriate scope of government regulation. Take the government agencies on pp. 74-75 in the textbook, and divide them into three lists—agencies that you consider clearly desirable, those that are clearly undesirable, and ones you are not sure about. (You are not required to put any particular number on any of the lists. One or two of the lists may be blank if there are no such agencies.) In each case, explain briefly why you put the agency on the list you did.

2. In most communities, the following services are provided by the local government:

   a. Police
   b. Elementary education
   c. Street cleaning
   d. Garbage collection

Could these be provided by private enterprise? Is there any advantage in having them provided by the government? Would there be any advantage in having them provided by the private sector?

3. What externalities are created by individuals:

   a. driving on a highway
   b. mowing their lawn
   c. smoking in a theater

In each case, do you think that the government should do anything to encourage or discourage the activity? If so, what, and why? If not, why not?

ANSWERS

Matching columns: 1 f, 2 d, 3 b, 4 a, 5 j, 6 i, 7 c, 8 h, 9 e, 10 g

True-False:
1 T (p. 67)
2 F (p. 67)
3 T (pp. 67-68)
4 F (p. 68)
5 T (p. 69)
6 F (p. 69)
7 F (p. 69)
8 F (p. 72)
9 F (p. 73)
10 F (p. 76)

Multiple Choice:
1 a (p. 67)
2 d (p. 68)
3 b (p. 68)
4 d (p. 68)
5 e (p. 68)
6 c (p. 69)
7 b (p. 69)
8 c (p. 69)
9 c (p. 69)
10 e (p. 70)
11 e (p. 70)
12 e (p. 70)
13 a (p. 71)
14 d (p. 72)
15 b (p. 73)
16 e (p. 74)
17 d (p. 76)
18 c (p. 76)
19 c (p. 76)
20 c (p. 76)

Exercises

1.   Tax A.
        Average rates: 15%, 15%, 15%, 15%.
        Marginal rates: 15%, 15%, 15%.
        The tax is proportional.

        Tax B.
        Average rates: 15%, 17.5%, 20%, 22.5%.
        Marginal rates: 20%, 25%, 30%.
        The tax is progressive.

2. $750, $1,500, greater.

PART 2

AN INTRODUCTION TO MACROECONOMICS:
High Employment And A Stable Price Level

CHAPTER 6

MEASURING NATIONAL PRODUCT AND NATIONAL INCOME

LEARNING OBJECTIVES

After you have studied this chapter in the textbook and study guide, you should be able to:

✔ State the relationship between gross investment, net investment, depreciation, and the change in the stock of capital

✔ State the major differences between GNP and NNP, between NNP and National income, between National income and Personal income, and between Personal income and Disposable personal income. (See Fig. 6-3 in the textbook)

✔ State the relationship between nominal GNP, real GNP, and the GNP deflator. That is, you should understand equation 6-6.

✔ Explain why the GNP deflator is not exactly the same as the consumer price index

✔ Explain why real GNP is a better measure of how we are doing than is nominal GNP

✔ Explain why real GNP is nevertheless not a very good way to measure how well we are doing

✔ Explain why it is so hard to calculate a more comprehensive measure of economic welfare

✔ Explain why the *underground economy* exists, why its size may have increased in recent years, and why this is of concern to economists

MAJOR PURPOSE

Macroeconomics is about the *overall magnitudes* in the economy—total output and the average level of prices. The main purpose of this chapter is to provide an introduction to macroeconomics by explaining how total output and the average level of prices are measured. In calculating total output—or GNP—we want to *count everything* that is produced *once, but only once*. This means that there is an important problem to be avoided—the problem of double counting. This problem can be avoided by counting only final products such as TV sets, and excluding intermediate products such as the wire and chips that went into the TV set.

Another important objective of the chapter is to draw a *distinction between nominal* (or current-dollar) *magnitudes and real* (or constant-dollar) *magnitudes.* Through time, GNP measured in dollar terms goes up rapidly. This rapid increase is the combined result of two things:

- there is an increase in the quantity of goods and services that we are producing, and

- the prices at which these goods and services are sold are going up.

The first of these is desirable; the second is not. To see what is happening in real terms, national product accountants eliminate the effects of inflation. They do this by measuring the GNP of each year in the prices of a single base year, 1982.

HIGHLIGHTS OF CHAPTER

This chapter explains how national product is measured, in both *real* and *nominal* terms. It also explains some of the limitations of GNP as a measure of economic welfare.

To calculate the total output of the nation, we must somehow add apples and oranges, steel and airplanes, haircuts and medical services. The only reasonable way to add up different goods and services is to add together the total amount of money spent on each of them. Thus, when we put together a measure of national product, we use *market prices* as a way of judging the comparative importance of each product. A car selling for $10,000 contributes as much to national product as do 20,000 bottles of Coca-Cola selling for $.50 each.

When we measure national product, we want to measure everything produced in the economy (except for illegal products). However, we have to be careful. If we took the value of all the cars produced in the economy, plus all the steel and all the tires, then we would be exaggerating our output. Why is that? The answer is: because much of the steel and many of the tires were used by car manufacturers to produce their cars. We didn't produce a car plus four tires, but the car into which the four tires went.

To *avoid double counting* of tires, steel, and other intermediate products, national product accountants concentrate on *final products*. These are placed in four main categories:

- consumer expenditures for goods and services,

- investment,

- government purchases of goods and services, and

- net exports (that is, exports minus imports).

Investment is perhaps the trickiest of these four to understand precisely. The first important point is that we are dealing with the production of capital goods—buildings, machines, etc.—and not what Wall Streeters mean by investment. That is, we do not include financial investments—such as the purchase of common stock—in the investment category of GNP. The reason is straightforward. When individual A buys 100 shares of common stock from B, there is simply a transfer of ownership, not a direct increase in production. (Of course, the ability of firms to issue stock or bonds may help them to finance new factories, and these new factories are included in GNP.) Recall that this distinction between financial capital (such as stocks and bonds) and capital goods (such as factories) was made back in Chapter 2.

A second complication with investment is that it includes some intermediate products, such as steel, tires, or wheat. Specifically, it includes the increases in our inventories of such products. These inventory increases are something we have produced during the year. They are not included elsewhere—for example, they have not yet been used in the production of consumer goods. They have not yet been included when we count consumer goods. Therefore, they are counted here, in the investment category.

The final complication is that, when we count all the factories and machines produced during the year, we are in an important sense exaggerating what we have produced. The reason is that existing factories and machines have been wearing out and becoming obsolete during the year. What we should be measuring is not the total production of capital goods during the year, but only the increase in our capital stock. In other words, it would make sense to include only the increase in the stock of equipment, plant, and residential buildings, just as we include only the increase in the stocks of inventories.

This leads to the distinction between net investment and gross investment. Gross investment (I_g) is total output of plant, equipment, residential buildings, and increases in inventories. Net investment (I_n) is just the increase in our stock of plant, equipment, residential buildings, and inventories. The difference between the two is depreciation (Figure 6-2). GNP includes gross investment; NNP includes net investment. Accordingly, the difference between GNP and NNP is also depreciation (Figure 6-3).

Other important magnitudes—national income, personal income, and disposable personal income—are also shown in Figure 6-3. While you should not try to memorize the numbers on that figure, you should know the differences between the five major measures. You should also have a general idea of the magnitudes. For example, you should know that personal saving is less than 10% of disposable income; it is not 20% or 30%.

We have seen that market prices provide a feasible way to add various products. But, when we use market prices, a complication arises. Today, a person can use $100 to buy food, or clothing, or other things. The relative prices of food, clothing, or other things represents the relative amounts that people pay for the various goods; it is a way of measuring their relative value. But a person can't shop now out of the Sears catalogue of 1970. A car bought for $10,000 now is not worth four times as much as the car that sold for $2,500 in 1965. Money has lost some of its value as a result of inflation.

This raises an important problem. We want to use GNP figures as one measure of how well the economy is performing, of how large the economy is now as compared to the way it was 5 or 10 years ago. If we simply used GNP measured at current prices, we would not know what to do with the comparison. Does a higher GNP today reflect success; are we producing more? Or does it simply reflect our failure to prevent inflation? In practice, it is likely to reflect both.

In order to separate the undesirable increase in prices from the desirable increase in output, national product accountants calculate constant-dollar GNP. That is, they calculate what GNP would have been if prices had remained what they were in a single base year. Such constant-dollar or real GNP figures represent what has been happening to output over time.

Although real GNP is an important measure of the performance of the economy, it has major defects which mean that we should not concentrate single-mindedly on increasing real GNP. A lot of important things don't appear in GNP—the quality of the physical environment, the stability of the political system, or the degree of social harmony, to name but a few. Because of limits of GNP as a measure of welfare, some economists have considered the possibility of a broader measure, to include important features of our economic performance that are left out of GNP. This attempt has not been very successful. The problems are apparently insoluble. In particular, it is not clear how leisure should be counted. In the period studied by Nordhaus and Tobin per capita real NNP rose 90%, while leisure per capita rose 22%. It is not clear what this means, in terms of an overall measure. Were we more than 90% better off, since we had 90% more goods and more leisure too? Or was the improvement only some average of the 90% and the 22%? The answer is not obvious. The most promising approach is therefore not to search for some comprehensive single measure of welfare, but to look at a number of measures simultaneously—for example, not only real NNP, but also literacy, life expectancy, infant mortality, etc.

IMPORTANT TERMS

Match the first column with the corresponding phrase in the second column.

_d_	1. GNP	a.	Personal income - [income taxes and other personal taxes]
_i_	2. NNP	b.	Good intended for resale or further processing
_f_	3. National Income	c.	Production of plant, equipment, and housing, and changes in inventories
_a_	4. Disposable income	d.	NNP + depreciation
_h_	5. Depreciation	e.	Remove the effects of inflation from a time series
_c_	6. Real investment	f.	NNP - sales taxes
_j_	7. Financial investment	g.	Unreported income
_b_	8. Intermediate product	h.	GNP - NNP
_k_	9. Value added	i.	$C + G + I_n + X - M$
_e_	10. Deflate	j.	Acquisition of bonds and corporate stocks
_g_	11. Underground economy	k.	Sales minus cost of intermediate products bought from outside suppliers

TRUE-FALSE

T   F   1.   The easiest way to calculate GNP is to add the sales of all corporations.

T   F   2.   Gross private domestic investment includes all the money spent on U.S. stock exchanges during the year, but it excludes money spent by Americans on foreign stock exchanges.

T   F   3.   It is possible for inventory investment to be negative during a year.

T   F   4.   It is possible for gross investment in plant and equipment to be negative during a year.

T   F   5.   GNP can be determined by adding sales taxes to NNP.

T   F   6.   It is possible for net exports to be negative during a year.

T   F   7.   Suppose that there are no sales taxes in an economy. Then personal income will be the same as national income.

T   F   8.   If real GNP has gone up and the price index has gone up, then we can be sure that nominal GNP has gone up.

MULTIPLE CHOICE

1.   Which of the following is the best example of an intermediate product?

   a. a road
   b. steel
   c. bread
   d. a TV set
   e. an automobile

2.   In the GNP accounts, which of the following is included as a final product

   a. a plane bought by the government
   b. government expenditures to resurface roads
   c. purchases of washing machines by households
   d. purchases of washing machines by laundromats
   e. all of the above

3.   Suppose that a firm sells its output for $40,000. It pays $22,000 in wages and salaries, $10,000 for materials bought from other firms, $3,000 for interest on its bonds, and it has profits of $5,000. Then its value added is:

   a. $18,000
   b. $22,000

   c. $30,000
   d. $35,000
   e. $37,000

4.   In the GNP accounts, increases in inventories are

   a. excluded, since they are made up mostly of intermediate goods
   b. included as part of the consumption category, since they are made up mostly of consumer goods
   c. included as part of the government category, together with other miscellaneous items
   d. included as part of the investment category
   e. included as an item separate from C, I, and G

5.   Suppose we know $C + I_g + G$. Then, to get GNP, we should:

   a. add depreciation
   b. subtract depreciation
   c. add the increase in inventories
   d. add sales taxes
   e. add exports and subtract imports

6. Last year, the XYZ manufacturing corporation issued $10 million in new common stock, and used $8 million of the proceeds to build a new factory. The other $2 billion was used to repay bank loans, and replenish XYZ's deposits at its banks. As a result, GNP went up by:

   a. the $8 million spent for the factory
   b. the $10 million in new common stock
   c. $12 million
   d. $18 million
   e. $20 million

7. The GNP statistics show that gross investment in 1988 was $766 billion, while depreciation was $506. We may conclude that:

   a. net investment was $1,272 billion
   b. net investment was $260 billion
   c. net investment was -$260 billion
   d. net investment was negative, but we don't know how much
   e. inventory accumulation was negative

8. Some years ago, the Department of Commerce published a statistical report that, in 1932, gross private domestic investment in the United States was $1.0 billion, while depreciation was $7.6 billion. What conclusion may we come to?

   a. net investment was larger than gross investment
   b. net investment was negative; the capital stock was smaller at the end of the year than at the beginning
   c. most investment was in the form of inventory accumulation
   d. imports were larger than exports
   e. there is something wrong with the statistics; maybe the Department of Commerce got gross investment and depreciation mixed up

9. Suppose that gross investment has been 10% of GNP, but then it falls to zero during the current year. In the current year:

   a. depreciation is the same size as inventory accumulation
   b. depreciation is the same size as gross investment
   c. depreciation is also zero
   d. net investment is also zero
   e. net investment is negative

10. Consider the following **incorrect** definition. National Income equals the sum of: wages and salaries, rent and interest, proprietors' income, net exports, and corporation profits. To make this statement **correct**, one item should be deleted. This item is:

    a. wages and salaries
    b. rent and interest
    c. proprietors' income
    d. net exports
    e. corporation profits

The next 6 questions are based on the following table, which shows national product in a simple economy with only guns and butter

	Production of guns	Price of guns	Production of consumer goods	Price of consumer goods
1982	200	$1,000	1,000	$500
1990	250	$2,000	2,000	$1,500

11. In this simple economy, current-dollar GNP in 1982 was:

    a. $700,000
    b. $1,250,000
    c. $1,900,000
    d. $3,500,000
    e. $4,200,000

12. In this simple economy, current-dollar GNP in 1990 is:

    a. $700,000
    b. $1,250,000
    c. $1,900,000
    d. $3,500,000
    e. $4,200,000

13. Suppose that 1982 is the base year in this simple economy. Real GNP in 1990 is:

    a. $700,000
    b. $1,250,000
    c. $1,900,000
    d. $3,500,000
    e. $4,200,000

14. Suppose that 1982 is the base year in this simple economy. In this economy, the GNP deflator in 1990 is:

    a. 162.5
    b. 250
    c. 271
    d. 280
    e. 300

    $$\frac{3,500,000 \times 100}{1,250,000}$$

15. In this economy, the average level of prices rose how much between 1982 and 1990?

    a. 150%
    b. 171%
    c. 180%
    d. 200%
    e. 280%

    $$\frac{C\ Price}{R\ Price} \times 100 = \frac{3,500,000}{1,250,000} \times 100$$
    $$= 280\%$$
    $$2\text{倍}=1982$$
    $$1.8\text{倍}=1982$$
    rose 180

16. In this economy, real GNP rose how much between 1982 and 1990?

    a. 52%
    b. 79%
    c. 152%
    d. 179%
    e. 204%

    $$\frac{RGNP_{1990}}{RGNP_{1982}} \times 100 = \frac{1,250,000}{700,000} \times 100$$
    $$= 178.5\%$$
    $$= 179\%$$
    rose 79%

17. This year's nominal GNP measures

    a. this year's output at base-year prices
    b. this year's output at this year's prices
    c. NNP less depreciation
    d. National income less depreciation
    e. NNP less sales taxes

18. Suppose that, since the base year, all prices have risen by 100%. This year's current-dollar GNP is $2,000 billion. Then constant-dollar GNP is

    a. $4,000 billion
    b. $3,000 billion
    c. $2,000 billion
    d. $1,000 billion
    e. $500 billion

19. Suppose we divide current-dollar GNP for 1986 by constant-dollar GNP for 1986. Then the resulting figure is a measure of

    a. inflation during 1986
    b. real output during 1986
    c. nominal output during 1986
    d. the GNP price deflator for 1986
    e. depreciation

20. Last year, Sam Brown spent each Saturday from May to November building a new wing on his family home. In last year's GNP:

    a. the full market value of the wing is included
    b. the lumber, windows, paint, and other materials he bought at the store were included, but the value of his labor was not
    c. the full market value of the wing was included, plus an additional 10% if the Commerce Department's survey found that he actually enjoyed building the wing
    d. the wing was not included at all, since it was not a market transaction
    e. the wing was not included at all, since it probably is not as good as one built by a professional builder

EXERCISES

1. Suppose you have the following incomplete data:

C	$900
I_g	400
Wages and salaries	800
Interest and rent	100
Corporate profits (after taxes)	250
Personal taxes	350
Depreciation	50
G	450
Corporate income taxes	150
Contributions to social security	0
Sales taxes	200
Transfer payments	200
Undistributed corporate profits — *Retained profits*	150
Proprietors' income	400

Compute the following:

NI _____
NNP _____
GNP _____
(X - M) _____
Personal income _____
Disposable personal income _____
I_n _____

2. Suppose a country produces two goods, a consumption good and an investment good. The first two rows of Table 6-1 give the current-dollar value of the total production of the two goods. Fill in the next row indicating nominal GNP each year. The next two rows indicate the market prices of the two goods each year. Fill in the next two rows giving the number of units of each good produced each year. Then fill in the final four rows, using 1982 as the base year.

Table 6-1

	1982	1985	1990
Current-dollar value of C production	200	450	600
Current-dollar value of I production	100	150	200
Nominal GNP			
Price of C	5	9	10
Price of I	20	25	40
Quantity of C production			
Quantity of I production			
Constant-dollar value of C production			
Constant-dollar value of I production			
Real GNP			
GNP deflator			

ESSAY QUESTIONS

1. In what ways does GNP **overstate** economic well-being? In what ways does it **understate** economic well-being? ① *If count intermediate product.* ② *underground economy*

2. Do the per-capita NNP figures of two countries give a measure of their relative economic welfare? Explain the major deficiencies of NNP as a way of comparing welfare in different countries.

3. "Transfer payments to the poor and the elderly are **not** included in the G segment of national product. But the assistance to the poor and elderly make very important contributions to economic welfare. Therefore, transfer payments should be added, to get a better measure of GNP." Do you agree or not? Explain why.

ANSWERS

Exercises

1.

NI	1,700
NNP	1,900
GNP	1,950
X - M	200
Personal income	1,600
Disposable personal income	1,250
I_n	350

2.

Table 6-1

	1982	1985	1990
Nominal GNP	300	600	800
Quantity of C production	40	50	60
Quantity of I production	5	6	5
Constant-dollar value of C production	200	250	300
Constant-dollar value of I production	100	120	100
Real GNP	300	370	400
GNP deflator	100	162	200

CHAPTER 7

FLUCTUATIONS IN ECONOMIC ACTIVITY

LEARNING OBJECTIVES

After you have studied this chapter in the textbook and study guide, you should be able to

✔ Describe the four phases of the business cycle

✔ Describe the major features of the Great Depression of the 1930s

✔ Explain the major features of recent business cycles — for example, what happens to profits, investment, and the purchase of consumer durables during recessions?

✔ Explain how the unemployment rate is calculated

✔ Explain why the unemployment rate may understate the problem of unemployment during a recession

✔ Explain why the productivity of labor is adversely affected by recessions

✔ State what Okun's Law is

✔ List the three major types of unemployment, and explain how they are different

✔ Explain potential GNP and the GNP gap

MAJOR PURPOSE

This chapter describes the two major macroeconomic problems — **unemployment** and **inflation**. These two problems are closely related to **economic fluctuations**. During recessions, when output is declining, fewer workers are needed by business and the unemployment rate increases. During a rapid expansion, when spending by businesses and consumers is rising rapidly,

inflation generally becomes more severe. Economic conditions were most unstable in the United States during the period between the two world wars. Between 1929 and 1933, output collapsed and the unemployment rate shot upward.

This chapter explains how the business cycle is divided into its four phases:

- **recession,**
- **trough,**
- **expansion,** and
- **peak.**

It also describes how unemployment rises, while output and profits decline during recessions. Inflation generally declines during the later part of recessions and during early recoveries.

This chapter explains how the unemployment rate is calculated, and the various major types of unemployment. **Cyclical** unemployment is the result of fluctuations in overall economic activity. Reducing this type of unemployment is one of the major objectives of economic policy. **Frictional** unemployment results from the normal turnover of the labor force; some amount of frictional unemployment is inevitable. **Structural** unemployment arises when the labor force does not have the type of skills needed for available jobs, or if workers live a long distance from available jobs. This type of unemployment is more severe than frictional unemployment. To escape structural unemployment, people must move or switch to different types of work.

The U.S. economy is quite flexible and changes rapidly. Even in the best of times, the unemployment rate does not get down to zero. It is not possible to identify any specific, unchanging unemployment rate as "full employment." During the 1960s, the government believed that it would be possible to lower the unemployment rate to 4% without generating strong inflationary pressures; 4% was therefore generally taken as the "full-employment target." During the 1970s, 4% seemed unachievable; discussions of full employment focussed on the unemployment range between 5.5% and 6%. During the 1980s, this figure has been revised downward.

The most important characteristics of recessions are higher unemployment and declining output. The shortfall of output below the economy's potential is known as the **GNP gap**; it is a measure of output lost because of slack in the economy.

HIGHLIGHTS OF CHAPTER

The business cycle has four phases. During a **recession**, economic activity declines, and the unemployment rate increases. Economic activity reaches its low point at the **trough**. This is followed by the **expansion** phase, which ends at the upper turning point or **peak**. The key to identifying a business cycle is to tell when a recession has occurred. Not every downward jiggle is called a recession; the downward movement must be significant. The National Bureau of Economic Research decides whether downturns are significant enough to be called recessions. Its starting point is historical: Is the downward slide as severe as the declines of the past which have been called recessions? A simpler rule of thumb has often been used as a quick and ready method of identifying a recession: Has real GNP declined for two or more quarters? While this rule of thumb can be used to identify most recessions, it is not foolproof. Output did not decline for two quarters during the recession of 1980.

The most severe downturn in history occurred between 1929 and 1933 as the economies of the United States and many other countries collapsed into the Great Depression. In this chapter, the main events of the Great Depression are summarized. Although the depression may seem like ancient history, it remains a lesson in how badly things can go wrong. It thus provides a reason for studying macroeconomics. If things can go this badly when macroeconomic policy is mismanaged, it is important to have some idea of what macroeconomic policy is all about.

Between 1929 and 1933, the unemployment rate in the United States rose to almost 25%, real GNP fell 30%, and the average level of prices declined more than 20%. The production of capital equipment, buildings, and consumer durables fell particularly sharply. On the farm, the depression caused a collapse of prices. On international markets, commodity prices also collapsed. International trade fell precipitously, by about two thirds in nominal terms between 1929 and 1933.

Recent recessions have been much *milder* than the downturn of 1929-33. Some have been very short and mild indeed — for example, the recession of early 1980. However, there has been no noticeable tendency for recessions to become progressively more mild over the past four decades. Two recent recessions were severe — those of 1973-75 and 1981-82.

The unemployment rate is calculated by the Bureau of Labor Statistics, as a percentage of the labor force. The unemployed are people who are out of work who

- are temporarily laid off but expect to be recalled,
- are waiting to report to a new job, or

- have been looking for work in the previous four weeks.

If people without jobs do not meet one of these conditions, they are considered to be out of the labor force. The labor force is made up of those with jobs, plus those who are unemployed according to the above criteria.

During recessions, it becomes harder to find a job. As a result, those out of work may become discouraged and stop looking for work. In this case, they drop out of the officially-measured labor force and out of the ranks of those who are counted as unemployed. Consequently, the unemployment rate may understate the unemployment problem during recessions. Nevertheless, the unemployment rate is one important indicator of what is happening during recessions.

During recessions, as sales of products fall, businesses lay off some employees. However, they are often reluctant to lay off highly skilled workers, since these workers may take jobs elsewhere and be unavailable when sales recover. Hence, employment does not fall as much as output. There is a decline in output per worker—that is, in the **productivity of labor**.

As the unemployment rate increases during recessions, so does the number of those who have been unemployed for a long period of time. Not only are more people unemployed, but the hardship faced by the average unemployed person also becomes more severe.

Not all groups are affected equally by unemployment. The unemployment rate for teenagers—particularly minority teenagers—is much higher than for adults.

No matter how prosperous the economy becomes, it is not possible to eliminate unemployment altogether. *Frictional* unemployment represents those who are temporarily unemployed because they are looking for a better job, or because of adjustments associated with a dynamic, changing economy. In a changing economy, there is always some frictional unemployment.

Thus, if full employment is to be a meaningful goal, it cannot be defined as an unemployment rate of zero. There is some debate over the unemployment rate that should be considered full employment. During the 1960s, an unemployment rate of 4% was frequently looked on as representing full employment. Most economists put the figure higher—at 6% or even 7%—during the 1970s. During the 1980s, the figure identified as full employment was reduced to the range between 5% and 5.5%. Chapters 13 and 14 will investigate the idea of full employment in detail.

Potential GNP is estimated as the GNP path along which the economy would move if there were no business cycles and a high level of employment were maintained continuously. The shortfall of actual GNP below the estimated potential is the **GNP gap**. It provides an estimate of the output lost because of recessions.

IMPORTANT TERMS

Match the first column with the corresponding phrase in the second column.

_b_ 1. Recession	
_f_ 2. Trough	
_j_ 3. Peak	
_i_ 4. Underemployed	
_c_ 5. Discouraged workers	
_e_ 6. Okun's Law	
_h_ 7. Frictional unemployment	
_a_ 8. Structural unemployment	
_k_ 9. Cyclical unemployment	
_g_ 10. Potential GNP	
_d_ 11. GNP gap	

a. To reduce this unemployment, people must move or acquire new skills

b. Downward movement of the economy, usually lasting two quarters or more

c. Those who have dropped out of the labor force because they were unable to find work

d. Potential output less actual output

e. Observation that unemployment rate moves less strongly than output during the business cycle

f. Turning point at the end of a recession

g. What output would be if the economy were at full employment

h. Unemployment associated with adjustments in a changing, dynamic economy

i. Discouraged workers plus those who are not kept busy because demand is low

j. Turning point as a recession is about to begin

k. Unemployment caused by recessions

TRUE-FALSE

T   F   1.   During the Great Depression, the prices of agricultural products fell much more than the prices of manufactured products.

T   F   2.   Recessions in the U.S. economy have become consistently less and less severe over the past three decades.

T   F   3.   Inflation responds to changes in business conditions. During rapid expansions of real output, the rate of inflation generally increases, and it generally decreased during recessions. However, inflation does not respond immediately; it responds with a lag.

T   F   4.   In percentage terms, investment fluctuates less than consumption, but more than total GNP, during the typical business cycle.

T   F   5.   During the business cycle, consumer spending for durable goods fluctuates more than consumer spending for nondurable goods.

T   F   6.   People temporarily laid off, but waiting to be recalled, are included among the unemployed.

T   F   7.   During a recession, as workers are laid off, the remaining workers can use the best equipment. Therefore, productivity of those remaining at work generally increases rapidly during a recession.

T   F   8.   According to Okun's Law, recessions occur regularly, at intervals of between 5 and 7 years.

MULTIPLE CHOICE

1. Between the peak of 1929 and the trough of the Great Depression in 1933, U.S. real GNP fell by approximately:

   a. 30%
   b. 15%
   c. 10%
   d. 5%
   e. 2%

2. Which of the following is a turning point in the business cycle?

   a. Expansion
   b. Recovery
   c. Peak
   d. Recession
   e. Depression

3. A simple, unofficial definition of recession has often been used by economists and journalists. According to this definition, a recession occurs when seasonally-adjusted real GNP falls for at least:

   a. one month
   b. two months
   c. three months
   d. two quarters
   e. four quarters

4. Between the peak of 1929 and the trough of the Great Depression in 1933, the prices of agricultural commodities:

   a. rose about 15%, in spite of the decline in the prices of most other goods
   b. remained stable, in spite of the decline in the prices of most other goods
   c. remained stable, in spite of the increase in the prices of most other goods
   d. fell about 10%, or slightly less than the average of other prices
   e. fell much more than the average of other prices

5. During the collapse into the Great Depression between 1929 and 1933, the imports of most countries:

   a. declined by a greater percentage than GNP
   b. declined by about the same percentage as GNP
   c. declined by a smaller percentage than GNP
   d. remained approximately constant
   e. increased, in spite of the general decline in GNP

6. During the typical recession,

   a. profits, wages, and prices all fall sharply (normally by 10% or more)
   b. profits fall sharply, while wages and prices respond only slowly
   c. wages fall sharply, while prices and profits respond only slowly
   d. prices fall sharply, while wages and profits respond only slowly
   e. profits, wages, and prices all normally rise by 10% or more

7. During the typical recession,

   a. government spending falls more than consumption
   b. government spending falls more than investment
   c. consumption falls more than investment
   d. investment falls more than consumption
   e. consumption and investment generally increase, but at a slow rate

8. During recent decades, one sector of GNP has accounted for much of the downward movement during recessions. Recent recessions are therefore often referred to as:

   a. export recessions
   b. import recessions
   c. inventory recessions
   d. government recessions
   e. consumption recessions

9. The labor force includes:

   a. only those who are employed
   b. those who are employed, plus the unemployed
   c. the total population, less retirees
   d. the total population, less retirees and students
   e. the total population, less retirees, students, and government workers

10. Assume that the population is 200 million, the labor force is 100 million, and 90 million people are employed. Then, the unemployment rate is:

   a. 4.5%
   b. 5%
   c. 9%
   d. 10%
   e. 55%

11. Which of the following groups is **not** counted as being unemployed?

   a. People who have left school and are still looking for their first job
   b. People who are reentering the labor force, and are still looking for jobs
   c. People who are on temporary layoff, but are not looking for jobs because they expect to be recalled in the near future
   d. People who have been recently fired, and are looking for new jobs
   e. Retired people

12. Suppose a person lost a factory job six months ago, spent 3 months in a fruitless search for work, and then stopped looking. In the collection of official statistics, such a person is considered:

   a. still employed in the factory job
   b. structurally unemployed
   c. cyclically unemployed
   d. frictionally unemployed
   e. out of the labor force

13. Who best fits into the category of the "underemployed"?

   a. College students
   b. High school students
   c. Government workers
   d. Executives of major corporations
   e. People who can only find part-time work when they want full-time work

14. The productivity of labor is:

   a. output divided by the number of hours of labor input
   b. the extra amount produced by skilled workers, as compared to unskilled workers
   c. the extra amount produced by people with colege degrees, as compared to those without degrees
   d. the increase in the amount produced by the typical factory worker during the twentieth century
   e. the increase in the amount produced by the typical farm worker during the twentieth century

15. Okun's Law refers to what phenomenon?

    a. Employment fluctuates by a greater percentage than output during the business cycle
    b. Output fluctuates by a greater percentage than employment during the business cycle
    c. Investment fluctuates by a greater percentage than consumption during the business cycle
    d. Inventories fluctuate by a greater percentage than gross investment during the business cycle
    e. Investment fluctuates by a greater percentage than government spending during the business cycle

16. During a recession, the number of long-term unemployed (more than 15 weeks):

    a. rises, by a greater percent than the overall number of unemployed
    b. rises, but by a smaller percent than the overall number of unemployed
    c. is quite stable, since some of the unemployed get work as the labor force is reshuffled
    d. falls, since some of the unemployed get work as the labor force is reshuffled
    e. falls, since the government is most willing to help the unemployed during recessions

17. According to the official definition of unemployment, which of the following groups has the highest unemployment rate?

    a. Men
    b. Women
    c. Teenagers

    d. College students aged 20 and over
    e. Retirees

18. A major objective of macroeconomic policy is to reduce:

    a. cyclical unemployment
    b. frictional unemployment
    c. labor mobility
    d. product innovations
    e. all of the above

19. During the past three decades, the unemployment rate generally considered to represent "full employment":

    a. has been stable at 0%; at no other rate is there "full employment"
    b. has been stable, at about 4%
    c. has fallen, from about 10% to about 4%, as the economy recovered from the Great Depression
    d. has fallen, from about 8% to about 4%
    e. first rose from about 4% to 6% or 7% during the 1970s, and then fell to about 5.5% during the 1980s

20. Suppose that the unemployment rate this month is 10%. Then we can conclude that:

    a. the economy is still declining into a recession
    b. the economy is at the trough
    c. the economy has passed the trough, and is now in a recovery
    d. actual GNP is less than potential GNP
    e. potential GNP is less than actual GNP

EXERCISES

1. During recessions, output declines. So does employment (by even more than output, but by less than output). The relationship between changes and output and changes in unemployment is known as (Keynes' Law, Okun's Law). This relationship is reflected in a (rapid rise in productivity, fall in productivity) during the typical recession.

When a recession becomes very severe, it is called a (depression, stagnation). This occurred during the 1930s. At that time, prices fell, particularly those of (manufactured goods, agricultural commodities). Output declined very sharply, especially the output of (manufactured goods, agricultural commodities). There was a particularly sharp decline in the output of (consumer goods, capital goods). At that time, (cyclical, frictional, structural) unemployment was very high.

2. Figure 7.1 shows fluctuations in real output. Recessions occurred during the time periods _A-B_ and _C D_, and expansions during the periods _B C_ and _D E_. Peaks occurred at _A_ and _C_, while troughs occurred at _B_ and _D_.

Figure 7-1

Real GNP

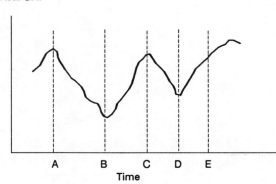

Time

ESSAY QUESTIONS

1. Explain why, during a recession:

   a. production of consumer durable goods decreases more than production of consumer nondurables
   b. production of capital goods decreases more than production of consumer nondurable goods
   c. output generally declines more than employment
   d. labor productivity generally declines

2. Explain the conceptual difference between structural and frictional unemployment. Explain also why it may be difficult in practice to distinguish whether specific unemployed individuals are part of "structural" or "frictional" unemployment. Might it also be difficult to tell if specific individuals are part of "frictional" or "cyclical" unemployment? Why or why not?

ANSWERS

Important terms: 1 b, 2 f, 3 j, 4 i, 5 c, 6 e, 7 h, 8 a, 9 k, 10 g, 11 d

True-False: 1 T (p. 103)
2 F (p. 103)
3 T (p. 105)
4 F (p. 107)
5 T (p. 107)
6 T (p. 108)
7 F (p. 109)
8 F (p. 110)

Multiple Choice:

1 a (p. 100)
2 c (p. 102)
3 d (p. 102)
4 e (p. 103)
5 a (p. 104)
6 b (p. 105)
7 d (p. 107)
8 c (p. 107)
9 b (p. 108)
10 d (p. 108)
11 e (p. 108)
12 e (p. 108)
13 e (p. 108)
14 a (p. 109)
15 b (p. 110)
16 a (p. 110)
17 c (p. 111)
18 a (p. 112)
19 e (p. 115)
20 d (pp. 115-116)

Exercises

1. but by less than output, Okun's Law, fall in productivity, depression, agricultural commodities, manufactured goods, capital goods, cyclical.

2. AB, CD, BC, DE, A, C, B, D.

CHAPTER 8

AGGREGATE DEMAND AND AGGREGATE SUPPLY:
Classical and Keynesian Equilibria

LEARNING OBJECTIVES

After you have studied this chapter in the textbook and study guide, you should be able to

✔ Explain why we should not just assume that aggregate demand and supply curves look like demand and supply curves for an individual product

✔ Draw the aggregate demand curve of classical economists, and explain why it slopes downward to the right

✔ Explain why classical economists drew the aggregate supply function as a vertical line

✔ Explain why the simple version of the Keynesian aggregate supply curve is a reversed L, and what the explanation is for the horizontal section

✔ List the four major components of aggregate demand that Keynesians consider in detail to determine what is happening to aggregate demand as a whole

✔ Explain why classical economists believed that equilibrium would occur at full employment, while Keynesian economists believed that equilibrium might occur either at full employment or with large-scale unemployment

✔ Summarize how classical economists explained the Great Depression of the 1930s

✔ Summarize the three major propositions in Keynes' *General Theory*, including his major policy conclusion

✔ Summarize the major points of agreement between Keynesians and those in the classical tradition, and the major points of disagreement

MAJOR PURPOSE

Chapter 7 provided an overview of macroeconomic problems—fluctuations in the overall level of production, periods of high unemployment, and the problem of inflation. The purpose of this chapter is to begin a study of *why* these macroeconomic problems arise. In explaining macroeconomic events, **aggregate supply** and **aggregate demand** are useful tools, just as supply and demand are useful in figuring out what is happening in the market for individual products such as hamburgers, shoes, or wheat.

The Great Depression of the 1930s was caused by a collapse in aggregate demand. The milder business cycles of recent decades have been caused primarily by more moderate fluctuations in aggregate demand. Thus, a more stable aggregate demand is the key to reducing fluctuations in output and employment.

HIGHLIGHTS OF CHAPTER

When studying the market for a specific good (such as apples or hamburgers), we use demand and supply curves. To study the overall behavior of the economy as a whole—changes in total output and the average level of prices—we likewise use aggregate demand and aggregate supply curves.

There are major differences between demand and supply in an individual market, and aggregate demand and aggregate supply for the economy as a whole. The major difference is that when drawing a demand or supply curve for, say, hamburgers, we are looking at what happens when *only* the price of this one good changes. (Recall the *ceteris paribus* assumption—that everything else remains unchanged.) Thus, an increase in the price of hamburgers represents a change in *relative* prices; the price of hamburgers rises *relative* to the prices of other goods. Consumers and producers respond to the change in relative prices. Consumers *switch* away from hamburgers and buy hot dogs or other products instead. Such switching is the major reason that the quantity of hamburgers is smaller when the price is higher. Similarly, producers have an incentive to switch. When the price of hamburgers rises, producers have an incentive to make hamburgers instead of other products. Their willingness to switch from other products, and to produce hamburgers instead, is the principal reason why the supply curve slopes upward to the right.

On the other hand, when we look at *aggregate* demand and aggregate supply, we are looking at the responses of buyers and sellers when the *overall* level of prices rises. In simple terms, we are looking at what happens when all prices rise by, say, 10%. Since *all* prices are rising, there is no change in relative prices. Thus, there is no reason for either buyers or sellers to switch as a result. Switching does *not* provide a reason for the slope of the aggregate demand or aggregate supply curve.

Nevertheless, classical economists believed that the aggregate supply curve sloped downward to the right. The reason was that a fall in the average level of prices would increase the purchasing power of money. When prices fell, people would be able to buy more goods and services with the money in their pockets and their bank accounts. Therefore, they would buy more.

However, classical economists did not draw the aggregate supply curve sloping upward to the right. Instead, they believed that it was vertical, at the full-employment or potential quantity of output. If, starting at full employment, all prices—including the price of raw materials and labor—were to increase by, say, 10%, then producers would have no incentive to produce more. They would get 10% more for their products, it is true, but they would have to pay 10% more for their inputs. Because they had the same incentive to produce, the total amount offered for sale would remain constant, regardless of the general level of prices.

Equilibrium occurred at the intersection of aggregate demand and aggregate supply. Because classical economists drew the aggregate supply curve as a vertical line at the full-employment output, they believed that there would be full employment whenever the economy was in equilibrium. This raised a question: How was the depression to be explained? Within the classical framework, large-scale unemployment could be caused by disturbances that resulted in a temporary **disequilibrium**. During the early 1930s, the economy moved away from its full employment equilibrium as a result of the reduction in the money stock and a fall in aggregate demand. Classical economists believed that full employment could be restored by a decrease in wages and prices, which would lead to a new equilibrium at a lower overall price level, or by an increase in the money stock, which would bring aggregate demand back up.

Keynes saw the world differently. He believed that there could be a *long-lasting equilibrium* with high unemployment. The simplest way to illustrate this is with the reversed-L aggregate supply function. In the horizontal range, prices and wages are downwardly rigid. If aggregate demand is so low that it leaves the economy in this horizontal range, then an unemployment equilibrium can persist. The solution to the depression, said Keynes, was to increase aggregate demand. The best way to get an increase would be through direct government action. The government had the responsibility, said Keynes, to increase its spending and thereby increase overall demand, leading the economy back toward full employment. (This major policy conclusion of Keynesian economics will be explained in detail in Chapter 10.)

The theoretical frameworks of both classical and Keynesian economics are still important, since they are both still used — in modified form — by present-day economists. In spite of the different approaches, there is a widespread agreement among economists on a number of central points:

- A sharp decline in aggregate demand can cause large-scale unemployment, as it did during the depression.

- More moderate fluctuations in aggregate demand can cause milder business cycles and temporary periods of high unemployment.

- If aggregate demand can be stabilized, the amplitude of business cycles can be reduced.

- When the economy is already at full employment, any large increase in aggregate demand will cause inflation.

Nevertheless, differences remain both in theoretical approach and in policy conclusions between Keynesian economists and those in the classical tradition. Most important are the following differences:

- Although most economists now believe that both monetary and fiscal policies are important, those in the classical tradition (monetarists) emphasize monetary policy, while those in the Keynesian tradition generally emphasize fiscal policies.

- Keynesians believe that the government has the responsibility to **manage aggregate demand** by changing fiscal and monetary policies from time to time, in order to stabilize demand and minimize business fluctuations. Monetarists believe that active management is more likely to destabilize than to stabilize aggregate demand. They generally advocate a **policy rule** — the authorities should aim for a slow, steady increase in the stock of money. They believe that this will result in a slow, steady increase in aggregate demand and keep the economy at or close to full employment, without causing inflation.

IMPORTANT TERMS

Match the first column with the corresponding phrase in the second column.

_e_	1.	Purchasing power of money
_i_	2.	Downward rigidity of prices
_k_	3.	Long run
_c_	4.	Classical aggregate supply
_j_	5.	Keynesian aggregate supply
_h_	6.	The classical equilibrium
_a_	7.	Cause of unemployment
_g_	8.	Cause of inflation
_f_	9.	Monetarist
_b_	10.	Monetarist policy
_d_	11.	Keynesian policy

a. Decline in aggregate demand
b. Money rule
c. Vertical line
d. Active demand management
e. What a dollar will buy
f. Present-day classicist
g. Too much aggregate demand
h. This occurs at full employment
i. This accounts for the horizontal section of Keynesian aggregate supply function
j. Reversed L
k. In classical economics, the period when prices and wages adjust to their equilibrium levels

TRUE-FALSE

T   F   1.   The aggregate demand curve slopes downward to the right because people switch way from services, and buy goods instead, when the average price of goods declines.

T   F   2.   Even if relative prices remain stable, the aggregate demand curve can nevertheless slope downward to the right.

T   F   3.   Classical economists explained the Great Depression as the result of a fall in the money stock, and downward stickiness of wages and prices.

T   F   4.   According to classical economists, brief recessions represented periods of disequilibrium, but the economy could be in an unemployment equilibrium during a major depression.

T   F   5.   According to classical economists, full employment could have been reestablished during the 1930s, but this would have required that both of two conditions be met: (1) a large increase in the money stock, and (2) flexibility of wages and prices.

T   F   6.   The major theoretical innovation in Keynes' *General Theory* was the proposition that the economy could reach an equilibrium with large-scale unemployment.

T   F   7.   Sticky wages and prices are the reason for the horizontal section of the Keynesian aggregate supply curve.

T   F   8.   One major shortcoming of Keynesian economics is that it assumes prices are permanently fixed. Inflation therefore cannot be explained within this theory.

T   F   9.   Those who believe that there should be a policy rule are most likely to advocate a slow, steady increase in the money stock.

T   F   10. Monetarists advocate a slow, steady increase in the money stock because they believe that the economy will work best with a slow, steady inflation.

MULTIPLE CHOICE

1. When we draw a classical aggregate demand curve, what do we put on the vertical axis?

    a. total quantity of goods demanded
    b. total quantity of goods and services demanded
    c. full-employment output
    d. the quantity of money
    e. the average level of prices

2. There is an important reason why we cannot conclude that the aggregate demand curve must slope downward to the right, just because the demand for an individual product slopes downward to the right. The reason is:

    a. there are no "other goods" for consumers to switch from
    b. relative prices rather than absolute prices are on the axis
    c. inflation-adjusted prices rather than relative prices are on the axis
    d. real prices rather than nominal prices are on the axis
    e. nominal prices rather than real prices are on the axis

3. According to the classical approach, people buy more goods and services when the price level falls (*ceteris paribus*) because:

   a. they switch among products when prices fall
   b. the purchasing power of their money has increased
   c. the purchasing power of their money has decreased
   d. the economy is coming out of a recession
   e. potential GNP has increased because of past investment

4. When the price level doubles, then the purchasing power of the dollar:

   a. also doubles
   b. increases, but only by 50%
   c. doesn't change much
   d. falls 50%
   e. falls 100%

5. Which of the following was put at the center of aggregate demand analysis by classical economists?

   a. money
   b. government spending
   c. the government's tax revenues
   d. tax rates
   e. investment

6. According to classical economists, the aggregate supply curve was:

   a. upward sloping, like the supply curve for wheat
   b. downward sloping, like the supply curve for wheat
   c. vertical, at potential GNP
   d. an L
   e. a reversed L

7. According to classical economists, when the economy was at equilibrium, then real GNP would be:

   a. about 10% above the level in the most recent recession
   b. above potential GNP
   c. at potential GNP
   d. below potential GNP
   e. either (c) or (d), but we can't tell which without information on aggregate demand

8. According to classical economists, the Great Depression represented:

   a. a disequilibrium caused by a fall in the quantity of money
   b. a disequilibrium caused by a fall in exports
   c. a disequilibrium with the twin problems of high inflation and high unemployment
   d. an equilibrium with the twin problems of high inflation and high unemployment
   e. an equilibrium with large-scale unemployment and falling prices

9. According to classical economists, if the economy suffers from a high level of unemployment, full employment can be reestablished by

   a. an increase in the productive capacity of the economy
   b. an increase in the price level
   c. a decrease in the price level
   d. an increase in the money stock
   e. either (c) or (d), or a combination of the two

10. According to classical economists, the best thing the government could do to prevent recessions and depressions would be to:

    a. cut government spending
    b. increase government spending
    c. provide a steady increase in the money stock
    d. promote investment
    e. promote imports

11. According to Keynes, the primary cause of large-scale unemployment is:

    a. high prices
    b. low prices
    c. high exports
    d. low exports
    e. inadequate aggregate demand

12. According to Keynes, when the economy was at equilibrium, then real GNP would be

    a. about 10% above the level in the most recent recession
    b. above potential GNP
    c. at potential GNP
    d. below potential GNP
    e. either (c) or (d), but we can't tell which without information on aggregate demand

13. In its simplest form, the Keynesian aggregate supply function was

    a. upward sloping, like the supply curve for wheat
    b. downward sloping, like the supply curve for wheat
    c. vertical, at potential GNP
    d. an L
    e. a reversed L

14. Consider the reversed L aggregate supply function of Keynesian economics. The effects of an increase in aggregate demand will differ, depending on where the economy begins. Specifically, an increase in aggregate demand will lead to:

    a. an increase in prices if the economy starts in the horizontal section, but an increase in output if it starts in the vertical section
    b. an increase in prices if the economy starts in the vertical section, but an increase in output if it starts in the horizontal section
    c. an increase in prices if the economy starts in the horizontal section, but a decrease in prices if it starts in the vertical section
    d. an increase in prices if the economy starts in the vertical section, but a decrease in prices if it starts in the horizontal section
    e. an increase in prices if the economy starts in the horizontal section, but a decrease in employment if it starts in the vertical section

15. The Keynesian and classical aggregate supply functions are similar in that they both

    a. have a horizontal range
    b. have an intermediate, upward-sloped range
    c. are based on the assumption of downward price rigidity
    d. are based on the assumption of price stickiness
    e. lead to the conclusion that a large increase in aggregate demand will cause inflation if the economy is already at full employment

16. According to Keynes,

    a. a collapse in investment demand was the primary cause of the depression, and an increase in investment demand provided the best hope of recovery
    b. a collapse in government spending was the primary cause of the depression, and an increase in government spending provided the best hope of recovery
    c. a collapse in investment demand was the primary cause of the depression, but an increase in government spending provided the best hope of recovery
    d. a collapse in government spending was the primary cause of the depression, but an increase in investment demand provided the best hope of recovery
    e. a collapse in government spending was the primary cause of the depression, but an increase in saving provided the best hope of recovery

17. The principal cause of the Great Depression of the 1930s was:

    a. a collapse in aggregate demand
    b. a collapse in aggregate supply
    c. a collapse in prices
    d. a collapse in government spending
    e. the outbreak of the Second World War

18. Those in the classical and Keynesian traditions agree that:

    a. a decline in aggregate demand was the principal cause of the Great Depression
    b. a decline in the money stock was the principal cause of the Great Depression
    c. a decline in investment demand was the principal cause of the Great Depression
    d. fluctuations in aggregate supply have been the major cause of fluctuations in output and employment in recent decades
    e. the government has the responsibility to manage aggregate demand actively

19. Shifts in aggregate demand, rather than shifts in aggregate supply, seem to be the primary reason for fluctuations in output. We come to that conclusion because declines in output are usually associated with:

    a. rising inflation
    b. declining inflation
    c. more unemployment
    d. less unemployment
    e. increases in government spending

20. Some macroeconomists propose that the authorities adhere to a *policy rule*. The most common proposal of the proponents of a rule is for a moderate, steady increase in:

    a. the quantity of money
    b. potential GNP
    c. the average level of prices
    d. tax rates
    e. government tax revenues

EXERCISES

1. In Figure 8.1, AS_1 represents the part of the aggregate supply function above point *A*. A classical economist completing this function would draw the dashed section shown as (AS_a, AS_b). However, a Keynesian economist would be more likely to complete it with (AS_a, AS_b).

    Suppose that AD_1 is the initial aggregate demand curve. Then the initial equilibrium will be at point _____, where the equilibrium quantity of output will be $OQ\_\_$. According to (classical, Keynesian, both) economists, there will be full employment at this initial equilibrium.

Figure 8.1

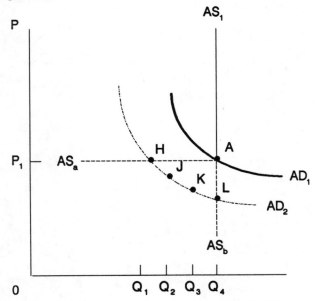

Now suppose that aggregate demand collapses to AD_2. According to classical economists, the economy will move in the short run to a point such as _____. However, this point does not represent a new equilibrium, since (the economy is not at full employment, prices are below P_1). If aggregate demand remains at AD_2, prices will (rise, fall), and the economy will move a new equilibrium at point _____. At this new equilibrium, there will be (full employment, large-scale unemployment).

In the face of a fall in aggregate demand from its initial AD_1 to AD_2, Keynesians see a different outcome. In the short run, the economy will move to point _____. If aggregate demand remains stable at AD_2, the long-run equilibrium will be at point _____, with output $OQ\_\_$. With this output, there will be (full employment, large-scale unemployment).

2. On many matters, Keynesian economists and those in the classical tradition agree. However, there are still some disagreements. Mark each of the views below with a **C** if it is more likely to be held with those in the classical tradition, or with **K** if it is more likely to be held by Keynesians:

_____ a. Money is by far the most important determinant of aggregate demand
_____ b. The government should manage aggregate demand to reduce cyclical swings in the economy
_____ c. Even when the unemployment rate is high, wages and prices will move down only slightly, if at all
_____ d. Following a rule, rather than periodically adjusting policies, is more likely to lead to a stable economy
_____ e. The best policy to follow is to increase the quantity of money at a slow, steady rate
_____ f. Large-scale unemployment represents a temporary disequilibrium.

ESSAY QUESTIONS

1. Using diagrams, explain briefly how classical economists drew the aggregate demand and aggregate supply curve. What might cause a depression? How might the economy move out of a depression and to full employment?

2. Summarize the three main points in Keynes' *General Theory*. Which points, if any, might a classical economist agree with?

ANSWERS

Important terms: 1 e, 2 i, 3 k, 4 c, 5 j, 6 h, 7 a, 8 g, 9 f, 10 b, 11 d

True-False: 1 F (p. 119)
                                  2 T (p. 120)
                                  3 T (p. 121)
                                  4 F (p. 123)
                                  5 F (p. 123)
                                  6 T (p. 124)
                                  7 T (p. 125)
                                  8 F (p. 125)
                                  9 T (p. 129)
                                  10 F (p. 129)

Multiple Choice: 1 e (p. 119)
                                  2 a (p. 119)
                                  3 b (p. 120)
                                  4 d (p. 120)
                                  5 a (p. 120)
                                  6 c (p. 121)
                                  7 c (p. 121)
                                  8 a (p. 123)
                                  9 e (p. 123)
                                  10 c (p. 124)
                                  11 e (p. 124)
                                  12 e (p. 125)
                                  13 e (p. 125)
                                  14 b (p. 125)
                                  15 e (p. 126)
                                  16 c (p. 127)
                                  17 a (p. 128)
                                  18 a (p. 128)
                                  19 b (p. 128-29)
                                  20 a (p. 129)

Exercises

1. AS_b, AS_a, *A*, OQ_4, both, *J*, the economy is not at full employment, fall, *L*, full employment, *H*, *H*, OQ_1, large-scale unemployment.

2.   a. C,   b. K,
            c. K,   d. C,
            e. C,   f. C.

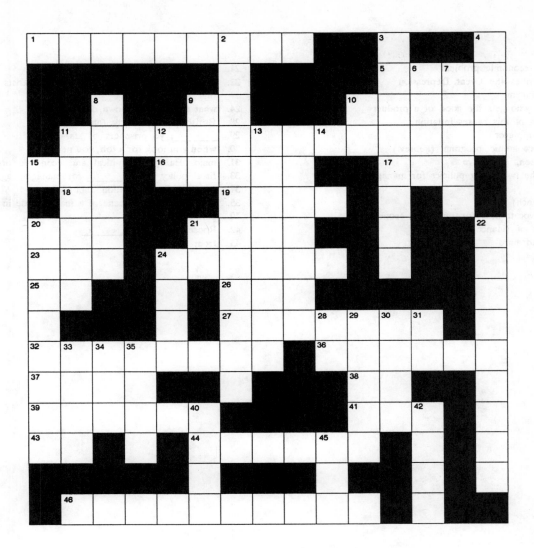

Across

1. to reduce fluctuations, some economists recommend this (2 words)
5. an early economist who was interested in money
9. not (French)
10. builder
11. an important economic objective (2 words)
15. a metal
16. a fruit, or a computer
17. before
18. road (abbrev.)
19. one of the three factors of production
20. in cards, it's either high or low
21. to banks or pension funds, this is important
23. where lawyers sometimes go, either during work or after
24. he revolutionized the study of macroeconomics
25. two directions (abbrev.)
26. peace (Russian)
27. according to Marx, capitalism would do this to workers
32, 36. according to classical economists, these were one reason why the depression lasted so long
37. Greek letter, now means something very small
38. third "person"
39. they decide who will be president
41. unhappy
43. the (Spanish)
44. according to Keynesians, this is the best type of policy
46. money has this type of power

Down

2. a major economic problem
3. this describes the Great Depression
4. type of income
6. someone who gets the good of a product
7. too much of this causes inflation
8. a football player
9. Lenin's economic program (abbrev.)
10. first person, possessive
11. one of the two major policies for managing aggregate demand
12. the (French)
13. some advocate this for managing economy
14. providers of finance
20. rough and hard

21. exist
22. the intellectual ancestors of the monetarists belonged to this school
24. what the guy in 8 down does
28. British political party (abbrev.)
29. _____, ye prisoners of starvation!
30. when you look for a job, you need this
31. major European political and economic organization
33. fiscal policy is a _____ for managing aggregate demand
34. major U.S. corporation (abbrev.)
35. a French city, the scene of a major battle in World War II
40. part of a window
42. Roosevelt's New _____
45. from (German)

CHAPTER 9

EQUILIBRIUM WITH UNEMPLOYMENT:
The Keynesian Approach

LEARNING OBJECTIVES

After you have studied this chapter in the textbook and study guide, you should be able to

✔ Explain the relationship between disposable income and consumer expenditures

✔ Explain what the MPC is, and why it is the same as the slope of the consumption function

✔ Explain why, when we put disposable income (or national product) on the horizontal axis, we can also measure disposable income (or national product) as the distance up to the 45° line

✔ Derive the saving function from the consumption function

✔ Explain the relationship between the MPC and the MPS

✔ Explain why equilibrium national product is found where the aggregate expenditures function cuts the 45° line

✔ Explain what will happen if national product is greater or less than this equilibrium quantity

✔ Explain the difference between a leakage and an injection, and give an illustration of each

✔ Express the equilibrium condition for national product in three different ways, and explain why these three different statements amount to the same thing

✔ Explain why there may be large-scale unemployment when the economy is in equilibrium

✔ Explain why an increase in investment has a multiplied effect on aggregate expenditures and national product

✔ Write the two equations for the multiplier in the simple economy with no taxes or international transactions

MAJOR PURPOSE

Chapter 8 presented the main outlines of Keynesian and classical economics. The purpose of this chapter is to explain the central proposition of Keynesian economics — **that the economy may reach an equilibrium with large-scale unemployment.** This happens when aggregate spending is too low to buy all the goods and services that could be produced by the economy at full employment. When aggregate spending is too low, businesses can't sell many of their products. Lacking sales, they cut back on production and lay off workers.

Aggregate demand is made up of four major components: personal consumption expenditures, investment demand, government purchases of goods and services, and net exports. In order to present the simplest explanation, this chapter deals with an economy with only consumption and investment — that is, the government and the foreign sectors are ignored in this chapter. (They are considered in Chapter 10.) Furthermore, investment demand is not explained here; we simply assume that investment demand exists, and see what happens when it changes. (The reasons for a change in investment demand will be studied in Chapter 17 and in the appendix to Chapter 18.)

Thus, consumption is the only type of spending studied in detail in this chapter. The main determinant of consumption is disposable income: When people have more income, they generally spend more. This has important implications for what happens when **investment** demand increases. People are put to work producing factories and machines. Their incomes rise. Therefore they consume more. Therefore, an increase in investment demand causes — or **induces** — an increase in consumption demand, too. As a result, an increase in investment demand has a *multiplier effect* — national product goes up by a multiple of the increase in investment.

HIGHLIGHTS OF CHAPTER

This chapter introduces the basic framework of Keynesian theory. The major innovation of Keynes was the proposition that the economy could reach an equilibrium with large-scale unemployment. National product would not automatically move to the full-employment level; it could stay much below that level if aggregate demand were low. This conclusion provided the reason for his policy conclusion: Since a policy of laissez faire might result in large-scale unemployment, it was up to the government to adopt policies designed to bring aggregate demand up to the full employment level. (This policy conclusion will be studied in Chapter 10.)

As we saw in Chapter 8, there are four components of aggregate demand:

- personal consumption expenditures,
- investment demand,
- government purchases of goods and services,
- and net exports.

However, to make things simple, this chapter deals with an economy with only consumption and investment.

Consumption expeditures (C) depend on disposable income (DI). The relationship between C and DI is known as the **consumption function.** This function has three main characteristics:

- As DI increases, so does consumption. This means that the consumption function *slopes upward*.

- The change in C (ΔC) is less than the change in DI (ΔDI). The change in C, as a *fraction* of the change in DI, is known as the **marginal propensity to consume** (MPC). This fraction, $\Delta C/\Delta$DI, is also the *slope* of the consumption function. Because the MPC is less than one, the slope of the consumption function is likewise less than one.

- At very low levels of DI, C is larger than DI. That is, people spend more than their incomes; they *dissave*. They do this by running down their assets or by borrowing.

These characteristics are illustrated in Figure 9-2 in the textbook.

In order to simplify the discussion, the consumption function is also given a fourth characteristic: It is drawn as a *straight line* in textbooks. This means that the MPC is constant. The evidence on consumer behavior shown in Figure 9-1 suggests that the MPC need not in fact be constant. Thus, we should file away in the back of our minds that we have made a simplifying assumption that is not necessarily correct.

Saving may be identified by drawing a 45° line on the consumption function diagram. The 45° line is equidistant from the two axes; measuring up to the 45° line gives the same number as measuring horizontally to the line. Because we measure disposable income on the horizontal axis, we may also measure disposable income in an upward direction; it is they height of the 45° line. Saving is zero at the point where C = DI — that is, the point where the consumption function and the 45° line intersect.

In simple terms, saving equals DI - C. (It is standard procedure to use this simple relationship, and ignore the interest paid to consumers shown on Figure 6-3 in the textbook.) Thus, a saving function can be derived directly from the consumption function. Specifically, the height of the saving function (Figure 9-3) is the vertical distance between the consumption function and the 45° line (Figure 9-2).

- As DI increases, so does saving. This means that the saving function *slopes upward*.

- The change in S (ΔS) is less than the change in DI (ΔDI). The change in S, as a *fraction* of the change in DI, is the **marginal propensity to save** (MPS). This fraction, $\Delta S / \Delta$DI, is also the *slope* of the saving function. Because the MPS is less than one, the slope of the saving function is likewise less than one.

- When people have very low incomes, S is negative. That is, people *dissave*.

Because each $1 of additional disposable income is either consumed or saved, MPC + MPS = 1.

To see a simple illustration of equilibrium, we look at a simple economy in which there is no depreciation, no government, and no international transactions. In such an economy GNP = NNP, and we can talk simply of national product, NP. Furthermore, in the absence of taxes and transfers, NP = NI = DI, and we can therefore redraw the consumption function with NP measured along the horizontal axis or up to the 45° line.

When we add investment demand (I^*) vertically to the consumption function, we get the **aggregate expenditures function**, which shows how aggregate spending depends on national product. Equilibrium occurs where AE = NP — that is, where the AE function cuts the 45° line. At this point, producers are able to sell what they produce. If national product were larger — say at L in Figure 9-5 in the textbook, then production would be greater than aggregate expenditures. Unsold goods would pile up in **undesired inventory accumulation**. In order to reduce their undesired inventories, businesses would cut back on orders from suppliers and reduce their production. Output would fall back to its equilibrium at K. At equilibrium, aggregate expenditures may fall below the level needed for full employment. That is, equilibrium national product K may be to the left of full-employment point F, as shown in Figure 9-5. Figure 9-5 is one of the half dozen most important diagrams in the book.

The circumstances under which there is equilibrium may be stated in three different ways, all of which amount to the same thing. Equilibrium occurs when:

- AE = NP, as shown by the intersection of AE and the 45° NP line in Figure 9-5. At this point of intersection, there is a demand for all the goods and services produced. That is:

- Undesired inventory accumulation equals zero, and $I = I^*$.

- $S = I^*$, as shown in Figure 9-6.

If investment demand increases, the additional investment demand is added vertically to the AE function; the AE function shifts upward. As a result, national product increases. As it does so, incomes increase. People spend more. Thus, a $1 increase in investment demand leads not only to $1 more in the output of capital goods; it leads to more output of consumer goods and services, too. Overall output increases by a multiple of the $1 increase in investment. This is the important *multiplier* concept. Specifically, the multiplier is equal to ΔNP/ΔI^*. In the simple economy, this equals 1/MPS. Details on the multiplier are given in Figure 9-11 in the textbook.

IMPORTANT TERMS

Match the first column with the corresponding phrase in the second column.

_e_	1. Marginal Propensity to Consume	a.	Saving
_h_	2. Marginal Propensity to Save	b.	NP = AE
_g_	3. Saving	c.	1/MPS
_b_	4. Equilibrium national product	d.	I minus I^*
_d_	5. Undesired inventory accumulation	e.	$\Delta C/\Delta DI$
_a_	6. A leakage	f.	I^*
_f_	7. An injection	g.	DI - C
_c_	8. Multiplier	h.	1 minus MPC

TRUE-FALSE

T   F   1. If the MPC is constant, then the MPS is equal to the MPC.

T   F   2. The slope of the aggregate expenditures function is equal to the MPS.

T   F   3. The slope of the saving function = 1 - MPC.

T   F   4. If the consumption function is a straight line, then the MPC is greater than 1.

T   F   5. Businesses respond to undesired inventory accumulation by increasing their orders for goods.

T   F   6. If national product is above its equilibrium, then actual investment is greater than desired investment.

T   F   7. If undesired inventory accumulation is positive, then actual national product exceeds equilibrium national product.

T   F   8. Because all goods must be demanded if they are to be produced, the slope of the aggregate expenditures schedule equals 45°.

T   F   9. The higher is the MPC, the larger is the multiplier.

MULTIPLE CHOICE

1. In Keynesian theory, aggregate demand is studied as the sum of four components, including each of the items below **except one**. Which one?

   a. Personal consumption expenditures
   b. Personal saving
   c. Investment demand
   d. Government purchases of goods and services
   e. Net exports

2. Saving equals zero when:

   a. $C + I^*$ = National Product
   b. $C + I^*$ = Aggregate expenditures
   c. Personal income = disposable income
   d. Consumption = disposable income
   e. MPC = 1

3. The slope of the consumption function is equal to

   a. the MPC
   b. the MPS
   c. the MPS + 1
   d. the multiplier
   e. 1/(the multiplier)

4. If the MPC is three quarters, then an increase in disposable income will cause:

   a. consumption to rise by three times the increase in disposable income
   b. consumption to rise by four times the increase in disposable income
   c. consumption to increase, while saving decreases
   d. consumption to decrease, while saving increases
   e. consumption and saving both to increase, with consumption increasing more than saving

5. Suppose that the consumption function is a straight line. Then:

   a. consumption is a constant fraction of income
   b. saving is a constant fraction of income
   c. the MPC is constant
   d. the MPC becomes smaller as income becomes smaller
   e. the MPS becomes smaller as income becomes smaller

6. If the slope of the consumption function rises, then we may conclude that:

   a. the slope of the saving function has fallen
   b. the marginal propensity to save has risen
   c. the marginal propensity to consume has fallen
   d. the multiplier has become smaller
   e. undesired inventory accumulation has become larger

7. The aggregate expenditure function shows how spending increases in real terms as:

   a. prices fall
   b. prices increase
   c. real national product increases
   d. saving increases
   e. unemployment increases

8. Actual investment minus investment demand equals:

   a. one
   b. zero
   c. inventory investment
   d. undesired inventory investment
   e. desired inventory investment

9. Suppose that, in a simple Keynesian system, national product exceeds its equilibrium quantity. Then:

   a. aggregate expenditures exceed national product
   b. investment demand exceeds saving

   c. actual investment exceeds investment demand
   d. the multiplier equals 1
   e. MPC = MPS - 1

10. National product is at its equilibrium when:

    a. aggregate expenditures = $C + I^* + G$
    b. aggregate expenditures = national product
    c. saving = undesired inventory accumulation
    d. saving = desired inventory accumulation
    e. government spending = tax revenues

11. When undesired inventory accumulation equals zero:

    a. S = 0
    b. I = 0
    c. $I^* = 0$
    d. government spending = tax revenues
    e. national product is at its equilibrium level

12. In *The General Theory*, Keynes argued that

    a. a market economy might reach equilibrium with large-scale unemployment
    b. large-scale unemployment is caused by inadequate aggregate demand
    c. the best way to cure large-scale unemployment is by increasing government spending
    d. all of the above
    e. none of the above

13. Suppose that saving is greater than investment demand. Then

    a. there must be full employment when the economy is in equilibrium
    b. there must be large-scale unemployment when the economy is in equilibrium
    c. national product is greater than the equilibrium
    d. national product is less than the equilibrium
    e. undesired inventory accumulation is negative

14. In the circular flow of spending:

    a. investment is an injection, and saving a leakage
    b. saving is an injection, and investment a leakage
    c. saving and investment are both leakages, and consumption is an injection
    d. saving and investment are both injections, and consumption is a leakage
    e. consumption and saving are both leakages, and investment is an injection

15. The condition for equilibrium may be stated in three different ways—in each of the following ways **except one**. Which is the exception?

    a. aggregate expenditures = national product
    b. $I = I^*$
    c. $S = I^*$
    d. $S = I$

16. When investment demand increases, which of the following functions shifts upward:

    a. aggregate supply
    b. aggregate expenditures
    c. consumption
    d. saving
    e. leakages

17. Consider a simple economy, with no government or international trade, and with an MPC of 0.9. According to the multiplier theory, if investment demand increases by $100 billion, equilibrium national product will rise by a multiple of the $100 billion. Specifically, equilibrium national product will rise by

    a. $1,000 billion, made up of the original $100 billion in investment plus an additional $900 billion of investment stimulated by the initial investment
    b. $1,000 billion, made up of the $100 billion in investment plus $900 billion in consumption as consumers move along the consumption function
    c. $500 billion, made up of $100 billion in investment plus $400 billion in consumption
    d. $500 billion, made up of the original $100 billion in investment plus an additional $400 billion of investment stimulated by the initial investment
    e. $500 billion, made up of $100 billion in investment, $200 billion of consumption, and $200 billion of government spending for goods and services

18. Consider a simple economy, with no government and no international trade. Then if the MPC = 0.9, the multiplier is:

    a. also 0.9
    b. 1
    c. 5
    d. 10
    e. 100

EXERCISES

1. Figure 9.1 below shows a simple economy with only two types of expenditure—consumption and investment. In this economy, equilibrium occurs at point _____, with national product of _____. At this national product, consumption is distance _____, desired investment is distance _____, actual investment is distance _____, saving is distance _____, and undesired inventory accumulation is _____. Now, suppose that national product is equal to OC. At this national product, consumption is distance _____, desired investment is distance _____, actual investment is distance _____, saving is distance _____, and undesired inventory accumulation is distance

_____.

In this diagram, we can also tell the size of the multiplier. If, from an initial point of equilibrium, investment were to fall to zero, the equilibrium point would move to _____. That is, when investment demand fell by distance _____, national product would fall by distance _____. Thus, the size of the multiplier is distance AB divided by distance

_____.

We can also tell the MPC in this diagram. Specifically, it is distance _____ divided by distance EF.

Figure 9.1

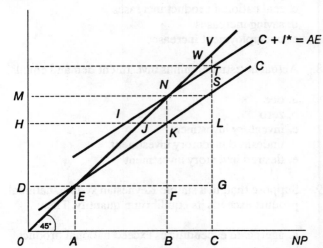

2. Table 9.1 below represents the same type of simple economy studied in this chapter. Suppose that the MPC = 0.8. Fill in the second column, giving the consumption expenditures at each level of disposable income DI. Suppose that desired investment is 40. Now fill in the third column, giving aggregate expenditures at each level of disposable income DI. Now fill in the fourth and fifth columns, giving (respectively) the amount of saving and the amount of undesired inventory accumulation at each quantity of national product. Then fill in the sixth column, giving S minus desired investment. What is the equilibrium national product in this economy?

Table 9.1

(1) DI(=NP)	(2) C	(3) Aggregate expenditures	(4) Saving	(5) Undesired inventory investment	(6) S minus desired investment
0	20	_____	_____	_____	_____
100	_____	_____	_____	_____	_____
200	_____	_____	_____	_____	_____
300	_____	_____	_____	_____	_____
400	_____	_____	_____	_____	_____
500	_____	_____	_____	_____	_____

3. Suppose that the consumption function is C = 25 + 0.75DI. In other words, if DI = 100, then C = 25 + 0.75x100 = 100. Plot the consumption function in Figure 9.2. Plot the corresponding saving function in Figure 9.3. Now suppose that desired investment is 25. Plot this investment in Figure 9.3, and plot the aggregate expenditures function and the 45° line in Figure 9.2. The MPC equals _____, the MPS equals _____, the multiplier equals _____, and the equilibrium national product is _____.

Now suppose that desired investment increases by 25; it is now 50. Plot the new aggregate expenditures function in Figure 9.2 and the new desired investment in Figure 9.3. The new equilibrium national product is _____. At the quantity of NP that used to be equilibrium, aggregate expenditures are now [more, less] than NP by quantity _____, saving is now [more, less] than desired investment by quantity _____, and undesired inventory accumulation equals _____.

Figure 9.2

Aggregate Expenditures

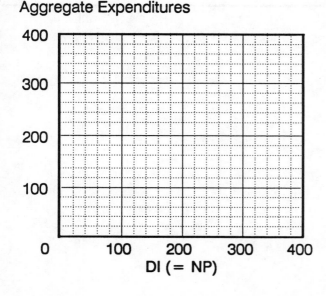

Figure 9.3

S,I

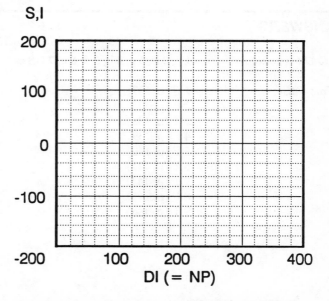

4. Suppose that the MPC is 0.5 and that investment expenditures increase by 400 (that is, desired investment increases by 400). In the first column of Table 9.2, fill in the expenditures at each round, as in the table accompanying Figure 9-11 on p. 147 in the text. In the second column, fill in the cumulative total of expenditures (investment plus consumption) up to and including that round. The total expenditures in *all* the rounds, if the series is continued indefinitely, will be _____.

Table 9.2

		(1) Change in aggregate expenditures	(2) Cumulative total
Fiirst round	Investment of		
Second round	Consumption of		
Third round	Consumption of		
Fourth round	Consumption of		
Fifth round	Consumption of		
Sixth round	Consumption of		
Seventh round	Consumption of		

ESSAY QUESTIONS

1. In the textbook, disposable income is the main determinant of consumption expenditures. But consumption can depend on other things, too. What other variables do you think are important, and why? (Hints: What beside disposable income determines the expenditures of a retiree in Florida? Does it make sense for a student to consume more than his or her disposable income? Why?)

2. In the textbook, the level of investment is initially assumed to be constant, and then it is assumed to change without explanation. What do you think would be the important determinants of investment? Would investment demand depend on national product? *If so*, how would this change the way in which Figures 9-5 and 9-6 were drawn in the textbook? Would it make the economy more or less stable through time? *If not*, why do you think other determinants are more important than national product?

ANSWERS

Matching columns: 1 e, 2 h, 3 g, 4 b, 5 d, 6 a, 7 f, 8 c

True-False: 1 F (p. 137)
2 F (pp. 138, 141)
3 T (p. 139)
4 F (p. 139)
5 F (p. 140)
6 T (p. 141)
7 T (p. 141)
8 F (p. 141)
9 T (p. 148)

Multiple Choice:

1 b (p. 134)	
2 d (p. 137)	
3 a (p. 138)	
4 e (pp. 138-139)	
5 c (p. 139)	
6 a (p. 139)	
7 c (p. 139)	
8 d (p. 140)	
9 c (p. 140)	
10 b (p. 141)	
11 e (p. 141)	
12 d (pp. 129, 142)	
13 c (p. 142)	
14 a (p. 143)	
15 d (p. 145)	
16 b (p. 146)	
17 b (pp. 146-148)	
18 d (p. 148)	

Exercises

1.   N, OB, BK, KN, KN, KN, zero. CS, ST, SV, SV, TV. E, KN, AB, KN. FK.

2.

Table 9.1 Completed:

(1) DI(=NP)	(2) C	(3) Aggregate expenditures	(4) Saving	(5) Undesired inventory investment	(6) S minus desired investment
0	20	60	−20	−60	−60
100	100	140	0	−40	−40
200	180	220	20	−20	−20
300	260	300	40	0	0
400	340	380	60	20	20
500	420	460	80	40	40

Equilibrium national product is 300.

3.   0.75, 0.25, 4, 200, 300, more, 25, less, 25, -25

4.

Table 9.2 Completed:

	(1)	(2)
First round Investment of	400	400
Second round Consumption of	200	600
Third round Consumption of	100	700
Fourth round Consumption of	50	750
Fifth round Consumption of	25	775
Sixth round Consumption of	12½	787½
Seventh round Consumption of	6¼	793¾

The total expenditures in all rounds will be 800.

Part 3

AGGREGATE DEMAND POLICIES

FISCAL POLICY

LEARNING OBJECTIVES

After you have studied this chapter in the textbook and study guide, you should be able to

✔ Explain why an increase in government spending causes an increase in aggregate expenditures

✔ Explain why a cut in tax rates causes an increase in aggregate expenditures

✔ Explain why a $100 change in government spending can have a more powerful effect on equilibrium national product than a $100 change in taxes

✔ Explain why taxes have nevertheless become the primary tool of fiscal policy

✔ Explain why an increase in tax rates causes the aggregate expenditures function to become flatter, thereby decreasing the size of the multiplier

✔ Give an illustration of an automatic stabilizer, and explain how it acts to stabilize the economy

✔ Describe how the full-employment budget is measured

✔ Explain what the full-employment budget is used for

✔ Explain why the government may destabilize the economy if it attempts to balance the budget every year

✔ Explain why a large and growing national debt can be a problem

MAJOR PURPOSE

The principal cause of recessions and depressions is the instability of aggregate expenditures. The authorities have two tools with which to stabilize aggregate expenditures — fiscal policy and monetary policy. Fiscal policy, in turn, can be subdivided under two headings — changes in government spending and changes in tax rates. The major purpose of this chapter is to explain how these two fiscal policy tools can be used to influence aggregate expenditures.

Government spending for goods and services constitutes one of the components of aggregate expenditures, and an increase in such spending therefore increases aggregate expenditures directly. If, during a depression, the government builds new roads, people will be put to work building the roads and providing materials to construction companies. The initial increase in output and employment will be followed by a multiplier effect, as those engaged in roadbuilding activities find that their incomes are higher and therefore buy more consumer goods.

A change in tax rates does not affect aggregate spending in the same way; taxes are not a component of aggregate expenditures. However, a cut in tax rates leaves the public with more disposable income, and therefore encourages consumption spending.

Ideally, the government should cut taxes to fight recessions and raise taxes to fight inflation, thereby stabilizing the path of demand. In practice, however, the U.S. government has had only partial success in using its fiscal policy tools.

HIGHLIGHTS OF CHAPTER

This chapter explains how the government can change its expenditures or tax policies in order to influence aggregate spending and equilibrium national product.

During a depression or severe recession, aggregate expenditures are below the full-employment output. If we look at the height of the aggregate expenditures function at the full-employment national product, we will find that it lies below the 45° line. The vertical distance between the two lines, measured at the full-employment NP, is the **recessionary gap**. This is the amount by which the aggregate expenditures curve should be shifted upward to get the economy to full employment. The government can eliminate a recessionary gap of, say, $10 billion by increasing its spending by that amount.

Government spending, like investment spending, contributes directly to aggregate expenditures. Furthermore, a change in government spending has the same multiplied effect on equilibrium national product as do changes in investment. Once government is included in the economy, the aggregate expenditures function represents the vertical addition of $C + I^* + G$.

Changes in tax rates also affect national product, but not in the same direct way, because taxes are not a component of aggregate expenditures. However, changes in taxes affect disposable income and therefore affect consumption. For example, an increase in tax rates reduces the disposable income of the public, thereby discouraging consumption. As a result, the consumption function is lowered, and the aggregate expenditures function is likewise lowered.

An increase in tax rates also has a second important effect on the consumption function and aggregate expenditures. Not only do these functions become *lower;* they also become *flatter.* The reason is that an increase of, say, 10% in taxes will take more income from the public if national product is large than if it is small. Therefore, the larger is national product — that is, the further we go to the right in the 45° diagram — the greater will be depressing effect of taxes on consumption.

In an economy with a high tax rate, the consumption function is quite flat, and this means that consumers respond weakly to a change in national product. A relatively small amount of consumption is induced by a change in investment or government spending. The multiplier is small. Fluctuations in investment have only a weak effect on aggregate expenditures. Because the existence of taxes means that the multiplier is smaller, the economy is **stabilized automatically**. Tax rates do not have to be adjusted for taxes to have a stabilizing effect. Automatic stabilizers mean that the government deficit *automatically* tends to increase during recessions.

While these automatic deficits help to stabilize the economy, they introduce two important complications into fiscal policy. First, they present a **trap** for the policy maker. If the government follows a superficially-plausible strategy of trying to balance the budget every year, it will end up destabilizing the economy. As the economy swings into recession, deficits will automatically appear. If the authorities raise taxes or cut spending in an attempt to balance the budget, they will be following precisely the wrong fiscal policy; they will be depressing aggregate expenditures further, and adding to the depth of the recession. President Hoover and the Congress fell into this trap in 1932 when they imposed a substantial tax increase. This added to the downward momentum of the economy. One of Keynes' major objectives was to warn against such blunders. He argued that it is important for fiscal policy to be **aimed at balancing the economy, not the budget**.

The second complication is the problem of **measuring** fiscal policy. Deficits automatically increase during a recession. Just because deficits rise during recessions, we should not conclude that the authorities are following counter-cyclical fiscal policies; they may be doing nothing. In order to determine what is happening to fiscal *policy,* some measure other than the actual budgetary surplus or deficit is needed. The **full-employment budget** provides such a measure. This budget gives a measure of the deficit or surplus that would occur with current tax rates and spending programs **if** the economy were at full employment. Because the full-employment budget is always measured at full employment (regardless of where actual output is), it does not automatically swing into deficit when the economy moves into a recession. However, the size of the deficit or surplus does change when tax rates or spending programs are changed. In brief, the full-employment budget changes when policies change; it does not change when the economy falls into recession. It therefore may be taken as a **measure of fiscal policy.**

Keynesian economists showed how the old objective of balancing the actual budget could lead to the wrong policies. But if the President and Congress are not held responsible for balancing the budget, what will restrain their spending? One possibility would be to have a guideline that would require restraint, while avoiding the trap of balancing the budget every year. Suggested guidelines include:

- balancing the full-employment budget every year,

- balancing the actual budget over the business cycle, with surpluses during prosperity to offset the deficits during recessions, or

- limiting federal government spending to, say, 21% of GNP.

While all of these options have been discussed, none has become a firm basis for policy. The question of restraint has become increasingly important in recent years. Government deficits grew rapidly during the 1980s, and are now running more than $100 billion per year.

When the government runs deficits, it borrows the difference between its expenditures and receipts. That is, it issues bonds or shorter-term securities. A $150 billion deficit therefore leads to a $150 billion increase in the national debt. The high deficits of recent years have made the national debt soar. A national debt is different from a personal or corporate debt, because we "owe most of it to ourselves." That is, even though we as taxpayers have to pay interest on the debt, we also receive most of the interest payments. We may not always be aware of this, because some of the interest payments are not obvious to us. For example, government bonds may be held by our pension funds, and the interest is paid into our pension funds without our necessarily being aware of the fact.

However, the national debt does raise a number of problems, particularly if it is increasing rapidly:

- Some of the debt may *not* represent what we owe to ourselves; some government bonds may be held by foreigners. In this case, the nation is less well off. In the future, we will be taxed to make interest payments to foreign countries. This aspect of the national debt has attracted much attention in recent years. Much of the increase in U.S. government debt has been purchased by foreigners. Only a few years ago, we were major international creditors. That is, U.S. assets abroad were much larger than foreign claims on the United States. However, by 1985, we had dissipated our creditor position; according to official statistics, we became net international debtors for the first time since 1914.

- Even when we own our government's bonds, and pay interest to ourselves, the debt is not problem-free. To pay the interest, the government levies taxes. The public has an incentive to alter its behavior to avoid the taxes. When this happens, the economy generally becomes less efficient. This decrease in efficiency is known as the *excess burden* of taxes.

- If the national debt rises high enough, the government may find it very difficult to collect enough taxes to pay the interest. It may simply borrow more and more, to service the ever-growing debt. In other words, the debt may *grow on itself.* Again, this is an issue which has attracted much greater attention during the 1980s because of the combination of rising debt and high interest rates. Interest on the national debt rose from 1.4% of GNP in 1975 to an estimated 3.3% by 1985. (See Table 10 -1 in the textbook.) Although this figure has leveled out, it remains much higher than it was at any time prior to 1980.

- Finally, as interest payments balloon, the government may be tempted to print money to meet these payments. If it does so to any great extent, this will add to inflationary pressures in the economy. (The government prints money via a complicated procedure. The U.S. Treasury issues bonds, and the Federal Reserve prints money to buy these bonds. This is a subject that will be studied in the next few chapters.)

IMPORTANT TERMS

Match the first column with the corresponding phrase in the second column.

<u>d</u> 1. Ressionary gap
<u>h</u> 2. Output gap
<u>b</u> 3. Excess burden of tax
<u>g</u> 4. An injection
<u>i</u> 5. A leakage
<u>a</u> 6. Deficit
<u>e</u> 7. Full-employment surplus
<u>c</u> 8. Automatic stabilizer
<u>f</u> 9. Policy trap

a. Negative surplus
b. The decrease in economic efficiency when people change their behavior to reduce their taxes
c. Any tax or spending program that makes the budgetary deficit rise during recession, even if no policy change is made
d. Vertical distance from the aggregate expenditures function up to the 45° line, measured at full-employment NP
e. $R_{FE} - G_{FE}$
f. The annually-balanced budget
g. Government purchases of goods and services
h. Full-employment NP - actual NP
i. Taxes

TRUE-FALSE

T F 1. An increase in government spending of $100 million will increase equilibrium national product by more than $100 million.

T F 2. An increase in tax rates reduces equilibrium national product.

T F 3. An across-the-board increase in income taxes by, say, 5% has an effect similar to an increase in a lump-sum tax: It causes the consumption function to move down, but it does not change its slope.

T F 4. An automatic stabilizer acts to stabilize the size of the government's surplus or deficit.

T F 5. A decline into recession causes an increase in the deficit in the actual budget.

T F 6. If the government tries to balance the full-employment budget every year, it will fall into a policy trap; it will increase the severity of recessions by raising tax rates or cutting spending during recessions.

T F 7. When the economy moves into a recession, the actual budget automatically moves toward deficit, but the full employment budget does not.

T F 8. An increase in government spending to build roads will move both the actual budget and the full-employment budget toward deficit.

T F 9. A cyclically balanced budget requires the full-employment budget to be balanced every year.

T F 10. Foreign held debt imposes no burden, because we pay foreigners with exports of goods and services, and exports make the economy stronger.

MULTIPLE CHOICE

1. The recessionary gap is:

   a. the amount by which actual GNP falls short of equilibrium GNP
   b. the amount by which actual GNP falls short of full-employment GNP
   c. the vertical distance from the aggregate expenditures line to the 45° line, measured at equilibrium national product
   d. the vertical distance from the aggregate expenditures line to the 45° line, measured at the full-employment national product
   e. the vertical distance from equilibrium national product to the aggregate expenditures function

2. When the economy is in equilibrium, the vertical distance between the aggregate expenditures function and the 45° line is equal to:

   a. the output gap
   b. the recessionary gap
   c. investment demand
   d. saving
   e. zero

3. Suppose that the recessionary gap is $10 billion, and it is expected to remain at that amount into the future if no action is taken. The appropriate policy to eliminate this $10 billion gap is:

   a. a cut in taxes of $10 billion
   b. a cut in government spending of $10 billion
   c. an increase in taxes of $10 billion
   d. an increase in government spending of $10 billion
   e. an increase in government spending of $10 billion x the multiplier

4. There is a relationship between the recessionary gap and the output gap. Specifically, the output gap is the recessionary gap:

   a. times the multiplier
   b. divided by the multiplier
   c. times the average tax rate
   d. divided by the average tax rate
   e. minus the average tax rate

5. Suppose that MPC equals 0.75 and that all taxes are lump-sum taxes. If national product is $3,000 billion and full-employment national product is $3,400 billion, then the output gap is:

   a. $100 billion
   b. $400 billion
   c. $600 billion
   d. $700 billion
   e. $1,600 billion

6. To stimulate aggregate expenditures during a severe recession, the appropriate fiscal policy is:

   a. an increase in taxes and/or an increase in government spending
   b. an increase in taxes and/or a decrease in government spending
   c. a decrease in taxes and/or an increase in government spending
   d. a decrease in taxes and/or a decrease in government spending
   e. a decrease in government purchases and/or a decrease in transfer payments

7. A $100 billion increase in government spending for goods and services has:

   a. the same effect on aggregate expenditures as a $100 billion increase in taxes
   b. the same effect on aggregate expenditures as a $100 billion cut in taxes
   c. a weaker effect on aggregate expenditures than a $100 billion cut in taxes
   d. a stronger effect on aggregate expenditures than a $100 billion cut in taxes
   e. no affect on aggregate expenditures; it effects only the "supply side" of the economy

8. In a diagram with aggregate expenditures on the vertical axis and national product on the horizontal axis, an across-the-board cut of one half in all income tax rates will cause the consumption function to become:

   a. lower, with no change in slope
   b. lower and flatter
   c. lower and steeper
   d. higher and flatter
   e. higher and steeper

9. An increase in income tax rates:

   a. makes the aggregate expenditures function steeper, and therefore lowers the size of the multiplier
   b. makes the aggregate expenditures function steeper, and therefore raises the size of the multiplier
   c. makes the aggregate expenditures function flatter, and therefore lowers the size of the multiplier
   d. makes the aggregate expenditures function flatter, and therefore raises the size of the multiplier
   e. lowers aggregate expenditures, but has no effect on the size of the multiplier

10. When we include international transactions in our model of the economy, the multiplier becomes:

   a. larger, because exports are an injection
   b. larger, because imports are an injection
   c. larger, because of the interaction between taxes and imports
   d. smaller, because the aggregate expenditures function now slopes downward
   e. smaller, because the leakage into imports increases as national product increases

11. When we include the government and international transactions in our model of the economy, equilibrium occurs when:

   a. $S + T + M = I* + G + X$
   b. $S + T + X = I* + G + M$
   c. $S + T + X + M = I* + G$
   d. $S + G + M = I* + T + X$
   e. $S + G + X = I* + T + M$

12. An illustration of the term "automatic stabilizer" is provided by:

   a. the tendency of tax collections to rise as the economy moves into a recession
   b. the tendency of tax collections to fall as the economy moves into a recession
   c. increases in tax rates as the economy moves into a recession
   d. decreases in tax rates as the economy moves into a recession
   e. public works designed to get the economy out of a depression

13. In which of the following cases does the government fall into a "policy trap" and make the economy more unstable?

   a. it cuts taxes as the economy falls into a recession, since its deficits will increase as a result
   b. it increases tax rates as the economy falls into a recession, since it will depress aggregate expenditures
   c. it increases spending as the economy falls into a recession, since its deficits will increase as a result
   d. it attempts to balance the full-employment budget every year, since this will strongly destabilize aggregate expenditures
   e. it moves toward a full-employment deficit during recessions, since this will strongly destabilize aggregate expenditures

14. The principal purpose of the full-employment budget is to measure:

   a. changes in fiscal policy
   b. the size of the recessionary gap
   c. the size of the output gap
   d. the cut in taxes needed to get the economy to full employment
   e. the increase in taxes needed to get the economy to full employment

15. The full-employment budget:

   a. differs from the actual budget because it does not include transfer payments
   b. differs from the actual budget because it includes transfer payments, whereas the actual budget does not
   c. is in surplus whenever the economy falls short of full employment
   d. is more likely to show a surplus than is the actual budget
   e. is less likely to show a surplus than is the actual budget

16. Since 1960, fiscal policy has:

    a. been strongly stabilizing, particularly in 1964-69, when increases in spending promoted a strong, non-inflationary recovery
    b. been strongly stabilizing, particularly in the early 1980s, when large tax increases were the reason for lower inflation
    c. been strongly destablizing, particularly in the early 1980s, when large tax increases caused surpluses and made the recessions worse
    d. been strongly destabilizing, particularly in 1975, when large tax cuts made the deficits bigger and made the recession worse
    e. had a mediocre record, sometimes stabilizing, and sometimes destabilizing the economy

17. Suppose that a tax cut improves the efficiency of the economy and shifts the aggregate supply curve to the right. The most likely results are:

    a. an increase in both output and inflation
    b. an increase in output, but lower inflation
    c. a decrease in output, but higher inflation
    d. a decrease in both output and inflation
    e. there is no basis for a conclusion; each of the above is equally likely

18. The term, "excess burden of taxes," refers to what?

    a. taxes become burdensome whenever they exceed 10% of GNP
    b. personal income taxes are more obvious, and therefore more burdensome, than taxes on corporate profits
    c. personal income taxes are more obvious, and therefore more burdensome, than sales taxes
    d. people may alter their behavior to avoid paying taxes, thereby reducing the efficiency of the economy
    e. taxes must be raised, not only to repay the principal on the government debt, but also to pay interest

19. The U.S. government cannot "go broke" because:

    a. it has the power to tax
    b. it has the power to issue bonds whenever needed to repay its debt
    c. it has the power to print money, and bonds are repayable in money
    d. it has gold stocks equivalent to its long-term debt outstanding
    e. the constitution limits the size of the debt

20. A number of guidelines have been proposed as a way of exerting restraint on the government. Which of the following possible guidelines provides the greatest opportunity for an active fiscal policy aimed at reducing the amplitude of business fluctuations?

    a. balance the actual budget every year
    b. balance the full-employment budget every year
    c. balance the actual budget over the business cycle
    d. allow the government to increase spending whenever an increase in tax receipts pushes the budget into surplus
    e. none of the above allow any active countercyclical fiscal policy

---

EXERCISES

1. Figure 10.1 below shows a consumption function in an economy with no taxes. Its equation is $C = 200 + 0.5DI$, where units are billions of dollars and DI stands for disposable income. In the no-tax economy, DI = NP. The MPC equals _____. Now suppose that the government imposes a *lump sum* tax of $200 billion is collected. When NP = $400 billion, DI = $_____ billion, and C = $_____ billion. When NP = $600 billion, DI = $_____ billion, and C = $_____ billion. Plot this consumption function in the same diagram. The new consumption function is (flatter than, steeper than, has the same slope as) the initial consumption function.

Figure 10.1

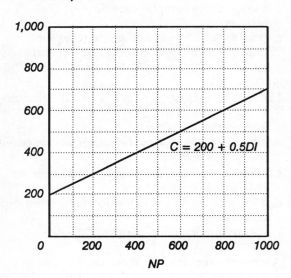

Consumption

$C = 200 + 0.5DI$

NP

Figure 10.2

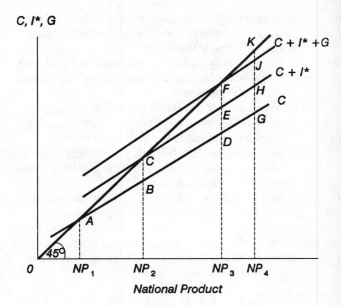

C, I*, G

National Product

Now suppose that the lump-sum tax is eliminated, and replaced with a proportional tax: T = (1/3)DI. The marginal tax rate is _____. When NP = $300 billion, T = $_____ billion, DI = $_____ billion, and C = $_____ billion. When NP = $600 billion, T = $_____ billion, DI = $_____ billion, and C = $_____ billion. Plot this new consumption function on the same diagram. This new consumption function is (flatter than, steeper than, has the same slope as) the initial consumption function. How do you account for the different behavior of the slope here, compared to what happened when a tax was imposed in the previous paragraph?

2. Figure 10.2 shows aggregate expenditures and its components. In this economy, equilibrium is at point _____, with national product = _____. At this equilibrium, government purchases of goods and services (G) amounts to distance _____, I* = _____, and I = _____. Personal saving (S) equals (DE, DF, we don't have enough information to say).

Now, suppose that national product is at the disequilibrium amount NP4. I* = _____, while I = _____, and undesired inventory (accumulation, decumulation) = _____.

Now, suppose that this disequilibrium quantity NP4 represents the full employment output. There is a recessionary gap equal to distance _____. The appropriate fiscal policy is an (increase, decrease) in government purchases of goods and services amounting to distance _____.

3. The government's tax revenues increase as national product increases, and fall during recessions. This means that the budget automatically tends to move into (surplus, deficit) during recession.

The automatic (surpluses, deficits) during recessions introduce two major complications into fiscal policy. First, they present a (opportunity, trap) for the policy maker. If the government follows a superficially-plausible strategy of trying to balance the budget (every year, over the business cycle), it will end up (stabilizing, destabilizing) the economy. As the economy swings into recession, (surpluses, deficits) will automatically appear. If the authorities (raise, lower) taxes or (raise, lower) spending in an attempt to balance the budget, they will be following the (correct, wrong) fiscal policy; they will be (slowing the decline of expenditures, depressing aggregate expenditures further), and (adding to, reducing) the depth of the recession.

This was illustrated most clearly in (1932, 1942, 1961, 1981) when tax rates were (increased, cut) substantially. This (reduced, added to) the downward momentum of the economy. One of Keynes' major objectives was to (show how fiscal policy could be used in this manner to restore full employment, warn against such blunders). He argued that it was important for fiscal policy to be aimed at balancing the (budget, economy, both, neither).

The second complication is the problem of measuring fiscal policy. (Surpluses, Deficits) *automatically* increase during a recession. Just because (surpluses, deficits) rise during recessions, we should not conclude that the authorities are following counter-cyclical fiscal policies; they may be doing nothing. In order to determine what is happening to fiscal *policy*, some measure other than the actual budgetary surplus or deficit is needed. The (actual, full-employment, long-term) budget provides such a measure. This budget gives a measure of the deficit or surplus that would occur with current tax rates and spending programs *if* the economy were at (equilibrium, full employment). Because it is always measured at (equilibrium, full

employment), this budget does not automatically swing into (surplus, deficit) when the economy moves into a recession. However, the size of the deficit or surplus does change when tax rates or spending programs are changed. In brief, this budget changes when policies change; it does not change when the economy falls into recession. It therefore may be taken as a measure of fiscal policy.

Keynesian economists showed how the old objective of balancing the (actual, full-employment) budget could lead to the wrong policies. But if the President and Congress are not held responsible for balancing this budget, what will restrain their spending? One possibility would be to have a guideline which would require restraint, while avoiding the trap of balancing the (actual, full-employment) budget every year. Suggested guidelines include

(1)_____

(2)_____
or
(3)_____

ESSAY QUESTIONS

1. For each of the following, state whether you agree or disagree, and explain why:

   a. A tax acts as an automatic stabilizer only if it makes the aggregate expenditures function flatter.
   b. Whenever the aggregate expenditures function becomes flatter, the multiplier is lower.
   c. Automatic stabilizers reduce the size of the multiplier.

2. Critically evaluate the following statement: "Any system of unemployment insurance will be completely useless as a way of reducing business cycles. Even though the payment of benefits to the unemployed will help to raise aggregate expenditures during recessions, the contributions (taxes) to support the system will lower aggregate expenditures."

ANSWERS

Matching columns: 1 d, 2 h, 3 b, 4 g, 5 i, 6 a, 7 e, 8 c, 9 f

True-False:

1 T (p. 164)
2 T (p. 166)
3 F (p. 168)
4 F (p. 171)
5 T (p. 171)
6 F (pp. 172-173)
7 T (p. 173)
8 T (p. 173)
9 F (pp. 173, 179)
10 F (p. 178)

Multiple Choice:

1 d (p. 165)
2 e (p. 165)
3 d (p. 165)
4 a (p. 165)
5 b (p. 165)
6 c (p. 167)
7 d (p. 167)
8 e (p. 168)
9 c (p. 168)
10 e (p. 170)
11 a (p. 170)
12 b (p. 170)
13 b (p. 171)
14 a (p. 172)
15 d (p. 173)
16 e (p. 173)
17 b (p. 175)
18 d (p. 177)
19 c (p. 178)
20 c (p. 179)

Exercises

1.   0.5, $200, $300, $400, $400, has the same slope as. 1/3, $100, $200, $300, $200, $400, $400, flatter than, here the tax increases with NP while it did not do so with the lump-sum tax in the previous paragraph.

2.   F, NP_3, EF, DE, DE, we don't have enough information to say [Note: the reason is that, in equilibrium, $I^* + G = S + T$. The diagram tells us what G and I^* are. But we can't tell what S is unless we also know T.] GH, GH + JK, accumulation, JK, JK, increase, JK.

3.   [Note: this exercise is based partly on the chapter highlights section.] deficit. deficits, trap, every year, destabilizing, deficits, raise, lower, wrong, depressing aggregate expenditures further, adding to, 1932, increased, added to, warn against such blunders, economy. Deficits, deficits, full-employment, full employment, full employment, deficit. actual, actual, (1) balancing the full-employment budget every year, (2) balancing the actual budget over the business cycle, with surpluses during prosperity to offset the deficits during recessions, or (3) limiting government spending to a fixed percentage of GNP.

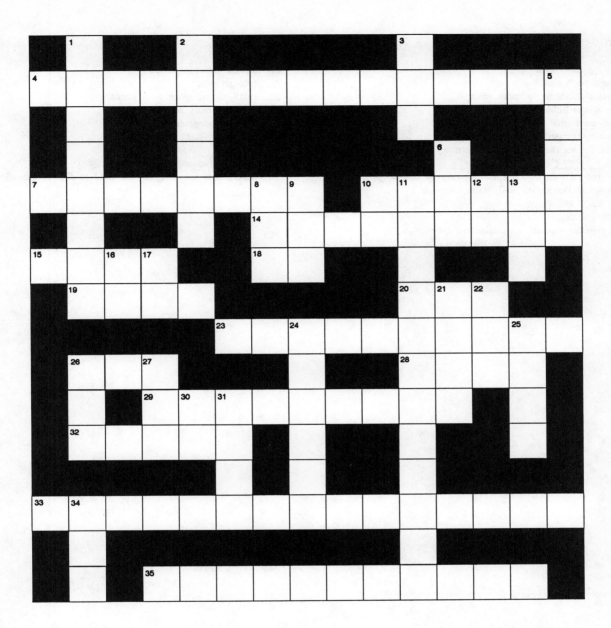

Across

4. a way to combat a depression (2 words)
7, 10. if the government aims for this every year, it may destabilize the economy
14. when NP exceeds its equilibrium, there is undesired _____ accumulation
15. when the government runs a deficit, the national _____ rises
18. a continent (abbrev.)
19. what you do with disposable income that you do not spend on consumption
20. change in saving, divided by change in disposable income
23. change in equlibrium national product, divided by change in government spending for goods and services
26. the party of George Bush
28. one of the factors of production
29. investment or government spending
32. a quantity theorist of the early 20th century (see inside cover of text)
33. fiscal and monetary policies can be used to manage this (2 words)
35. largest component of national product

Down

1. saving and taxes
2. huge bodies of water
3. national income + sales taxes
5. he was a billionaire
6. an insecticide
8. one (German)
9. this carries the code of life (abbrev.)
10. to _____, or not to _____
11. to reduce this, deficit spending may be desirable
12. between Boardwalk and Baltic Avenue
13. make a mistake
16. college degree
17. a popular type of entertainment (abbrev.)

21. should precede action
22. transgression
24. small picture worn as a pendant
25. remove errors from a manuscript
26. NNP + depreciation
27. a medium-sized mammal
30. not so
31. famous student of psychology
34. government spending can be used to fill the recessionary _____

Chapter 10   Fiscal Policy

114

CHAPTER 11

MONEY AND THE BANKING SYSTEM

LEARNING OBJECTIVES

After you have studied this chapter in the textbook and study guide, you should be able to

✔ Describe the three basic functions of money

✔ Explain the differences between M1 and M2

✔ Explain why a bank might want to hold only fractional reserves, rather than reserves equal to 100% of its deposit liabilities

✔ Explain why fractional-reserve banking leads to the risk of a bank run, and why no bank can withstand a severe run without outside help

✔ Explain in detail how an individual bank responds to an increase in its reserves, and how the overall banking system can increase money by a multiple of the increase in reserves. (The explanation requires use of balance sheets.)

✔ State the formula for the deposit multiplier

✔ Give two reasons why the actual expansion of deposits is likely to be less than indicated by this formula

MAJOR PURPOSE

The major purpose of this chapter is to explain how the banking system creates money. The details of money creation, as set out in the various tables in this chapter, are important. A number of specific conclusions are also important:

- Even though the banking system can create money equal to a multiple of its reserves, an individual bank cannot do so.

- Instead, an individual bank receiving a deposit of $100 can create money by lending only a fraction of this $100 (specifically, $100 x 0.8, if the required reserve ratio is 0.2).

- The bank sees nothing particularly magical or peculiar about such loans, even though they result in an increase in the money stock.

- Fractional-reserve banking developed as a natural result of the desire to make profits.

- Fractional-reserve banks can be subject to runs. Because each bank holds reserves equal to only a fraction of its deposit liabilities, no bank can withstand an all-out run without outside help, no matter how sound the bank was originally.

- Bank runs are not only unfortunate for the banks and individual depositors who are too late to get their funds; they also can have strong adverse effects on the economy. Because reserves are being withdrawn from the base of the monetary pyramid, bank runs cause strong downward pressures on the money stock. One of the major tasks of the monetary authorities is to prevent bank runs and instability of the monetary supply, as we shall see in the next chapter.

HIGHLIGHTS OF CHAPTER

This chapter introduces the basic concepts of money and banking, as a background for studying monetary policy in the next chapter.

Money performs three interrelated functions:

- It is a **medium of exchange**; that is, it is used to buy goods and services.

- It is a **standard of value**; that is, we keep accounts, quote prices, and sign contracts in dollar terms.

- It is a **store of value**; that is, you can hold money for future purchases rather than spending it right away.

The basic definition of the money stock, M1, includes items which are used as money in everyday transactions—coins, paper currency, checking accounts in banks and similar financial institutions, and travelers' checks. Each of these items represents wealth to the holder; if you have $100 in your pocket, you are better off than you would be without it. In this way, money is different from a credit card, which represents a convenient way to run up debt, rather than an asset. Thus, even though credit cards (and the corresponding lines of credit) are often used to make purchases, lines of credit are not included in the money stock.

M2 includes M1 plus noncheckable savings deposits, small time deposits, money market deposits, and money market mutual funds. Although such assets are not used in an unrestricted way to make purchases,

they can be quickly switched into M1. Thus, they can have a powerful effect on people's spending behavior. When we are concerned about the relationship between "money" and aggregate demand, we often use the broader definition of money, M2.

Commercial banks and similar financial institutions—such as savings and loan associations—accept deposits, using most of the proceeds to make loans. They hold reserves equal to only a fraction of their deposit liabilities. **Fractional-reserve banking** developed centuries ago, when financial institutions realized that they could cover their costs and make profits from the interest on loans. Through history, fractional-reserve banks have been plagued by the problem of runs, which have not only been dangerous for them, but have also disrupted the economy. One conspicuous example occurred in 1932-33, when the U.S. banking system collapsed, adding to the downslide into the depression.

Even in olden times, when there were no required reserve ratios, banks kept reserves to use as working balances and to meet unexpected withdrawals; such reserves provided some protection against a run. Now, the function of reserves is not to provide protection against a run. Rather, it is to give the authorities control over the money stock. The Federal Reserve, which is the central bank of the United States, is empowered to set reserve requirements within limits specified by Congress. If the required reserve ratio is, say, 0.10, then a $100 withdrawal from a bank deposit will reduce the required reserves by only $10. The other $90 will have to be obtained elsewhere by the bank, most likely by reducing its portfolio of loans or bonds. In other words, reserves in this case would only provide one tenth of the funds needed to meet the withdrawal.

If there is a required reserve ratio specified by law, then the banking system as a whole can increase its deposit liabilities by as much as 1/R times any increase in its reserves. Tables 11-4 to 11-9 in the text explain in detail how banks do this. These tables are not repeated here, but they are of central importance in any study of the monetary system. They often appear on examinations. Students should go over them particularly carefully, together with the balance sheets in the exercises below. Warning: **The the multiple expansion of bank deposits is one of the most important and difficult concepts in introductory economics.**

The deposit multiplier, D = 1/R, shows the *maximum* increase in deposits that can occur when the banking system acquires additional reserves. In practice, the actual increase is likely to be much less, for two reasons. Most important is that, as people acquire more checking deposit money, they are likely to want to hold some of the additional money in the form of currency. When they make withdrawals from their banks, the reserves of banks are reduced. The second reason is that banks may hold excess reserves rather than lending all they are permitted. In recent years, excess reserves have been very small, and this second point represents only a minor complication. However, it was quite important back in the 1930s, when excess reserves at times amounted to almost half of total reserves. There were two reasons for the very large holdings of excess reserves. Interest rates were very low, which meant that bankers didn't forego much interest when they kept excess reserves. Second, bankers were frightened to lend to businesses, since so many businesses were going bankrupt. The failure of banks to lend more of their excess reserves was unfortunate, since more lending and more money would have promoted economic recovery.

We here have one illustration of the difference between what is good for an individual or an institution and what is good for the economy as a whole. Risky bank lending would have increased the money stock and contributed to economic recovery. But it could have meant financial suicide for any bank making risky loans. Bankers cannot be expected to commit suicide for the public good. It is up to the Federal Reserve, not up to individual banks, to see that the money stock is at the right level to keep aggregate demand close to its desired path. How the Fed does this will be studied in the next chapter.

(A second example of the conflict between what is good for the individual and what is good for the overall economy occurs during a bank run. Each individual has an incentive to be first in line. But severe bank runs can disrupt the economy.)

IMPORTANT TERMS

Match the first column with the corresponding phrase in the second column.

_____ 1. Currency
_____ 2. M1
_____ 3. Liquid assets
_____ 4. Liabilities
_____ 5. What a single bank can prudently lend
_____ 6. Required reserves
_____ 7. Maximum increase in deposits
_____ 8. Fractional-reserve banking

a. Assets - net worth
b. Deposit liabilities x *R*
c. Major reason for risk of runs
d. Actual reserves - required reserves
e. Coins, paper currency, and checking deposits
f. Increase in reserves x 1/*R*
g. Short-term government securities
h. Coins and paper currency

TRUE-FALSE

T   F   1. Checking deposits held by manufacturing corporations – such as General Motors – are included in the money stock (M1).

T   F   2. Reserve deposits held by the Chase Manhattan bank are included in the money stock (M1).

T   F   3. Fractional reserve banking was invented by the Federal Reserve.

T   F   4. In the modern U.S. banking system, most commercial banks reserves are held in the form of gold.

T   F   5. When General Motors deposits $100,000 in the Chase Manhattan bank, the resulting deposit appears as an asset on the G.M. balance sheet, and the same deposit appears as a liability on the Chase Manhattan balance sheet.

T   F   6. If a commercial bank receives a deposit of currency, then its actual reserves and excess reserves both increase by the same amount (specifically, by the amount of the deposit).

T   F   7. If a commercial bank receives the deposit of a check drawn against an account in another bank, then its actual reserves and its excess reserves both increase as a consequence.

T F 8. A bank may prudently lend the amount of its excess reserves x 1/R.

T F 9. Banks are more likely to hold excess reserves during a depression than during prosperity.

T F 10. Bank deposits are normally equal to reserves x 1/R. However, they can be larger than that during depressions, when more money is needed to stimulate recovery.

MULTIPLE CHOICE

1. Between 1929 and 1933, during the early part of the Great Depression:

    a. the quantity of money rose, but aggregate demand nonetheless collapsed
    b. the quantity of money fell, but prices nevertheless rose moderately
    c. there was hyperinflation, even though the money stock fell
    d. the quantity of money fell, and this contributed to the downturn
    e. the quantity of money increased at a slow, steady rate, as advocated by monetarists, but the depression nevertheless occurred

2. Even though credit cards are used by many people in making purchases, they are not included in M1. A major reason is that:

    a. credit cards are a way of going into debt, whereas the components of M1 represent assets
    b. credit cards had not yet been invented when money was defined
    c. some credit cards are issued by stores (such as Sears), whereas all money is issued by banks
    d. credit cards are much less liquid than M1
    e. credit cards don't affect consumer expenditures, whereas M1 does

3. Checking deposits make up approximately what fraction of the money stock (M1) in the United States:

    a. 1%
    b. 10%
    c. 25%
    d. 50%
    e. 70%

4. Checking deposits are included in the money stock M1:

    a. only if they are owned by individuals
    b. if they are owned by individuals or non-bank corporations (such as IBM or a local car dealer)
    c. if they are owned by individuals, other banks, or the Federal Reserve

    d. if they are owned by individuals, other banks, or the U.S. Treasury
    e. if they are owned by individuals, the Federal Reserve, or the U.S. Treasury

5. Suppose we know M1, and want to calculate M2. To do so, which of the following do we add to M1?

    a. coins
    b. paper currency
    c. checking deposits
    d. noncheckable savings deposits
    e. Treasury bills

6. In the balance sheet of a business:

    a. Assets = Liabilities
    b. Assets = Liabilities + Net Worth
    c. Assets = Liabilities - Net Worth
    d. Liabilities = Assets + Net Worth
    e. Any of the above may be correct; it depends on the health of the business

7. The primary reason why the activities of early goldsmiths developed into "fractional reserve banking" was the desire to:

    a. keep the money stock down to a fraction of its earlier level, in order to restrain inflation
    b. increase the quantity of money, in order to finance the growth of trade
    c. provide a more stable money system, in order to reduce the size of business fluctuations
    d. provide a broader range of financial services to their customers
    e. increase profits, by lending out some of the gold deposited with them

8. A bank run is most likely to occur at a time when:

    a. government surpluses are high
    b. tax rates are high
    c. many non-bank businesses are going bankrupt
    d. investment by non-bank businesses is large
    e. banks have reserves equal to 100% of their deposit liabilities

9. During a bank run, there can be a conflict between the interests of the individual and the interests of the society as a whole. Specifically:

   a. each depositor has an incentive to get in line, even though bank runs can weaken the economy
   b. each depositor has an incentive to make additional deposits because of the high interest rates, but high interest rates are undesirable for the society as a whole
   c. it is even more important for society than for the individual depositor that unsound banks be closed down
   d. even though a run at a specific bank causes a contraction at that bank, the overall economy nevertheless expands because of the improved competitive position of other banks
   e. all of the above

10. The Federal Reserve performs all the following functions *except one*. Which is the exception? The Fed:

    a. issues paper currency
    b. conducts fiscal policy
    c. controls the quantity of money in the United States
    d. acts as the federal govermment's bank
    e. acts as a bankers' bank

11. In the balance sheet of the typical commercial bank, the largest asset is:

    a. reserve deposits
    b. loans
    c. checking deposits
    d. time deposits
    e. net worth

12. Commercial banks are required by law to hold reserves. These reserves are specified as percentages of a bank's:

    a. total assets
    b. total liabilities
    c. deposit liabilities
    d. holdings of government securities
    e. net worth

13. Suppose that the required reserve ratio is 10% and that a person deposits $100 of currency in his or her bank. Then that single bank can create

    a. $80 in additional money by lending $80
    b. $90 in additional money by lending $90
    c. $100 in additional money by lending $100
    d. $1,000 in additional money by lending $1,000
    e. no additional money; it takes the actions of the whole banking system to create more money, not just one bank

14. Suppose that the required reserve ratio of a commercial bank is represented by the fraction R. Suppose that this commercial bank receives a deposit of currency of $100. Then, as a result, *this single commercial bank* can make a loan of as much as:

    a. $100 / R
    b. $100 x R
    c. $100 / (1-R)
    d. $100 x (1-R)

15. When a commercial bank makes a loan to the local drug store

    a. the bank's assets increase
    b. the bank's liabilities increase
    c. the money stock increases
    d. the amount of checking deposits increases
    e. all of the above

16. Suppose that someone in New York, who banks at the Citibank, sends a check for $1,000 to someone in California, who deposits it in the Bank of America. The required reserve ratio is R. In the process of check clearing, the reserves of Citibank will:

    a. increase by $1,000, while those of the Bank of America will decrease by $1,000
    b. decrease by $1,000, while those of the Bank of America will increase by $1,000
    c. increase by $1,000 x R, while those of the Bank of America will decrease by $1,000 x R
    d. decrease by $1,000 x R, while those of the Bank of America will increase by $1,000 x R
    e. increase by $1,000 divided by R, while those of the Bank of America will decrease by $1,000 divided by R

17. An increase in the required reserve ratio on checking deposits would most likely cause:

    a. an increase in M1
    b. a decrease in M1
    c. an increase in checking deposits
    d. an increase in bank profits
    e. an increase in the checking deposit multiplier

18. The monetary system is sometimes said to form an inverted pyramid. By this, we mean that:

    a. a large quantity of checking deposit money can be built on a small quantity of reserves

    b. a large quantity of reserves can be built on a small quantity of checking deposit money

    c. a large quantity of currency can be built on a small quantity of checking deposit money

    d. checking deposits are the largest component of M1

    e. currency is the largest component of M1

19. The deposit multiplier, 1/R, represents the *maximum* amount by which the banking system may increase deposits as a result of an initial increase in bank reserves. (R is the required reserve ratio.) In practice, the actual increase is likely to be less than shown by this multiplier, since:

    a. a single bank can increase deposits by less than can the banking system as a whole

    b. a single bank can increase deposits by more than can the banking system as a whole

    c. as the banks expand their loans, the public will decide to deposit more currency in their bank accounts

    d. banks may hold less than the required reserve ratio; with a smaller actual reserve ratio, the expansion of deposits is likewise smaller

    e. banks may hold excess reserves, and the public may decide to hold more currency as the quantity of money increases

20. Banks are most likely to hold significant quantities of excess reserves when:

    a. their profits are high

    b. the economy is in a boom

    c. the economy is growing slowly and steadily

    d. the economy is in a mild recession

    e. the economy is in a depression

EXERCISES

1. a. If I deposit $100,000 in currency into a checking deposit in bank A and the required reserve ratio is 20%, then the immediate increase in bank A's total reserves is $_____ and the immediate increase in bank A's required reserves is $_____. Thus, the immediate increase in bank A's excess reserves is $_____. As a result of this transaction, the total amount of currency in the hands of the public has [increased by $_____, decreased by $_____, not changed], the total amount of checking deposits held by the public has [increased by $_____, decreased by $_____, not changed], and the total amount of M1 has [increased by $_____, decreased by $_____, not changed].

    b. Suppose bank A now lends all its new excess reserves. The borrower writes a check against the proceeds of the loan, and this check is deposited in a checking deposit in bank B. When this loan is made and this check is deposited and cleared, the effect is to make bank A's total reserves [increase by $_____, decrease by $_____, remain unchanged], to make bank A's required reserves [increase by $_____, decrease by $_____, remain unchanged], to make bank A's excess reserves [increase by $_____, decrease by $_____, remain unchanged], to make bank B's total reserves [increase by $_____, decrease by $_____, remain unchanged], to make bank B's required reserves [increase by $_____, decrease by $_____, remain unchanged], and to make bank B's excess reserves [increase by $_____, decrease by $_____, remain unchanged]. As a result of this loan, the total amount of checking deposits has [increased by $_____, decreased by $_____, not changed].

    c. If the process of lending continues until all excess reserves have been eliminated throughout the banking system, then as a result of the whole process, starting with my initial deposit, the total quantity of currency in the hands of the public will have [increased by $_____, decreased by $_____, not changed], the total quantity of checking deposits in the hands of the public will have [increased by $_____, decreased by $_____, not changed], the total quantity of M1 in the hands of the public will have [increased by $_____, decreased by $_____, not changed], and the total quantity of M2 in the hands of the public will have [increased by $_____, decreased by $_____, not changed].

2. Show what happens as a direct result of each of the following transactions by filling in the appropriate numbers for that transaction in the balance sheet. Each balance sheet should represent the **change** in assets and liabilities of *all* banks as a group. In each case, suppose that the required reserve ratio on checking deposits is 20% and on all other deposits is 10%. Each transaction should be considered separately from all the others.

a. Someone deposits $25,000 in currency into a checking deposit.

b. Someone withdraws $100,000 in currency from a noncheckable savings account.

c. Someone switches $200,000 from a checking deposit to a noncheckable savings deposit.

d. A bank lends $40,000 to someone who immediately takes the proceeds of the loan in the form of currency.

e. A bank lends $100,000 to someone who uses that $100,000 to pay off a loan to someone who puts the $100,000 into a noncheckable savings deposit.

Balance Sheet a

Change in assets		Change in liabilities	
Loans	_____		
Total reserves	_____		
Required reserves	_____	Checking deposits	_____
		Other deposits	_____
Excess reserves	_____		

Balance Sheet b

Change in assets		Change in liabilities	
Loans	_____		
Total reserves	_____		
Required reserves	_____	Checking deposits	_____
		Other deposits	_____
Excess reserves	_____		

Balance Sheet c

Change in assets		Change in liabilities	
Loans	_____		
Total reserves	_____		
Required reserves	_____	Checking deposits	_____
		Other deposits	_____
Excess reserves	_____		

Balance Sheet d

Change in assets		Change in liabilities	
Loans	_____		
Total reserves	_____		
Required reserves	_____	Checking deposits	_____
Excess reserves	_____	Other deposits	_____

Balance Sheet e

Change in assets		Change in liabilities	
Loans	_____		
Total reserves	_____		
Required reserves	_____	Checking deposits	_____
Excess reserves	_____	Other deposits	_____

ESSAY QUESTIONS

1. Why are bank runs most likely to occur during a depression or severe recession? Are bank runs most damaging to the economy at such times, or would they be more damaging during a period of prosperity? Why?

2. Deposits in most banks and S&Ls are now covered by federal insurance. If your bank doesn't have the money, the federal government will make good, up to a maximum of $100,000 per deposit. As a result, runs on banks and other financial institutions have been *much* less common than they were during the 1930s, prior to federal deposit insurance. Nevertheless, runs still occasionally occur. Why do you suppose they still do?

3. By his term "invisible hand," Adam Smith suggested that self-interested actions tend to benefit society. This chapter has explained two cases where pursuit of self-interest lead to undesirable results for the society as a whole. What are these two cases, and why does self-interest lead to socially undesirable outcomes? Can you think of any way to deal with these problems?

4. Individual bankers often argue, "We don't create money; we just lend money that has already been deposited with us." Is this correct? If so, explain why. If not, explain why not.

ANSWERS

Matching columns: **1 h, 2 e, 3 g, 4 a, 5 d, 6 b, 7 f, 8 c**

True-False:
1 T (p. 189)
2 F (p. 189)
3 F (p. 191)
4 F (p. 194)
5 T (p. 196)
6 F (p. 196)
7 T (p. 197)
8 F (p. 198)
9 T (p. 202)
10 F (p. 201-202)

Multiple Choice:
1 d (p. 187)
2 a (p. 188)
3 e (p. 189)
4 b (p. 189)
5 d (p. 190)
6 b (p. 191)
7 e (p. 192)
8 c (p. 193)
9 a (p. 193)
10 b (p. 193)
11 b (p. 194)
12 c (p. 194)
13 b (pp. 195-198)
14 d (pp. 195-198)
15 e (p. 196)
16 b (p. 197)
17 b (p. 201)
18 a (p. 202)
19 e (p. 202)
20 e (p. 202)

Exercises

1   a. $100,000, $20,000, $80,000, decreased by $100,000, increased by $100,000, not changed.
     b.   decrease by $80,000, remain unchanged, decrease by $80,000, increase by $80,000, increase by $16,000, increase by $64,000, increased by $80,000.
     c.   decreased by $100,000, increased by $500,000, increased by $400,000, increased by $400,000 (note: M1 is included in M2).

Balance Sheet a

Change in assets			Change in liabilities	
Loans		0		
Total reserves		25,000		
Required reserves	5,000		Checking deposits	25,000
Excess reserves	20,000		Other deposits	0

Balance Sheet b

Change in assets			Change in liabilities	
Loans		0		
Total reserves		− 100,000		
Required reserves	− 10,000		Checking deposits	0
Excess reserves	− 90,000		Other deposits	− 100,000

Balance Sheet c

Change in assets			Change in liabilities	
Loans		0		
Total reserves		0		
Required reserves	− 20,000		Checking deposits	− 200,000
Excess reserves	+ 20,000		Other deposits	+ 200,000

Balance Sheet d

Change in assets			Change in liabilities	
Loans		+ 40,000		
Total reserves		− 40,000		
Required reserves	0		Checking deposits	0
Excess reserves	− 40,000		Other deposits	0

Balance Sheet e

Change in assets			Change in liabilities	
Loans		100,000		
Total reserves		0		
Required reserves	+10,000		Checking deposits	0
Excess reserves	−10,000		Other deposits	100,000

CHAPTER 12

THE FEDERAL RESERVE AND THE TOOLS OF MONETARY POLICY

LEARNING OBJECTIVES

After you have studied this chapter in the textbook and study guide, you should be able to

✔ Describe the organization of the Federal Reserve

✔ Describe how the Fed can use each of its three major tools to affect the size of the money stock

✔ Explain how open market operations change the balance sheets of the commercial banks and the Federal Reserve

✔ Explain how open market operations affect not only the size of the money stock, but also interest rates

✔ Give an example which shows why the yield (interest rate) on a treasury bill falls when its price rises

✔ Explain why a restrictive monetary policy usually does not involve an open market sale, but rather just a reduction in the rate of purchases on the open market

✔ Explain why large changes in the required reserve ratio would be very disruptive, and give an historical example

✔ Explain why a margin requirement may add to the stability of the stock market, even if the margin requirement is never changed

✔ Explain why federal deposit insurance reduces the risk of a run on banks

✔ Explain why stabilization of the interest rate may be a "trap" for the Federal Reserve, just as aiming for an annually balanced budget may be a trap for fiscal policymakers

---

MAJOR PURPOSE

There are two major tools for controlling aggregate demand—fiscal policy and monetary policy. Fiscal policy, which involves changes in tax rates and in government spending, is in the hands of the Congress and the President. Monetary policy, which involves changes in the rate of growth of the money stock, is in the hands of the Federal Reserve. The major purpose of this chapter is to explain how the Federal Reserve (the "Fed") can influence the money stock.

As we saw in Chapter 11, most of the money stock consists of checking deposits in banks and other similar institutions. The amount of money that banks can create depends on the quantity of reserves that they own and on the required reserve ratio. The Federal Reserve has three principal tools with which it can influence the quantity of money:

- It can **purchase securities on the open market.** When it does so, it increases the reserves of the banks.

- It can **change the discount rate,** changing the banks' desire to borrow from the Fed. Since the reserves of banks increase when they borrow from the Fed, changes in the discount rate influence the total quantity of reserves that the banks hold.

- It can **change the required reserve ratio,** thereby changing the quantity of deposits that can be created on any given reserve base.

HIGHLIGHTS OF CHAPTER

The Federal Reserve is the central bank of the United States. It is the "bankers' bank," and it is responsible for controlling the quantity of money. When the Federal Reserve was established, there were deep concerns over the power of centralized financial institutions, and therefore the Fed is decentralized. There are twelve Federal Reserve districts, with a Federal Reserve Bank in each district. In Washington, there is a Board of Governors with seven members. The most important policy body of the Fed—the Federal Open Market Committee (FOMC)—is made up of seven members of the Board, plus five of the presidents of the regional Federal Reserve Banks. At meetings of the FOMC, these five presidents explain to the other members of the FOMC the economic and financial conditions in their districts. (So do the other regional bank presidents, who are non-voting members of the FOMC.) Thus, conditions in the various regions are considered as the FOMC develops monetary policy.

The Fed has three major tools with which it can affect the quantity of money:

- **open market operations**

- **changes in the discount rate,** and

- **changes in the required reserve ratios.**

Open market operations are the most important tool; they are used for the every-day, "bread and butter" activities of the Fed.

When the Fed buys securities worth, say, $10 million on the open market, bank reserves increase by the same $10 million. Because the banks have additional excess reserves, they are able to make loans; the money stock can increase by a multiple of the $10 million. As we saw in Chapter 11, the *maximum* increase in the money stock is the $10 million times $1/R$, where R is the required reserve ratio. However, in practice, the actual increase is not likely to be this great. As banks make loans and the quantity of money increases, the public is likely to want not only more checking deposits, but more currency too. People therefore withdraw some currency from their bank accounts. When they do so, the reserves of banks decline and the amount of money they can create likewise declines.

The maximum increase in the money stock depends on the size of the open market operation ($10 million in the above example) and on the required reserve ratio. It does not depend on whether a commercial bank, a non-bank corporation, or an individual sells the securities to the Fed. However, the details of the way in which the money supply increases will vary, depending on who the seller is. If a non-bank corporation—such as IBM—or an individual is the seller, then the money stock will go up immediately as a result of the open market purchase. For example, if IBM sells the $10 million in securities which the Fed buys, IBM will deposit the proceeds from the sale in its checking deposit, and its holdings of money will therefore increase by $10 million. IBM's bank will now have larger deposit liabilities, and its required reserves will rise—by $10 million times the required reserve ratio. If this ratio is, say, 15%, the bank will have $8.5 million of excess reserves (the $10 addition to reserves less the increase of $1.5 million in required reserves). It will safely be able to lend the $8.5 million. There will be a series of expansions: $10 million + ($10 x 0.85) million + ($10 x 0.85^2) million, and so on.

On the other hand, if a commercial bank sells the $10 million in securities, there is no initial increase in the quantity of money, since the checking deposits held by the public have not been affected. Required reserves likewise remain unchanged, but the banks have $10 million in excess reserves. They can therefore lend the full $10 million, again initiating an expansion of $10 million + ($10 x 0.85) million + ($10 x 0.85^2) million, and so on. Although the initial, first round effects of the two types of transaction are different, their ultimate effects on the money stock will be the same.

Thus, when the Fed buys securities on the open market, the money stock increases. If the Fed sold securities on the open market, it would likewise cause a multiple decrease in the money stock. However, this would cause *very* tight monetary conditions. In our growing economy, the money stock can grow at a moderate rate without causing inflation. Therefore, when the Fed wants to tighten monetary conditions, it normally does not sell securities. Instead, it simply *reduces the rate of purchases* on the open market.

When it buys securities on the open market, the Fed bids their prices *up*. But this is just another way of saying that it bids interest rates *down*. As a result of the Fed's purchase, the banks have excess reserves. As they make loans or buy bonds with these reserves, the banks bid interest rates down even further.

Changes in the discount rate are the second major tool of the Fed. By cutting the discount rate, the Fed encourages banks to borrow more. When they borrow more, their reserves increase. Thus, a cut in the discount rate is an expansionary policy; increases in the rate are a restrictive policy. The Fed is sometimes spoken of as the **lender of last resort**; the banks can go to the Fed to borrow reserves if they are temporarily short and cannot get funds elsewhere.

The third major tool of the Fed is a change in the required reserve ratio. As we have seen in Chapter 11, checking deposits can be as much as $1/R$ times reserves, where R is the required reserve ratio. By changing R, the Fed can thus change the size of the deposit multiplier. Relatively small changes in R can have a powerful effect on the size of the money stock. In order to avoid disruption of monetary conditions, the Fed is now careful to make only small changes when it does adjust R.

The Fed also has a number of other ways of influencing monetary and financial conditions. It imposes **margin requirements**, limiting the amount that can be borrowed by those who are buying stocks or bonds. The Fed has the power to adjust these requirements, but it has in fact kept the rate on stocks stable at 50% in recent years. For requirements to have a stabilizing effect, it is not necessary that they be adjusted. A steady 50% rate means that stockholders will not be wiped out by moderate reverses in the stock market, and will not be forced to dump their stocks. If they had been able to borrow, say, 90% of the value of the stock, their rush to get out of the stock market could change a small retreat into a stock market collapse.

Finally, the Fed can influence bank behavior by **moral suasion** — suggestions to bankers regarding appropriate policy.

When the Fed purchases securities on the open market, it creates money "out of thin air." Our money is not backed by gold. Money retains its value because the Fed limits its supply; money is scarce. Checking deposits are backed not only by the assets of the banks, but also by the Federal Deposit Insurance Corporation. Insurance is important for individual depositors; it offers them protection. It is also important for the stability of the system as a whole: Federal insurance greatly reduces the risk of a run on banks.

At times in our history, money has also been backed by **gold** (and silver). This system had one great advantage, in that it limited the amount of money that could be created, and thus acted as a restraint on reckless, inflationary expansions in the money stock. However, it had two great defects.

- Increases in the quantity of gold played a function similar to open market purchases in the present system; they increased bank reserves, and permitted a multiple increase in the money stock. However, there was no assurance that the amount of gold mined or imported from abroad would provide the amount of money needed for a full-employment, non-inflationary economy.

- The banking system was vulnerable to runs. Whenever gold reserves were withdrawn from the base of the monetary pyramid, there was a powerful contractionary effect on the quantity of money. In other words, the gold standard could make financial crises and recessions worse — as it did in the early 1930s. This was the major reason for the abandonment of the gold standard.

Finally, this chapter explains how the Fed faces a **policy trap**, somewhat similar to the fiscal trap of attempting to balance the budget every year. If the Fed follows a policy of stabilizing interest rates, its policy is **passive**. It increases the money stock in response to rising demands from the public for funds. Responding in such a passive way can be a great mistake. The money supply may go up particularly rapidly during prosperity, when people are clamoring for loans. This can make the prosperity turn into an inflationary boom. A passive response can also add to a downturn.

IMPORTANT TERMS

*Match the first column with the corresponding phrase in the
second column.*

___f___ 1. The Federal Reserve
___i___ 2. Open market operation
___l___ 3. Example of restrictive policy
___h___ 4. Example of the expansive policy
___k___ 5. U.S. Treasury
___c___ 6. Discount rate
___j___ 7. Prime rate
___e___ 8. Price of a treasury bill
___b___ 9. Margin requirement
___d___ 10. Legal tender
___a___ 11. Fiat money
___g___ 12. Attempt to stabilize interest rates

a. Money unbacked by gold or silver; it is money because the government says so
b. Helps to stabilize stock market
c. Interest rate on Fed's loans to commercial banks
d. Creditors must accept this money in repayment of debts
e. This rises when interest rate falls
f. Central bank of the United States
g. Possibly, a monetary policy trap
h. Reduction of discount rate
i. Purchase or sale of government securities by the Fed
j. A bank's publicly-announced interest rate for short-term loans
k. This institution initially issued securities bought or sold in open market operations
l. Increase in the required reserve ratio

TRUE-FALSE

T   F   1.   Although the Federal Reserve is technically independent of the President, in fact the Fed is closely influenced by the President because the members of the board are appointed by the President for four-year terms which coincide with the presidential term.

T   F   2.   Open market policy is determined by the Federal Open Market Committee, which meets in Washington However, actual open market operations are carried out by the New York Federal Reserve Bank.

T   F   3.   If the required reserve ratio of the commercial banks is 10%, then an open market purchase of $1 million by the Federal Reserve permits the banks to increase their checking deposits by a maximum of $10 million.

T   F   4.   The appropriate strategy for the Federal Reserve during a depression is to sell government bonds, to make low-risk, sound assets available for the commercial banks to buy.

T   F   5.   When commercial banks repay their discounts (borrowings from the Fed), the result is an increase in their excess reserves.

T   F   6.   When the Fed sells securities to the commercial banks, it increases their earning assets, and thus makes possible an increase in the money stock.

T   F   7.   When the Fed increases its purchases of government securities, it is engaging in an expansionary act; when it sells government securities, it is engaging in a restrictive act.

T   F   8.   If the interest rate doubles, then the price of a treasury bill falls by 50%.

T   F   9.   Federal Reserve notes (the paper currency of the United States) are backed dollar for dollar with gold held by the Fed.

T   F   10.   The existence of federal insurance for bank depositors reduces the danger of bank runs. Indeed, one of the major purposes of such insurance is to reduce this danger.

MULTIPLE CHOICE

1. The Federal Reserve *cannot* do one of the following. Which one?

   a. change the tax rate on profits
   b. change the discount rate
   c. change the required reserve ratio
   d. change margin requirements
   e. buy securities on the open market

2. When the Fed purchases securities on the open market, the securities it buys are:

   a. common stock of the U.S. corporations whose stocks are included in the Dow-Jones industrial average
   b. corporate bonds
   c. securities issued by state governments
   d. securities issued by the federal government
   e. any of the above; since it is a transaction on "the open market," the Fed buys whatever is offered for sale at the best price

3. As a result of an open market operation by the Fed, the amount of checking-deposit creation will be larger, the higher is the:

   a. required reserve ratio
   b. discount rate
   c. fraction of securities purchased from commercial banks, rather than the general public
   d. fraction of securities purchased from the general public, rather than from commercial banks
   e. volume of securities purchased by the Fed

4. If the Fed purchases $100,000 of government securities on the open market and the required reserve ratio is 20%, then the maximum increase in commercial bank reserves is:

   a. $20,000
   b. $100,000
   c. $200,000
   d. $400,000
   e. $500,000

5. When the Fed purchases a $100,000 Treasury bill from a manufacturing corporation, and that cor-

poration deposits the proceeds in a checking deposit in its bank (Bank A), then:

   a. Bank A's total reserves rise by $100,000
   b. Bank A's excess reserves rise by $100,000
   c. Bank A can safely lend $100,000
   d. the liabilities of the Fed increase by $500,000
   e. all of the above

6. Suppose that (a) the Fed purchases a $100,000 government security on the open market, (b) the required reserve ratio is 20%, (c) IBM sells the security, and (d) IBM deposits the proceeds from the sale in its commercial bank. The effect of this single transaction will be to increase the *excess* reserves of the commercial banking system banks by:

   a. $20,000
   b. $80,000
   c. $100,000
   d. $200,000
   e. $500,000

7. Suppose that *(a)* the Fed purchases a $100,000 government security on the open market, *(b)* the required reserve ratio is 20%, *(c)* IBM sells the security, and *(d)* IBM deposits the proceeds from the sale in its commercial bank. The effect of this single transaction will be to increase the money stock by:

   a. zero
   b. $20,000
   c. $100,000
   d. $200,000
   e. $500,000

8. When the Fed purchases a $100,000 Treasury bill from a commercial bank, as a result:

   a. the bank's total reserves rise by $100,000
   b. the bank's excess reserves rise by $100,000
   c. the bank can safely lend $100,000
   d. the Fed's assets increase by $100,000
   e. all of the above

9. During a depression, the best strategy of the Federal Reserve is to:

   a. sell government bonds, to make low-risk, sound assets available for commercial banks to buy
   b. sell government bonds, in order to reduce the size of the government's deficits
   c. sell government bonds, in order to increase aggregate demand
   d. buy government securities
   e. exhort banks not to lend to businesses, in order to reduce their risks of loss

10. The Fed *tightens* monetary conditions by *lowering*:

    a. required reserve ratios
    b. the margin requirements on stocks
    c. the discount rate
    d. the interest rate on Treasury bills
    e. the rate at which it is buying securities on the open market

11. The discount rate refers to:

    a. the penalty paid by risky bank borrowers; that is, the amount of interest they pay in excess of the prime rate
    b. the rate at which banks write off bad loans
    c. the rate at which assets lose their real value as a result of inflation
    d. the rate at which money loses its value as a result of inflation
    e. the rate of interest that the Fed charges on loans to commercial banks

12. If the required reserve ratio is 20%, and if commercial banks borrow $100 million from the Federal Reserve, then the effect on commercial bank reserves is:

    a. an increase of $100 million
    b. an increase of $500 million
    c. a decrease of $100 million
    d. a decrease of $500 million
    e. no change

13. If the price of a Treasury bill falls, then

    a. all interest rates certainly fall
    b. all interest rates probably fall

    c. the interest rate on this bill certainly falls
    d. the interest rate on this bill probably rises
    e. the interest rate on this bill certainly rises

14. If the price of a $100,000 Treasury bill with 1 month to maturity is $99,000, then the annual yield on that bill is approximately:

    a 1%
    b. 3%
    c. 4%
    d. 6%
    e. 12%

15. When the Fed purchases Treasury bills on the open market:

    a. the quantity of bank reserves falls
    b. the interest rate on Treasury bills rises
    c. the price of Treasury bills rises
    d. the risk premium on business loans usually rises
    e. required reserves of banks fall

16. In 1936 and 1937, the Fed doubled required reserve ratios. This action:

    a. helped speed up the recovery then under way
    b. was the single most important reason for the recovery from the Great Depression
    c. would have promoted recovery, if it had been backed up with open market sales
    d. was a cause of a recession within the Great Depression
    e. had no effect because banks held excess reserves

17. A margin requirement tends to make the stock market less unstable:

    a. only if it is backed up by open market operations
    b. only if the margin requirement is increased during an upswing in stock prices, and decreased during a downswing in stock prices
    c. only if the margin requirement is decreased during an upswing in stock prices, and increased during a downswing in stock prices
    d. only if the margin requirement is decreased whenever the rate of business bankruptcy increases
    e. even if it is kept perfectly stable, at (say) 50%

18. The Federal Reserve issues paper currency which acts as money in the United States. It is most accurate to say that this money is "backed" by Federal Reserve assets in the form of:

    a. loans to member banks
    b. U.S. government securities
    c. gold
    d. required reserves of the commercial banks
    e. the value of Federal Reserve buildings

19. Under the old gold standard system (such as that in the United States in the 1920s):

    a. the need for gold reserves limited the creation of money
    b. the knowledge that money was backed 100% by gold created confidence
    c. the knowledge that money was backed partly by gold created confidence and prevented runs on banks

    d. the government was forbidden to issue bonds unless it held 100% backing for those bonds in the form of gold
    e. the money stock was just a small fraction of the quantity of gold

20. There are two traps facing macroeconomic policy makers. Specifically, they are quite likely to destabilize aggregate demand if they attempt to:

    a. balance the full employment budget every year, and stabilize interest rates
    b. balance the actual budget every year, and stabilize interest rates
    c. balance the full employment budget every year, and stabilize the money stock
    d. balance the actual budget every year, and stabilize the money stock
    e. stabilize the growth in reserves and in the money stock

EXERCISES

1. Suppose that the required reserve ratio on all deposits is 20 percent.

   a. In balance sheets A, show the initial effects of an open market purchase of $10 million in government securities by the Fed. The seller is a manufacturing corporation that deposits the proceeds immediately in its bank.

   b. In balance sheets B, show the ultimate effects of the above transaction after the maximum expansion of loans and deposits. Assume that banks keep all increases in reserves in the form of deposits in the Fed.

   c. In balance sheets C, show the initial effects of an open market purchase of $10 million in government securities by the Fed. The seller is a commercial bank. (Is the initial change in the money stock the same as in part a? Why or why not?)

   d. In balance sheets B, show the ultimate effects of the transaction in part c, after the maximum expansion of loans and deposits. Assume that banks keep all increases in reserves in the form of deposits in the Fed. (Compare the results with the results in b.)

Balance Sheets A

Federal Reserve System		All commercial banks	
Federal government securities _____	Federal Reserve notes _____ Deposits of banks _____ Net worth _____	Loans _____ Total reserves _____ Required reserves _____ Excess reserves _____	Deposits _____

Balance Sheets B

Federal Reserve System		All commercial banks	
Federal government securities _____	Federal Reserve notes _____ Deposits of banks _____ Net worth _____	Loans _____ Total reserves _____ Required reserves _____ Excess reserves _____	Deposits _____

Balance Sheets C

Federal Reserve System		All commercial banks	
Federal government securities _____	Federal Reserve notes _____ Deposits of banks _____ Net worth _____	Loans _____ Gov. securities _____ Total reserves _____ Required reserves _____ Excess reserves _____	Deposits _____

Balance Sheets D

Federal Reserve System		All commercial banks	
Federal government securities _____	Federal Reserve notes _____ Deposits of banks _____ Net worth _____	Loans _____ Gov. securities _____ Total reserves _____ Required reserves _____ Excess reserves _____	Deposits _____

2. (This exercise is only for those who have studied Box 12-1 in the textbook.) Consider a bond with a face value of $100 and with an annual coupon of $10. In the table below, fill in the approximate price of the bond under different assumptions regarding its term to maturity and current market rates of interest. What does this example suggest regarding the relationship between (a) the term to maturity and (b) the size of price changes in response to a change in interest rates?

Term to maturity

Rate of interest	1 year	2 years	Perpetuity
8%	_____	_____	_____
10%	_____	_____	_____
12%	_____	_____	_____

ESSAY QUESTIONS

1. With an example, show how, if you buy shares on 50% margin, your gains would be higher if the price doubles than if you bought for cash. (Ignore brokerage fees, interest on the loan, and dividends on the stock). What would happen if the price fell by 50%?

2. (This question is especially for those who have studied Box 12-2 in the text and also exercise 2 in this Study Guide). Savings and loan associations (S&Ls) have traditionally held most of their assets in the form of mortgages on homes, with initial terms of 25 or 30 years. Suppose that many mortgages are made when interest rates are 8%. Then suppose that interest rates in the financial markets rise to 12%. What happens to the value of the mortgages held by an S&L? Suppose the S&L continues to offer low interest rates to depositors, because that is all it can afford to pay since it is receiving low interest on mortgages made in previous years. Will any difficulties arise for such an S&L?

ANSWERS

Matching columns: **1** f, **2** i, **3** l, **4** h, **5** k, **6** c, **7** j, **8** e, **9** b, **10** d, **11** a, **12** g

True-False:
1 F (p. 207)
2 T (p. 208)
3 T (p. 209)
4 F (pp. 210-211)
5 F (p. 211)
6 F (p. 211)
7 T (p. 211)
8 F (p. 212)
9 F (p. 215)
10 T (p. 217)

Multiple Choice:
1 a (p. 206)
2 d (p. 206)
3 e (pp. 206-207)
4 b (pp. 208-209)
5 a (p. 209)
6 b (p. 209)
7 c (p. 209)
8 e (p. 210)
9 d
10 e (p. 211)
11 e (p. 211)
12 a (p. 211)
13 e (p. 212)
14 e (p. 212)
15 c (p. 212)
16 d (p. 212)
17 e (p. 214)
18 b (p. 215)
19 a (p. 217)
20 b (p. 220)

Exercises:

1. Balance Sheets A

Federal Reserve System		All commercial banks	
Federal government securities $10 million	Federal Reserve notes 0	Loans 0	Deposits $10 million
	Deposits of banks $10 million	Total reserves $10 million	
		Required reserves $2 million	
	Net worth 0	Excess reserves $8 million	

Balance Sheets B

Federal Reserve System		All commercial banks	
Federal government securities $10 million	Federal Reserve notes 0	Loans $40 million	Deposits $50 million
	Deposits of banks $10 million	Total reserves $10 million	
		Required reserves $10 million	
	Net worth 0	Excess reserves 0	

Balance Sheets C

Federal Reserve System		All commercial banks	
Federal government securities $10 million	Federal Reserve notes 0	Loans 0	Deposits 0
	Deposits of banks $10 million	Government securities −$10 million	
		Total reserves $10 million	
	Net worth 0	Required reserves 0	
		Excess reserves $10 million	

Balance Sheets D

Federal Reserve System		All commercial banks	
Federal government securities $10 million	Federal Reserve notes 0	Loans $50 million	Deposits $50 million
	Deposits of banks $10 million	Government securities −$10 million	
		Total reserves $10 million	
	Net worth 0	Required reserves $10 million	
		Excess reserves 0	

2.　　The exact answers are:

Term to maturity			
Rate of interest	1 year	2 years	Perpetuity
8%	$101.85	$103.57	$125.00
10%	$100.00	$100.00	$100.00
12%	$ 98.21	$ 96.62	$ 83.33

The longer the term to maturity, the greater is the change in price of the bond for any given change in market interest rates. (Note: market interest rates on long-term bonds generally fluctuate much less than market rates on shorter term securities. This dampens the fluctuations in long-term bond prices somewhat. Nevertheless, long-term bond prices still fluctuate much more than the prices of shorter-term securities.)

Across

1, 7, 8, 9. the principal tool for controlling the quantity of money
11. what we do with income we don't spend
12. each
14. checking deposits form an inverted _____ on a base of bank reserves
17. third person
18, 19. central bank of the United States
21. not (French)
22. unbacked paper currency is _____ money
24. a university degree
26, 28. by changing this, the Federal Reserve can have a powerful effect on the quantity of money
29. by raising this, the Federal Reserve can discourage banks from borrowing (2 words)

Down

2. by keeping money _____, the Federal Reserve can protect its value
3. part of the foot
4, 28. if the Fed tries to stabilize this, it may destabilize the economy
5. one of the functions of money is to act as a _____ of value
6. in the early days of the Federal Reserve, this was at the base of the inverted monetary pyramid
9. mother
10. useless; of no _____
11. if the Fed lets the quantity of money _____, the result is rapid inflation
13. Dr. Jekyll's alter ego
14. it's mightier than the sword
15. regarding
16. a university degree
17. Alan Greenspan is the _____ of the Federal Reserve
19. be carried or transported by
20. a type of income
23. fearless and daring
25. the Fed sometimes engages in jawboning, or _____ suasion
26. interest rates generally are high on bonds with a high _____
27. bankers fear this

Part 4

GREAT MACROECONOMIC ISSUES:
Aggregate Supply

CHAPTER 13

HOW CAN INFLATION AND UNEMPLOYMENT COEXIST?

LEARNING OBJECTIVES

After you have studied this chapter in the textbook and study guide, you should be able to

✔ Summarize the experience of the United States with inflation and unemployment since 1960

✔ Explain why demand-management authorities sometimes feel that they face a policy dilemma

✔ Explain the two major reasons why the (short-run) Phillips curve can shift upward   *wages↑, cost↑ I↑*

✔ Explain the difference between cost-push inflation and demand-pull inflation, and explain why cost-push inflation can lead to higher prices and higher unemployment

✔ Explain why demand-management authorities face a very difficult problem when there is a large upward shift in the Phillips curve (such as in 1973-1974 and 1979-1980)

✔ Explain why inflation can accelerate to higher and higher rates if the authorities try to keep unemployment below the natural rate

✔ Explain why many economists believe that the long-run Phillips curve is vertical

✔ Explain why Milton Friedman argues that, "There is *always* a *temporary tradeoff* between inflation and unemployment; there is *no permanent tradeoff*."

✔ Explain why the process of reducing inflation can be painful   *Uemp ↑*

MAJOR PURPOSE

For several decades following the Great Depression, macroeconomists concentrated on the management of aggregate demand. When the economy was declining into a recession, they advocated expansive demand policies to keep output and employment at high levels. When inflationary pressures were strong, they advocated tighter policies to restrain demand and keep inflation down.

However, during the past two decades, the economy has from time to time given conflicting signals. There have been bouts of **stagflation**—that is, periods when high unemployment was combined with rapid inflation. The high unemployment suggested that demand should be expanded; the rapid inflation indicated the opposite. To understand this complex economy, we must look not only at aggregate demand, but also at aggregate supply. Our purpose in Chapter 13 is to study aggregate supply and, in doing so, to explore stagflation.

The simplest way to approach aggregate supply is the one presented earlier, in a diagram with real national product on the horizontal axis and the average level of prices on the vertical axis. However, this is not the approach most commonly used. Instead, economists generally begin with a diagram with the two macroeconomic problems—unemployment and inflation—on the axes. The smooth curve traced out by historical data during some periods, such as the 1960s, is known as a **Phillips curve**. However, the Phillips curve has not been stable in recent decades. One of the major purposes of this chapter is to try to explain why the Phillips curve shifts.

HIGHLIGHTS OF CHAPTER

When the demand for a specific commodity—such as wheat—changes, there is a movement *along* the supply curve (as illustrated in Figure 4-7 on p. 56 of the textbook). Similarly, when *aggregate* demand changes, the economy moves along the *aggregate* supply curve. Thus, when we study aggregate supply in this chapter, we are studying how the economy responds to a change in aggregate demand. This is an important and puzzling topic. From time to time, the economy has suffered from **stagflation**— a combination of high unemployment and high inflation. In such circumstances, it is not clear what the authorities should do. If they take steps to increase aggregate demand in an attempt to increase output and employment, they may get more inflation instead. If they restrain demand in an attempt to reduce inflation, they may get more unemployment. Making sense of the aggregate supply puzzle is an important topic; it is the main purpose of this chapter.

To study aggregate supply, it is possible to use the aggregate supply curve introduced in Chapter 8, with real national product (Q) on the horizontal axis and the average level of prices (P) on the horizontal axis. However, this is not the approach most commonly used. Instead, economists generally begin with a diagram with the two macroeconomic problems—unemployment and inflation—on the axes.

When historical data are plotted on such a diagram in Figure 13-3, two main conclusions stand out:

- Between 1961 and 1969, the points trace out a smooth curve, sloping upward to the left. This is known as a **Phillips curve**.

- Since 1970, the observations have been above and to the right of that Phillips curve. We have gotten more unemployment *and* more inflation. Strong movements in a "northeast" direction (upward and to the right) occurred between 1969 and 1970, between 1973 and 1975, and between 1978 and 1980.

During the 1960s, when most economists believed that the Phillips curve being traced out by the data represented a stable relationship, authorities felt trapped on the horns of a **dilemma**. If they expanded aggregate demand briskly, they would get more output and employment. But inflation would rise. On the other hand, if they restrained demand in order to keep inflation down, the unemployment rate would remain at high. They hoped to escape from this dilemma by using expansive aggregate demand policies to reduce unemployment, and incomes policies to directly restrain inflation. (Incomes policies will be studied in Chapter 14.) They were not entirely successful. Inflation in fact did increase as output expanded and unemployment declined. The economy in fact did move upward as it moved to the left in Figure 13-3 in the text.

Shifts in the Phillips Curve

Even worse problems were to come in the 1970s, as both inflation and unemployment increased. Two of the three strong movements to the "northeast" in Figure 13-3 coincided with the spiralling price of oil on the international markets. This suggests one explanation for the stagflation since 1970: Rising oil prices shifted the Phillips curve upward, and meant more inflation combined with more unemployment. Inflation was caused by the *upward push of costs*.

Oil prices certainly do not provide the whole explanation, however. The first major movement to the northeast, between 1969 and 1970, occurred while international oil prices were stable at a very low level. In fact, there was something of a glut on the international oil market.

To explain this early episode of stagflation, we must look elsewhere. The **accelerationist theory** provides the most generally accepted explanation.

The Accelerationist Theory

The accelerationist theory, put forward in the late 1960s by Ned Phelps and Milton Friedman, has one core idea. The Phillips curve—such as that observed in the 1960s—is fundamentally unstable. If the authorities attempt to reduce the unemployment rate to a very low level, they will succeed, but *only temporarily*. In particular, they will succeed only during the interval between the time when demand is expanded and the time when contracts are renegotiated to take the resulting inflation into account. When people renegotiate contracts, they will demand compensation for inflation; wages and other contractual prices will be adjusted upward. Inflation will accelerate; a **wage-price spiral** will gain momentum. This is illustrated by points H, J, and K in Figure 13-7 of the text. At each of these points, actual inflation is higher than people expected when they negotiated contracts. For example, at H, people expected zero inflation (as illustrated by the Phillips curve), but get 2% instead. They then renegotiate contracts on the expectation of 2% inflation. But, with higher costs, businesses raise prices; the economy moves to J. People expect 2% inflation; they get 4% instead.

How, then, can we return to macroeconomic equilibrium, once the wage-price spiral has begun? **Equilibrium occurs only when people get the amount of inflation they expected**. This happens if the rate of inflation stabilizes. For inflation to stabilize, the authorities must depart from their single-minded attempt to keep unemployment low; they must introduce a degree of restraint in aggregate demand policies. As restraint occurs, businesses will find it hard to raise prices more and more rapidly; inflation will indeed level off. However, as it becomes harder to sell goods, output will increase more slowly and the unemployment rate will rise.

Once people get the amount of inflation they expect, the unemployment rate will move back to its **natural** or **equilibrium** rate, illustrated by point N in Figure 13-8 of the text. A central proposition of the accelerationist theory is that this equilibrium rate of unemployment doesn't depend on the rate of inflation; once people adjust completely to inflation, the inflation rate doesn't affect their behavior. They are neither more nor less willing to work, and businesses are neither more nor less willing to hire them. Because the equilibrium rate of unemployment isn't affected by inflation—once people have gotten used to it—the *long run Phillips curve is vertical* (Figure 13-9, p. 236). In the short run, the central bank can lower the rate of unemployment by an inflationary policy. But in the long run, their willingness to accept an inflation rate of, say, 6% will not result in any gain in output and employment. There is a **short-run tradeoff** between the goals of low inflation and low unemployment, but there is **no long-run tradeoff**.

Just as low unemployment is associated with an acceleration of inflaton, so high unemployment is associated with a deceleration of inflation. If aggregate demand is too low to buy the goods and services being offered at the current rate of inflation, output will fall and businesses will settle for smaller increases in price. This is illustrated by point V in Figure 13-10 of the text (p. 238). V is not a good place to be; the unemployed are being used as cannon fodder in the war against inflation. In order to avoid painful periods at points like V, it is important to stop the inflationary spiral from gathering momentum in the first place. To those who asked in the 1970s how we might get out of stagflation, there was only one easy—although unsatisfactory—answer: Go back to 1965 and do it right this time. Stop inflation from accelerating in the first place. But, of course, we could not go back to 1965 again. The economy was in fact dragged through the severe recession of 1982 before the inflation rate was brought down to 4%—a rate that was still much higher than that of the period from 1955 to 1965.

IMPORTANT TERMS

Match the first column with the corresponding phrase in the second column.

_h_ 1. Phillips curve _h_
_d_ 2. Tradeoff _d_
_f_ 3. Stagflation _f_
_j_ 4. Cost-push inflation _j_
_g_ 5. Natural rate of unemployment _g_
_b_ 6. Accelerationist theory _b_
_i_ 7. Market power inflation _i_
_c_ 8. A likely cost of reducing inflation _c_
_e_ 9. Wage-price guideposts _e_
_a_ 10. Gradualism _a_

a. A policy of the President Nixon
b. View that there is tradeoff in the short run, but not in the long run
c. Unemployment greater than the natural rate
d. Choice between conflicting goals
e. A policy of Presidents Kennedy and Johnson
f. High unemployment combined with high inflation
g. Equilibrium rate of unemployment
h. Relationship between inflation and unemployment
i. Another term for cost-push inflation
j. The rise in the international price of oil is an example

TRUE-FALSE

T F 1. According to the aggregate supply function of simple Keynesian theory, large-scale unemployment *or* rapid inflation can exist, but not both simultaneously.

T F 2. U.S. data for the 1960s trace out a reasonably smooth Phillips curve, but the data for the 1970s do not.

T F 3. The Kennedy administration imposed wage-price guideposts in an attempt to shift the Phillips curve to the right.

T F 4. Those who emphasize cost-push inflation are more likely to believe that market power is important than are advocates of the accelerationist theory.

T F 5. Even when the unemployment rate is at its natural level, there is still frictional unemployment.

T F 6. A high point on the long-run Phillips curve represents a higher rate of inflation than does a low point.

T F 7. A high point on the long-run Phillips curve represents a higher rate of unemployment than does a low point.

T F 8. According to the accelerationist theory, the economy can be in equilibrium only when the inflation rate is zero; any positive rate of inflation will tend to accelerate.

T F 9. If the long-run Phillips curve is vertical, then there is no long-run tradeoff between the objectives of price stability and high employment. A low unemployment rate cannot be "bought" over the long run by a willingness to accept inflation.

MULTIPLE CHOICE

1. In the horizontal range of the Keynesian aggregate supply function, the rate of inflation is:

   a. zero
   b. rising
   c. high and constant
   d. equal to the natural rate
   e. less than the natural rate

2. If we compare the U.S. experience since 1970s with that of the 1960s, we find that, on average:

   a. the rate of unemployment and the rate of inflation have both been lower since 1970 than during the 1960s
   b. the rate of unemployment has been lower since 1970 than during the 1960s, but the rate of inflation has been higher
   c. the rate of inflation has been lower since 1970 than during the 1960s, but the rate of unemployment has been higher
   d. the rate of unemployment and the rate of inflation have both been higher since 1970 than during the 1960s

3. In the United States, "double digit" inflation (that is, inflation of 10% or more) occurred in:

   a. every year from 1966 to 1975
   b. every year from 1973 to 1981
   c. 1971, 1972, and 1973
   d. 1971, 1972, and 1982
   e. 1974, 1979, and 1980

4. The Phillips curve traced out by the U.S. data of the 1960s suggested that there was a policy "tradeoff." Specifically, there seemed to be a conflict between achieving the goal of high employment and the goal of:

   a. an equitable distribution of income
   b. allocative efficiency
   c. technological efficiency
   d. high growth
   e. low inflation

5. Cost-push inflation is different from demand-pull inflation because:

   a. demand-pull inflation involves a rise in every price, whereas cost-push inflation involves a rise in prices only in industries with monopoly power
   b. demand-pull inflation involves a rise in every price, whereas cost-push inflation involves only a rise in the prices of goods, not services
   c. when demand-pull inflation begins, it represents a movement along a short-run Phillips curve, but cost-push inflation is an upward shift of the short-run Phillips curve
   d. demand-pull inflation is accompanied by a rise in unemployment rate, but cost-push inflation by a fall in unemployment
   e. demand-pull inflation is accompanied by a fall in output, but cost-push inflation by an increase in output

6. Economists are most likely to conclude that "cost push" inflation is occurring when a rise in the rate of inflation is accompanied by an increase in:

   a. output
   b. the rate of growth of output
   c. the unemployment rate
   d. an increase in government deficits
   e. an increase in the money stock

7. Which of the following is an important assumption of cost-push theories of inflation?

   a. there is perfect competition
   b. market power is an important feature of the economy
   c. unemployment is below the natural rate
   d. an increase in the money stock is the most important cause of inflation
   e. government deficits are the most important cause of inflation

8. A point to the left of the long-run Phillips curve is unstable because:

   a. workers and others have underestimated inflation; they will demand higher wages and prices when new contracts are written
   b. workers and others have overestimated inflation; they will be willing to settle for lower wages and prices when new contracts are written
   c. monetary policy is unsustainably tight
   d. fiscal policy is unsustainably tight
   e. the unemployment rate is above its natural rate

9. Suppose two points, A and B, are on the long-run Phillips curve. B is higher than A. Then the *real* wage at B is:

a. higher than at A
b. the same as at A
c. lower than at A
c. falling, and so is the real wage at A and every other point on the long-run Phillips curve
e. rising, even though the real wage is falling at A

10. According to the accelerationist theory (that is, the natural rate hypotheses), the short-run Phillips curve shifts whenever there is a change in:

a. the natural rate of inflation
b. the natural rate of acceleration of inflation
c. expectations of inflation
d. the degree of unionization of the labor force
e. the rate at which innovations are being used by businesses

11. According to the accelerationist theory, equilibrium can exist only when:

a. the unemployment rate is at its natural rate
b. the inflation rate is zero, since any non-zero rate of inflation will tend to accelerate
c. the expected inflation rate is zero, since inflation will accelerate otherwise
d. the growth of the money stock is zero, since inflation will accelerate otherwise
e. all of the above conditions are met

12. Which of the following is an assumption of the accelationist theory of inflation?

a. there is downward rigidity in nominal wages
b. inflation is caused mainly by unions
c. inflation is caused mainly by OPEC
d. inflation is caused mainly by an acceleration in investment
e. people's expectations of inflation have an important effect on the contracts they negotiate

13. Suppose we draw a diagram with both a short-run Phillips curve and a long-run Phillips curve. At the point where they intersect:

a. the inflation rate is zero
b. the unemployment rate is zero

c. actual inflation is the same as expected inflation
d. inflation is accelerating
e. the rate of unemployment is rising

THE NEXT THREE QUESTIONS ARE BASED ON FIGURE 13.1

Figure 13.1

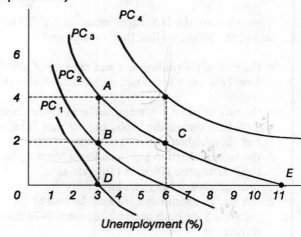

14. In Figure 13.1, the natural rate of unemployment is 6%. Which of the points represents an equilibrium?

a. A
b. B
c. C
d. D
e. E

15. In Figure 13.1, the natural rate of unemployment is 6%. Suppose that the economy is at point A on Phillips curve PC3. To get to that point, contracts have been based on an expected rate of inflation of:

a. zero
b. 2%
c. 3%
d. 4%
e. 6%

16. In Figure 13.1, the natural rate of unemployment is 6%. Last year, the economy was at point A on short run Phillips curve PC3. If contracts are now renegotiated, which of the short-run Phillips curves is most likely to result?

  a. PC$_1$
  b. PC$_2$
  c. PC$_3$
  d. PC$_4$
  e. either PC$_1$ or PC$_2$, but we can't be sure which

17. According to the accelerationist theory, the unemployment rate will be greater than the natural rate when inflation is:

  a. greater than people expected
  b. less than people expected
  c. low and steady
  d. high and steady
  e. zero

18. According to the accelerationist theory (that is, the natural rate hypotheses),

  a. inflation will accelerate whenever the unemployment rate deviates from the natural rate
  b. the short-run and long-run Phillips curves are both vertical
  c. there is a trade-off between inflation and unemployment in the long run, but not the short
  d. aggregate demand policies should be fine tuned in order to prevent inflation from accelerating
  e. an attempt to reduce inflation with more restrictive monetary policies will result in above-normal unemployment during a transition period

EXERCISES

1. Figure 13.2, shown here, represents the Phillips curve for year 1, when the expected rate of inflation is zero. The natural rate of unemployment is _____%. If unemployment is at the natural rate, the rate of inflation will be _____ in year 1. If, alternatively, the unemployment rate is 3%, the actual rate of inflation will be (more, less) than the expected rate by _____%.

Figure 13.2

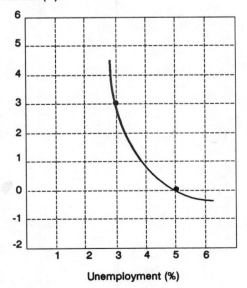

Suppose now that the expected rate of inflation is 2% in year 2. Draw the Phillips curve for year 2 in Figure 13.2. If the rate of unemployment is still 3% in year 2, the rate of inflation will be _____%.

If, on the other hand, inflation is 3% in year 2, the rate of unemployment will be about _____%. Now suppose that the rate of inflation is kept at 3% indefinitely, into years 3, 4, 5.... The expected rate of inflation will eventually become _____%, and the rate of unemployment will move to _____%. Alternatively, if aggregate demand policies are aimed at keeping the unemployment rate at 3%, the rate of inflation will _____.

2 a. Suppose that the economy is initially at point A on Phillips curve 1 in Figure 13.3. Then the curve shifts to Phillips curve 2. If policymakers pursue restrictive monetary and fiscal policies that keep the rate of inflation from increasing, then unemployment will (increase, decrease) by amount _____. If, on the other hand, they keep the rate of unemployment stable by following more expansive policies, then inflation will (increase, decrease), by amount _____.

Figure 13.3

Inflation

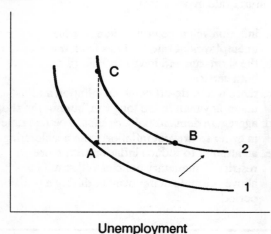

Unemployment

b. Suppose this shift in the Phillips curve is caused by workers observing a rate of inflation higher than they expected. Then, according to the natural rate theory, the rate of unemployment at *A* was (more than, less than, the same as) the natural rate. The attempt by the policymakers to go to point *C* will cause the Phillips curve to _____ when contracts are renegotiated.

ESSAY QUESTIONS

1. According to the accelerationist theory, the rate of unemployment cannot be kept permanently below the natural rate by an expansive aggregate demand policy. Explain why. Can the rate be kept permanently above the natural rate by a restrictive aggregate demand policy? Explain why or why not.

2. The short-run Phillips curve indicates that when unemployment rises, inflation should fall. But in some years, both inflation *and* unemployment rise. How would an accelerationist explain this? Is there any other explanation?

ANSWERS

Important terms: **1 h, 2 d, 3 f, 4 j, 5 g, 6 b, 7 i, 8 c, 9 e, 10 a**

True-False: **1 T (p. 226)**
2 T (p. 229)
3 F (p. 230)
4 T (pp. 232, 234)
5 T (pp. 233-236)
6 T (p. 236)
7 F (p. 236)
8 F (p. 236)
9 T (p. 237)

Multiple Choice: **1 a (p. 226)**
2 d (p. 229)
3 e (p. 229)
4 e (p. 230)
5 c (p. 231)
6 c (p. 231)
7 b (p. 232)
8 a (pp. 234-236)
9 b (pp. 235-236)
10 c (p. 236)
11 a (p. 236)
12 e (p. 236)
13 c (p. 236)

Exercises

1.   5, 0, more, 3, 5, 4, 3, 5, become more and more rapid.

Figure 13.2 Completed:

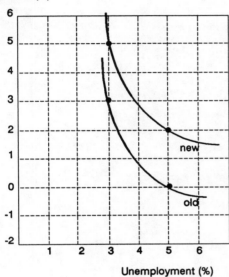

2   a. increase, *AB*, increase, *AC*

        b. less than, shift further up

CHAPTER 14

HOW DO WE DEAL WITH THE INFLATION-UNEMPLOYMENT DILEMMA?

LEARNING OBJECTIVES

After you have studied this chapter in the textbook and study guide, you should be able to

✔ Explain why the natural rate of unemployment can change

✔ List the policies that have been suggested to reduce the natural rate of unemployment

✔ Explain the major purposes of incomes policies

✔ Describe briefly the incomes policies of the past 30 years

✔ Explain the pros and cons of an incomes policy

✔ Explain why the indexation of wages may permit the authorities to reduce the rate of inflation without causing a long period of high unemployment

✔ Explain why the indexation of wages may nevertheless make the inflation problem worse

✔ Explain how profit sharing might make the economy more flexible, and reduce the severity of unemployment during recessions

✔ Explain what can happen if people anticipate the effects of policies, specifically why *(1)* the wage-price spiral might be speeded up, and *(2)* why the adjustment to a lower rate of inflation might be speeded up and made less painful

✔ Explain why it is important for the Federal Reserve to maintain credibility

✔ Explain the difference between adaptive expectations and rational expectations

✔ Explain why aggregate demand policies might become ineffective if people's expecations are rational

✔ Criticize the conclusions of rational expectations theorists

✔ Describe briefly how European experience with unemployment has differed from U.S. experience over the past three decades

MAJOR PURPOSE

The previous chapter explained how unemployment and inflation could coexist. Chapter 14 explains the policy issues raised by the desired to achieve low unemployment and low inflation simultaneously. One approach is to try to reduce the equilibrium or natural rate of unemployment by steps aimed at improving the flexibility and efficiency of the labor market. (Even though the long-run Phillips curve is vertical, it is not set in concrete. The equilibrium rate of unemployment can change if labor market institutions change.) The chapter reviews efforts to keep the inflation rate down by **incomes policies** — that is, by direct restraints on wages and prices.

This chapter also elaborates one of the conclusions of the previous chapter — that the short-run Phillips curve can shift when people's expectations change. If people try to anticipate the effects of policies, the wage-price spiral may be greatly speeded up, thus weakening the power of aggregate demand policies to bring down the unemployment rate, even in the short run.

HIGHLIGHTS OF CHAPTER

This chapter explains some of the policy issues raised by the short-run and long-run Phillips curves. The chapter covers four main topics:

- Policies to **reduce the natural rate** of unemployment

- Incomes policies to **control inflation** without creating high unemployment

- Other policies to **ease the transition** to lower inflation

- The ways in which **expectations** may be formed, and how the inflation-unemployment tradeoff depends on expectations.

Policies to Reduce the Natural Rate of Unemployment

The natural rate of unemployment need not be constant; it rose between the 1960s and 1970s and has fallen over the past decade. A number of proposals have been made to reduce the natural rate.

- **Abolish the minimum wage?** Critics of the minimum wage point out that it raises the cost of hiring unskilled teenagers and therefore reduces the number of jobs offered to them. Proponents of the minimum wage argue that it is only fair to pay a reasonable wage to workers. It is unlikely that congress would take the strong symbolic step of abolishing the minimum wage. However, as the wage is set in dollars ($3.35 per hour), it is eroded by inflation. The real minimum wage declined during the 1980s, and this worked to reduce the natural rate of unemployment.

- **A two-tiered minimum wage?** A two tiered minimum wage is sometimes suggested as a way to reduce the negative effect on employment: Employers could pay less while workers are learning their jobs. This proposal was endorsed by President Bush and was included in 1989 legislation to raise the minimum wage. However, the president vetoed the legislation on the ground that the increase in the minimum wage would create unemployment.

- **Less discrimination.** This would reduce the unemployment rate, as well as making the economy more fair. (Note that the objectives of fairness and low unemployment may be in conflict when a higher minimum wage is being considered. However, a reduction in discrimination raises no such conflict — steps toward fairness also reduce the unemployment rate.)

- **Training programs** that help the unskilled prepare for jobs.

- The government as the **employer of last resort?** This proposal would mean a major change in the way the labor market works: The government would offer a job to anyone who could not get one in the private sector of the economy. This proposal is very controversial; it could be quite expensive and could cause a less efficient economy. There is much less support for this proposal now than there was during the 1970s.

Incomes Policies

Incomes policies are sometimes used in an effort to ease the transition to a lower rate of inflation. For example, the wage-price freeze of the Nixon administration was intended to break inflationary expectations without an extended period of high unemployment. At other times, incomes policies are used to stop inflation from gathering momentum in the first place—for example, the wage-price guideposts of the Kennedy and Johnson administrations.

Incomes policies are controversial. Proponents say that they are the only compassionate way to deal with the inflationary problem—the only alternative is to use the unemployed as draftees in the war against inflation. Opponents say that incomes policies may do more harm than good. For example, by suppressing inflationary pressures temporarily, they may provide the illusion of success, with the authorities unwittingly continuing expansive policies as underlying inflationary pressures build up. The result can be an explosion of inflation. Critics also point out that, by interfering with the price system, incomes policies can reduce the efficiency of the economy. Proponents agree that incomes policies may create some problems, but these problems are minor compared to the unemployment caused if inflation is fought solely by restraints on aggregate demand.

Other Policies to Ease the Transition to Lower Inflation

During the 1970s, some economists suggested that the economy could move to a lower rate of inflation without high and persistent unemployment if wages were indexed. If wages are indexed, they are adjusted for changes in the cost of living. Wage indexation became much more common during the 1970s, when inflation was becoming both higher and more erratic.

Indexation may make it easier to unwind inflation without long periods of unemployment; money wages are more flexible, and respond more quickly to restrictive aggregate demand policies. But they are a two-edged sword. They can speed up a wage-price spiral. Indexation—which represents a way in which labor tries to protect itself from erratic inflation—tends to make inflation even more erratic.

Indexation is aimed at adjusting nominal wages in order to stabilize real wages. In contrast, profit sharing introduces flexibility into real wages. If workers receive a signficant share of their income in the form of bonuses tied to profits, labor costs move with the business cycle. During recessions, profits and bonuses—and therefore labor costs—fall, encouraging businesses to cut prices in order to maintain sales and output.

Expectations

To explain the basics of the acceleration theory, the last chapter used a very simple assumption—people expect the inflation of today to continue into the future. But expectations can be more complicated. If people not only respond to current inflation, but also anticipate the effects of policies, a wage-price spiral can be greatly speeded up. In negotiating their contracts, people do not simply compensate for past inflation; they compensate for expected future inflation, which can exceed the present rate. The result can be a very rapid upward shift in the short-run Phillips curve (Figure 14-1 in the text).

During a period of restraint, the short-run Phillips curve can also shift very rapidly, but now in a downard direction. People take into account not only the reduction in inflation that has already occurred, but the reduction expected for the future. The rapid downward shift of the short-run Phillips curve can cause a much quicker transition to low inflation, thus reducing the overall cost in terms of unemployment.

Therefore, credibility is important in macroeconomic policy. When tight policies are being followed, people will adjust relatively quickly if they believe that the policies will be firmly pursued. Paradoxically, the way to stop inflation without long periods of high unemployment is to convince the public that the Federal Reserve will firmly pursue a policy of restraint, even if it does cause unemployment.

If expectations are rational, people make the best forecasts possible with available information on what the authorities are doing and how the economy works. Available information is, however, not perfect; people still make mistakes. But they do not keep making the same mistake. Their mistakes are random numbers. (In contrast, people did keep making the same mistake in the simple acceleration theory presented back in Figure 13-7 on p. 234 of the text.)

Some rational expectations theorists argue that demand management policies are useless as a way of reducing cyclical unemployment because, if followed consistently, they will be anticipated by the public. The only way the Fed can affect real output is by creating a surprise — that is, by trickery. But surprises mean that the Fed is behaving in an unpredictable (erratic?) way. As a result, the public is less able to figure out what is going on, and fluctuations in unemployment become larger. It is important for the Fed to *minimize* uncertainty. This, say many rational expectations theorists, can be done if the Fed follows a monetary rule, with a steady, moderate growth in the money stock.

The theory of rational expectations has provided important perceptions regarding some of the limits of policy. However, the conclusions of the rational expectations theorists are subject to two major criticisms (others are given on p. 255 of the text):

- The facts don't fit the theory. According to the main body of rational expectations theory, deviations from the natural rate of unemployment should be random, relatively brief occurances. But this was not true during the deep recession of 1981-1982. And it most decidedly was not the case during the Great Depression of the 1930s.

- A monetary rule does not necessarily lead to the most predictable outcome. If the Fed can identify and offset fluctuations in the economy, it can make the economy more predictable. Therefore, rational expectations theory has left the old question, to be considered in detail in chapter 18: *Can* the Fed best stabilize the economy by a rule, or by active management?

IMPORTANT TERMS

Match the first column with the corresponding phrase in the second column.

b 1. Wage-price guideposts	a. Way to provide flexibility in real wages
h 2. Wage-price freeze	b. Incomes policy of President Kennedy
f 3. TIP	c. These mean that people do not make systematic mistakes
i 4. Escalator clause	d. Failure to go back to the original condition
j 5. Supply shock	e. The Federal Reserve should guard this
a 6. Profit sharing	f. Incomes policy backed with tax incentives
g 7. Adaptive expectations	g. These are based on the inflation actually observed
c 8. Rational expectations	h. Incomes policy of President Nixon
k 9. Ineffective policies	i. Way to stabilize real wages in the face of inflation
e 10. Credibility	j. With indexed wages, this can be a big problem
d 11. Hysteresis	k. Possible result of rational expectations

TRUE-FALSE

T   F   1.   Between the 1970s and the late 1980s, the natural rate of unemployment rose substantially.

T   F   2.   Suppose that money wages were constant through time. Then it would be possible to have a continuous downward trend in prices, if productivity rises.

T   F   3.   Under the wage-price guideposts of the Kennedy-Johnson years, wage increases were to be kept to 3.2% per year. The 3.2% was the estimated amount needed to compensate labor for the inflation of the previous decade.

T   F   4.   The TIP proposal was supposed to work by stimulating aggregate demand.

T   F   5.   Wage indexation reduces uncertainty about real wage rates, but increases uncertainty about nominal wage rates.

T	F	6.	A COLA clause in an indexed wage contract provides a fixed amount to cover an increase in the cost-of-living, no matter what the rate of inflation.
T	F	7.	Wage indexation speeds up the response of inflation to an increase in aggregate demand.
T	F	8.	Profit sharing has been adopted in some segments of U.S. business, including parts of the automobile and steel industries.
T	F	9.	If expectations of inflation are *adaptive*, they are correct.
T	F	10.	According to the theory of rational expectations, people can make mistakes, but their mistakes are random.

MULTIPLE CHOICE

1. Which of the following is likely to reduce the natural rate of unemployment?

   a. a fall in the proportion of teenagers in the labor force
   b. more emphasis on fiscal policy, and less on monetary policy
   c. more generous unemployment insurance benefits
   d. a rise in the minimum wage
   e. all of the above

2. Some people have proposed introducing two "tiers" into the minimum wage, with a lower wage for those who are newly hired. Proponents argue that, if their proposal were adopted, the result would be:

   a. less teenage unemployment
   b. less unemployment by older workers who might be replaced by teenagers
   c. a rightward shift of the long-run Phillips curve
   d. higher profits
   e. lower profits

3. If the government acted as the *employer of last resort*, it would:

   a. hire people when they completed college
   b. hire people in over 60 years of age who were unable to find jobs
   c. offer a job to anyone who could not find a job elsewhere
   d. require businesses to hire at least 10% more workers whenever the economy was in a recession
   e. all of the above

4. President Carter proposed "real wage insurance." Taxes of workers would be cut if prices increased by more than 7%, provided the workers had agreed to limit their wage increases to 7%. One criticism of this proposal is that it would tend to:

   a. make the income tax sytem less progressive
   b. cause a recession by introducing unexpected changes in fiscal policy
   c. cancel or offset the automatic stabilizing function of taxes by cutting taxes when inflation became more severe
   d. cause undue reliance on fiscal policy, rather than a reasonable combination of fiscal and monetary policies
   e. cause undue reliance on monetary policy, rather than a reasonable combination of fiscal and monetary policies

5. Which of the following policies is most likely to cause black markets?

   a. a tax-based incomes policies
   b. real wage insurance
   c. wage-price guideposts
   d. a price freeze accompanied by restrictive monetary policies
   e. a price freeze accompanied by expansive monetary policies

6. Price controls sometimes create shortages. Shortages are most likely in the markets for:

   a. luxuries, since their prices are likely to be controlled most tightly
   b. necessities, since their prices are likely to be controlled most tightly
   c. luxuries, since producers will realize that they're not very important socially, and cut back on their production
   d. necessities, since there is a tendency for the demand for necessities to increase at the most rapid rate
   e. services, since their prices are harder to control than goods

7. The major case for wage-price guideposts or controls is that:

a. they are the only way to stop inflation
b. they are the only way to keep profits from falling when labor unions bargain aggressively for higher wages
c. they are essential if income is to be distributed in a more equitable way
d. they help to shift the long-run Phillips curve to the right
e. if we avoid guideposts or controls and rely solely on tight aggregate demand policies to restrain inflation, there will be a high cost in terms of unemployment

8. Wage indexation *reduces*

a. the variability of inflation
b. the response of inflation to a change in aggregate demand
c. uncertainty about nominal wage rates
d. uncertainty about real wage rates
e. both (c) and (d)

9. One argument in favor of the indexation of wages is that it:

a. means that foreign producers of oil can't make Americans bear the costs of a higher oil price
b. generally leads to a more stable, predictable rate of inflation
c. keeps the unemployment rate below the natural rate
d. keeps the inflation rate below the natural rate
e. makes possible a quicker, less painful reduction in the rate of inflation

10. Which of the following is the strongest argument against the indexation of wages? Wage indexation:

a. makes the real wage rate more volatile
b. makes the rate of inflation more volatile
c. causes the rich to become richer and the poor poorer
d. increases the costs, in terms of unemployment, of an anti-inflationary policy
e. keeps the unemployment rate permanently above the natural rate

11. The term "profit sharing" usually applies to which of the following ideas

a. the granting of bonuses to workers when profits are high or rising
b. charitable giving by corporations
c. the taxation of profits of rich corporations, combined with grants to corporations suffering losses
d. a proportional profits tax, which takes twice as much from corporations when their profits are twice as high
e. a progressive income tax, which redistributes profits across the economy

12. Proponents of profit sharing support it on the ground that it would

a. make the real incomes of labor more flexible, and thus reduce the rate of unemployment during recessions
b. make the real incomes of labor more flexible, and thus reduce the average rate of unemployment over long periods of time
c. increase incentives to be more efficient, and thus reduce the rate of inflation during periods of prosperity
d. increase incentives to be more efficient, and thus reduce the average rate of inflation over long periods of time
e. all of the above

13. If people anticipate the inflationary or anti-inflationary effects of changes in aggregate demand policies (rather than simply responding to past inflation), the likely result will be

a. a more unstable inflation rate
b. a more rapid acceleration of inflation when expansive policies are followed
c. a more rapid deceleration of inflation when restrictive policies are followed
d. all of the above
e. none of the above; anticipations will change the natural rate of unemployment, not the inflation rate

14. If people anticipate the inflationary or anti-inflationary effects of changes in aggregate demand policies (rather than simply responding to past inflation), then

   a. a policy aimed at keeping the unemployment rate above the natural rate will quickly lead to an explosive wage-price spiral
   b. a policy aimed at keeping the unemployment rate below the natural rate will quickly lead to an explosive wage-price spiral
   c. an expansive aggregate demand policy will lead to a permanent reduction in the natural rate of unemployment
   d. an expansive aggregate demand policy will lead to a permanent increase in the natural rate of unemployment
   e. the economy will have a natural rate of inflation, as well as a natural rate of unemployment, because people will have a better idea of what is going on

15. Some economists argue that *credibility* of a restrictive monetary policy is the key to a quick unwinding of inflation. This conclusion is based on the idea that credibility will cause:

   a. the long-run Phillips curve to shift leftward
   b. the long-run Phillips curve to slope upward to the right
   c. the long-run Phillips curve to slope downward to the right, like a short-run Phillips curve
   d. the short-run Phillips curve to shift downward more quickly when restrictive policies are followed
   e. the short-run Phillips curve to become flatter

16. If expectations of inflation are *rational*, people may make mistakes, but

   a. they make mistakes only about the rate of inflation, not about the unemployment rate
   b. they make mistakes only about the actual rate of unemployment, not about the inflation rate
   c. they make mistakes only about the natural rate of unemployment
   d. their mistakes are solely the result of uncertainty about how the economy works, not the result of uncertainty about what the Federal Reserve will do
   e. their mistakes are random

17. According to the theory of rational expectations, if a policy of expanding aggregate demand is foreseen and understood by the public, it will affect:

   a. real GNP extremely strongly, since businesses will have time to prepare new investment projects
   b. prices, but not real GNP
   c. real GNP, but not prices
   d. both prices and real GNP
   e. neither prices nor real GNP, since the Fed can affect output and prices only by trickery

18. According to some proponents of the theory of rational expectations, aggregate demand policies are *worthless* as a way of

   a. lowering the unemployment rate
   b. lowering the rate of inflation
   c. changing people's expectations of inflation
   d. all of the above

19. According to rational expectations theorists, periods when the unemployment rate exceeds the natural rate

   a. cannot exist, because the economy is always on the long-run Phillips curve
   b. cannot exist, because the economy is always a short-run Phillips curve
   c. will be brief
   d. will be very long, if the Fed follows a restrictive policy that the public understands
   e. will be associated with an inflation rate that is higher than expected

20. According to some rational expectations theorists, the Federal Reserve can temporarily reduce unemployment below the natural rate by trickery. However, the Federal Reserve should not do so. The main reason is that a policy of trickery

   a. is dishonest
   b. will increase uncertainty over future policies, and therefore increase future fluctuations in unemployment
   c. will paradoxically decrease uncertainty over future policies, and therefore increase future fluctuations in unemployment
   d. will cause the long-run Phillips curve to shift sharply to the right
   e. will cause the long-run Phillips curve to shift sharply to the left

EXERCISES

1. Suppose labor productivity in an economy increases by 3% per year; the average worker produces 3% more than in the previous year. Assume also that the labor force and population both grow by 1% per year. The nominal wage [can rise by 3% per year without causing inflation, can rise by 4% per year without causing inflation, cannot rise without causing inflation]. If the inflation rate is zero, nominal GNP will rise by an average of _____% per year over the long run, and real GNP will rise by an average of _____% per year.

2 a. In Figure 14.1, an economy in equilibrium with zero inflation is at point _____. After some time at this point, suppose that aggregate demand unexpectedly increases. In the short run, the economy will move to point _____. This is on short run Phillips curve _____, which reflects expectations of inflation of _____ per year.

Figure 14.1

Inflation (percent per annum)

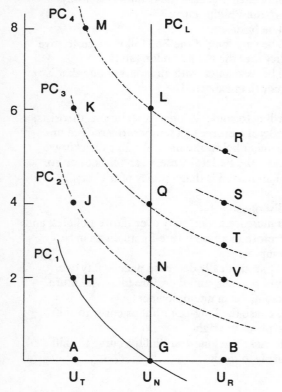

Unemployment rate (percent)

Now suppose that people expect the current rate of inflation of _____ per year to continue. Contracts will be renegotiated, causing the short-run Phillips curve to shift (upward, downward) to _____. If the authorities now expand demand in an effort to keep the unemployment rate at U_T, the economy will move in the short run to point _____. If people continue to expect the current rate of inflation—whatever it might be—to continue, then a demand management policy aimed at keeping the unemployment rate at U_T, will cause the economy to move to point _____ and then to point _____.

b. Suppose that, once the economy has gotten to point J by the process described in part (a), people no longer expect the current rate of inflation to continue, but rather anticipate an acceleration of inflation to 6%. When new contracts are negotiated, the short-run Phillips curve will shift upward from its present position at _____ to _____. Now, policy makers will be able to choose among points _____, _____, and _____, depending on the aggregate demand policies they pursue.

c. Finally, let us go back to starting point G. Suppose now that people have rational expectations. After an extended policy debate, the Federal Reserve decides that it would like to move the economy to point H by and expansive policy. As it pursues an expansive policy aimed at point H, the economy does not move there. Instead, it moves in the short run to point _____—provided that people's expectations are not only rational but correct. If, however, people make errors in forecasting the effects of the Fed's policy, they will move to point _____ or point _____.

ESSAY QUESTIONS

1. Critics argue that the use of wage-price controls is like trying to cure a sick person by using a thermometer that won't register higher than 98.6°. Why? How can wage-price controls lead to a "sicker" economic patient? How would the defenders of wage-price controls respond?

2. List the major criticisms of incomes policies. Now explain whether these criticisms apply more strongly to wage-price guideposts or to a wage-price freeze.

3. Do you believe that profit sharing is desirable? Explain why or why not.

ANSWERS

Important terms: **1** b, **2** h, **3** f, **4** i, **5** j, **6** a, **7** g, **8** c, **9** k, **10** e, **11** d

True-False:
1 F (p. 243)
2 T (p. 246)
3 F (p. 246)
4 F (p. 247)
5 T (pp. 248-249)
6 F (p. 249)
7 T (p. 249)
8 T (p. 250)
9 F (p. 251)
10 T (p. 253)

Multiple Choice:
1 a (p. 244)
2 a (p. 244)
3 c (p. 245)
4 c (p. 246)
5 e (p. 248)
6 b (p. 248)
7 e (p. 248)
8 d (p. 249)
9 e (p. 249)
10 b (p. 249)
11 a (p. 250)
12 e (p. 250)
13 d (p. 251)
14 b (p. 252)
15 d (pp. 252-253)
16 e (p. 253)
17 b (p. 254)
18 a (pp. 253-254)
19 c (pp. 253-255)
20 b (pp. 255)

Exercises

1.   can rise by 3% per year without causing inflation, 4%, 4%

2   a. G, H, PC_1, 0%, 2%, upward, PC_2, J, K, M.

      b. PC_2, PC_4, M, L, R.

      c. Q (note: Q, not N because the aggregate demand which is sufficient to move to H is more than sufficient for point N; the high demand causes a move to Q rather than N), K, T.

CHAPTER 15

HOW DOES INFLATION AFFECT THE ECONOMY?

LEARNING OBJECTIVES

After you have studied this chapter in the textbook and study guide, you should be able to

✔ Explain why unanticipated inflation has much stronger effects on the economy than anticipated inflation

✔ Give examples of those who lose from unanticipated inflation, and those who gain

✔ Explain how the real rate of interest is related to the nominal rate of interest and the expected rate of inflation (equation 15-1)

✔ Explain how the behavior of borrowers and lenders tends to stabilize real interest rates

✔ Give an example of how the after-tax real rate of interest may be negative, even though the pre-tax real rate has remained constant in the face of higher inflation

✔ Explain how borrowers—and particularly purchasers of first homes—can be adversely affected by inflation, even if the real rate of interest remains constant

✔ Explain the difference between a variable rate mortgage and a graduated payment mortgage, and explain how they are designed to deal with different problems

✔ Explain why a high, uncertain rate of inflation can cause problems in the bond market

✔ Explain the problems that can arise if the government uses the real government deficit as a measure of fiscal policy, or if the Fed uses the real quantity of money as a measure of monetary policy

MAJOR PURPOSE

In Chapter 13, we have seen how wage contracts can be adjusted to take account of inflation. The theory of the vertical Phillips curve is based on the view that inflation won't have any affect on the unemployment rate, once people get used to the inflation and adjust to it. This chapter deals with the way in which individuals, businesses, and the government adjust to an inflationary environment. By adjusting, they reduce the effects of inflation on real magnitudes, such as real output and real wages. However, even after two and a half decades of rather rapid inflation, the economy has not adjusted fully to inflation; inflation has significant real consequences. The purpose of this chapter is to study the ways in which the economy does and does not adjust to inflation.

One important set of adjustments is in the market for bonds and other debt instruments. Unanticipated inflation hurts bondholders; they are repaid in less valuable dollars. If they anticipate inflation, however, they can adjust for it. They can withdraw from the bond market until interest rates rise to compensate for inflation. However, even if this happens, with real interest rates remaining constant, inflation can still have important consequences for borrowers and lenders. In particular, the combination of high inflation and high nominal rates of interest means that debt is front-loaded — payments in the early years are high, in real terms. As a result, young people have difficulty buying their first homes.

HIGHLIGHTS OF CHAPTER

In Chapter 13, we began to see how the economy can adjust to inflation. As inflation continues, people come to expect it and change their behavior accordingly. For example, labor unions bargain for a higher nominal wages to compensate for the increase they have come to expect in the cost of living. If people's expectations are accurate, then the inflation need not affect real wages; it will be taken into account by both workers (who will demand higher money wages) and employers (who will be willing to pay higher money wages). In addition, the rate of unemployment may be unaffected; this was the idea behind the vertical long-run Phillips curve of Chapter 13.

The Real Rate of Interest

Adjustments like this may occur not only in the labor market, but also in other markets. Among the most important markets affected by inflation are the markets for corporate bonds, government bonds, mortgages, and other debt instruments. Owners of bonds can be severely hurt by inflation; they are repaid in dollars with smaller value. If they anticipate inflation, they can take steps to protect themselves. They can switch out of bonds and into other assets, such as common stock or real estate. When they do so, bond prices fall; that is, interest rates rise. The rise in interest rates is reinforced by the eagerness of borrowers. Because they will be able to repay in less valuable dollars, they have an incentive to borrow more as inflation increases.

The **real rate of interest** is the rate of interest after account is taken of inflation. It is (approximately) the nominal rate of interest less the expected rate of inflation. For example, if the nominal interest rate is 10%, someone lending $100 today will be repaid $110 in one year's time. If the rate of inflation is 10% during that year, the $110 will buy no more than the $100 would have bought originally. In real terms, the lender has no gain. The nominal interest rate of 10% is no more than enough to compensate for the 10% inflation; the real interest rate is zero (10%-10%). This is not very good from the lender's viewpoint. Lenders are therefore reluctant to make loans, causing a further rise in interest rate. When this happens, the real interest rate becomes positive. Many observers of financial markets believe that the behavior of lenders and borrowers will act to stabilize the real interest rate. Until the early 1970s, evidence suggested that the real interest rate was in fact quite stable. In the early 1980s, however, the real interest rate was high by historical standards.

Even if the real interest rates is constant and inflation is perfectly anticipated, a combination of high inflation and a high nominal interest rate can have an important effect on borrowers and lenders. There are two main reasons for this. One has to do with front loading; the other has to do with the tax system.

The Duration of Debt: Front Loading

Bonds, mortgages, and other types of debt usually specify a constant nominal rate of interest. In a world of zero inflation, a nominal interest rate of 3% represents a real rate of 3%. Someone who has issued a bond with a face value of $100,000 will pay $3,000 in interest each year.

Suppose now that inflation accelerates to 10%, with the *nominal* rate of interest keeping step at 13%. Someone issuing a $100,000 bond now has to pay $13,000 in interest per year. This $13,000 includes $10,000 to compensate for the loss of value by the $100,000 principal over the year. The remaining $3,000 represents a real interest payment. In a sense, $10,000 of the $13,000 may be looked on as a partial repayment of principal. In real terms, the borrower is not only paying interest, but is also repaying part of the principal each year. Payments in early years are very high—the $13,000 represents a lot in the first year, since prices have not yet risen much. The debt is **front loaded**.

During periods of rapid inflation and high nominal interest rates, mortgages are similarly front loaded. As a result, it is very difficult for first-time buyers to afford homes. If they take out a mortgage now, they may face a crushing burden in the early years. This problem would be solved if mortgage payments were graduated—that is, if nominal payments rose through the years to keep real payments stable. Such graduated mortgages are not generally available, nor are they likely to become available. One reason is that they would lead to a rise in the burden of mortgage payments through time if inflation unexpectedly slowed down.

Taxation and Inflation

Taxation is another reason that inflation can have lasting real consequences, even if it is perfectly anticipated. People pay taxes on their *nominal* interest, and can generally deduct their nominal interest payments from their taxable income. In the earlier example, with $13,000 interest on a $100,000 bond, the taxpayer in the 25% bracket would pay a quarter of the $13,000 in taxes, leaving only $9,750, or 9.75% after taxes. This is not enough to compensate for the 10% inflation. The **after-tax real rate of interest** is negative.

Inflation and Uncertainty

Uncertainty is another complication that prevents perfect adjustment to inflation. Periods of *rapid* inflation also tend to be periods of *erratic* inflation. Thus, bond buyers are taking a risk. High nominal interest rates may compensate for the inflation they expected when they bought the bond. But suppose that inflation speeds up unexpectedly. The bondholder will lose. Similarly, there are risks for the borrower: If inflation unexpectedly slows down, the real burden of interest payments increases. Because erratic inflation poses risks for both borrowers

and lenders, a high, erratic inflation may cause the long-term bond market to dry up.

One way to deal with the problem of uncertainty is to have periodic adjustments in interest during the period of the loan. For example, most new mortgages in the United States now have adjustable rates. With the introduction of adjustable rate mortgages, the mortgage market has dealt quite effectively with the problem of *erratic* inflation. But it has not been able to deal with the front-loading problem associated with *high* rates of inflation and interest. Graduated mortgages are unavailable.

Real Magnitudes and Fiscal and Monetary Policies

Finally, this chapter considers how the government itself might respond to an inflationary situation. One question is how we should measure fiscal policy. Some argue that we should look at the changes in the real deficit of the government. When inflation is rapid—say, at 10%—then the first 10% in interest doesn't really represent interest; it represents a partial repayment of the real value of the debt. Thus, a government with a $1 trillion debt and a $100 billion deficit is not running a deficit at all. In real terms, its budget is balanced; the real value of its debt is constant.

This is a rather interesting idea, but it presents a problem. Indeed, it represents a trap that can be added to the earlier list of traps (that is, an annually balanced budget or a monetary policy aimed at a stable nominal rate of interest). Specifically, if inflation increases, the real value of the debt declines. This causes a swing toward surplus in the real budget. If we take the real budget as our guide, we may respond by increasing government spending or cutting taxes. But these steps will increase aggregate demand and make inflation worse.

Similarly, it would be a trap for the Fed to focus on the real quantity of money. During periods of inflation, the real value of the outstanding money stock declines. If the Fed responds by increasing the amount of money in order to restore the real quantity, it will make inflation worse.

Nevertheless, the real debt and the real quantity of money are important. For example, the real quantity of money is an important determinant of how much people will buy. The problem is that real measures must be used *very* cautiously by policymakers. One of the problems with inflation is that it introduces an element of confusion and chaos into the debate over aggregate demand policies.

IMPORTANT TERMS

Match the first column with the corresponding phrase in the second column.

_____ 1. Anticipated inflation
_____ 2. Unanticipated inflation
_____ 3. The real rate of interest
_____ 4. Front loading
_____ 5. Graduated-payment mortgage
_____ 6. Adjustable-rate mortgage
_____ 7. Indexation
_____ 8. Cap

a. A way of dealing with the problem of front loading
b. A limit on indexation
c. This type of inflation has relatively small real effects
d. Automatic adjustment for inflation, as in wages
e. The nominal rate less the expected rate of inflation
f. A way of dealing with the problem of erratic inflation
g. An effect of inflation, even if real interest rates are constant
h. This type of inflation has large real effects

TRUE-FALSE

T   F   1.   People who have borrowed large sums gain from inflation, particularly when it is unanticipated.

T   F   2.   People who hold government bonds usually lose from inflation, particularly when it is accurately anticipated.

T   F   3.   Inflation makes lenders more eager to lend, and borrowers less eager to borrow.

T   F   4.   It is possible for the real rate of interest on a short-term government bill to be negative, but not the nominal rate of interest.

T   F   5.   Inflation provides one incentive for borrowers to borrow. The tax system provides another.

T   F   6.   When nominal interest rates rise, a new mortgage is "front loaded" as a result, if monthly payments on that mortgage are constant in dollar terms throughout the life of the mortgage.

T   F   7.   A variable-rate mortgage eliminates the "front loading" of mortgages.

MULTIPLE CHOICE

1.   Someone who has taken out a mortgage to buy a house will probably

   a. lose from inflation, especially if it was unexpected when the house was bought
   b. lose from inflation, especially if it was expected when the house was bought
   c. gain from inflation, especially if it was unexpected when the house was bought
   d. gain from inflation, especially if it was expected when the house was bought
   e. lose from inflation, but only if there is no mortgage on the house

2.   If the nominal rate of interest is 12% and the real rate of interest is 3%, then the expected rate of inflation is:

   a. 18%
   b. 15%
   c. 12%
   d. 9%
   e. 3%

3. Which of the following can be negative?

   a. the nominal rate of interest on short-term securities
   b. the nominal rate of interest on long-term securities
   c. the before-tax real rate of interest on short-term securities
   d. the after-tax real rate of interest on short-term securities
   e. (c) and (d), but not (a) or (b)

4. Between 1981 and 1985, real interest rates were high. The most plausible explanation for the high real rates has been:

   a. the acceleration of inflation between 1981 and 1985
   b. high unemployment
   c. a collapsing stock market
   d. rising tax rates
   e. large government deficits

5. Consider someone in the 25% tax bracket, holding a bank account paying 8% interest. The rate of inflation is 6%. Then the after-tax real return to that individual is:

   a. -2%
   b. 0
   c. 2%
   d. 4%
   e. 6%

6. During periods of rapid inflation, the real value of trading on the long-term bond market generally:

   a. is high, because after-tax real interest rates are high
   b. is high, because nominal interest rates are high
   c. is low, because the real return on bonds is unpredictable
   d. is low, because the real return on bonds is low relative to the real return on short-term securities
   e. increases while inflation is accelerating, but then decreases when inflation levels out

7. Adjustable-rate mortgages are aimed primarily at dealing with the problem created by:

   a. the tendency of homes to depreciate
   b. high inflation
   c. erratic inflation
   d. the combined effects of inflation and taxation

   e. the tendency for real rates of interest to vary with the business cycle

8. A mortgage is most likely to be front loaded if:

   a. nominal interest rates are high, reflecting a high rate of inflation
   b. real interest rates are high
   c. real interest rates are low
   d. inflation decelerates after the house is bought
   e. taxes rise after the house is bought

9. If you had a "graduated-payment" mortgage:

   a. real payments would rise when prices rose
   b. real payments would rise when your real income rose
   c. real payments would rise when the value of the home rose
   d. nominal payments would rise during periods of inflation, keeping real payments stable
   e. nominal payments would rise when your nominal income rose, keeping payments at a constant fraction of your income

10. Suppose that the rate of inflation is steady at 7% per annum. Then over a period of 20 years, the average price level will:

    a. double
    b. treble
    c. quadruple
    d. increase by 500%
    e. increase by 700%

11. "Graduated payment" mortgages (GPM) and "adjustable rate" mortgages (ARM) are aimed at easing two different problems. Specifically, a:

    a. GPM is aimed at reducing the problem of front loading caused by *high* inflation, while an ARM is aimed at the problems created by *erratic* inflation
    b. GPM is aimed at reducing the problems caused by *erratic* inflation, while an ARM is aimed at the problems created by *high* inflation
    c. GPM is aimed at keeping *after-tax* interest rates stable, while an ARM is aimed at keeping *before-tax* interest rates stable
    d. GPM is aimed at keeping *before-tax* interest rates stable, while an ARM is aimed at keeping *after-tax* interest rates stable
    e. GPM is aimed at keeping *nominal* interest rates stable, while an ARM is aimed at keeping *real* interest rates stable

12. The rule of thumb most likely to stabilize real economic activity and prices is:

a. a slow, steady increase in the real quantity of money

b. a slow, steady increase in the nominal quantity of money

c. a slow, steady increase in the real value of the government's debt

d. a balanced budget every year

e. a stable nominal rate of interest

EXERCISES

1. a. Suppose that you put $200 into a savings account and keep it there for 1 year, at which time it has grown to $220. Then the nominal rate of interest is _____%. If you expected inflation to be 4% during the year, you anticipated a real rate of interest of _____%. Suppose that inflation turned out to be 6% instead. Then, after the year, you would find that your real return was only _____%.

   b. If you are in a 40% tax bracket, you will pay $_____ in taxes. Your after-tax nominal rate of interest will be _____%, and your after-tax real return will be _____%

2. Figure 15.1 shows the demand and supply for loanable funds in a non-inflationary situation. The equilibrium rate of interest is _____%. In the same diagram, draw the supply and demand curves that would exist if everyone expected 2% inflation and the economy had adjusted completely to this rate of inflation. The equilibrium nominal rate of interest is now _____%, and the equilibrium real rate _____%. The equilibrium quantity of funds, in real terms, is now (more than, less than, the same as) in the initial situation.

Figure 15.1

Nominal rate of interest (%)

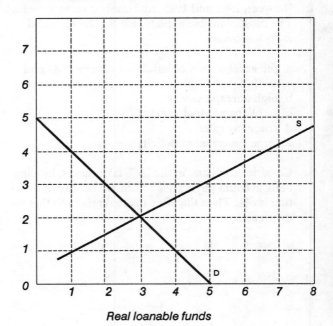

Real loanable funds

ANSWERS

Important terms: **1** c, **2** h, **3** e, **4** g, **5** a, **6** f, **7** d, **8** b

True-False:
1 T (p. 263)
2 F (pp. 263-266)
3 F (p. 264)
4 T (p. 265)
5 T (p. 267)
6 T (p. 270)
7 F (p. 271)

Multiple Choice:
1 c (p. 263)
2 d (p. 265)
3 e (pp. 264-267)
4 e (p. 266)
5 b (p. 267)
6 c (p. 269)
7 c (p. 269)
8 a (p. 270)
9 d (p. 271)
10 c (p. 271 Box)
11 a (p. 271)
12 b (pp. 272-275)

Exercises

1   a.   10, 6, 4
      b.   8, 6, 0

2.   2, 4, 2, the same as

Figure 15.1 completed:

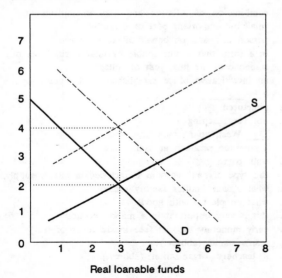

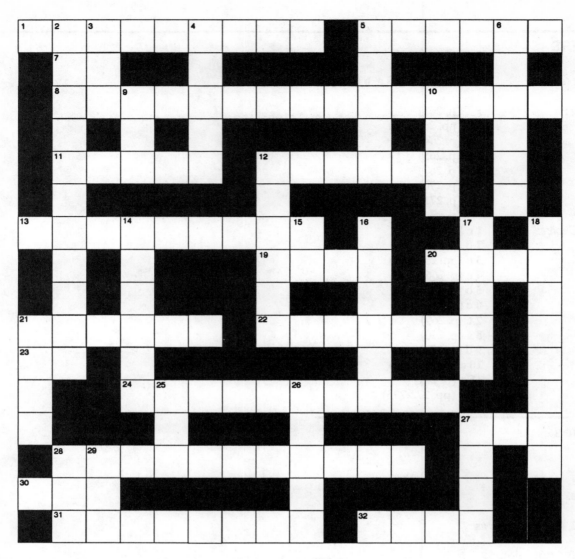

Across

1, 5. unions may use this as a protection against unexpected inflation

7. common preposition

8. the Federal Reserve influences this (2 words)

11, 12. a characteristic of mortgages when inflation and nominal interest rates are high

13. wage-price guideposts may require this

19, 20. a type of inflation

21, 22. policymakers often face this

23. on the interior of

24. used by Presidents Kennedy and Johnson to restrain inflation

27. title given to senior government leaders (abbrev.)

28. during inflation, workers want this done to their wages

30. a source of minerals

31, 32. a way the bond market may respond to erratic inflation

Down

2. combination of inflation and high unemployment

3. small but important part of a machine

4. person who acts on behalf of someone else

5. in a form that is unreadable by unauthorized persons

6. someone in the final year of college

9. an investigative office established by Congress

10. a la _____

12. punctured

14. not very exciting

15. ____ West, young man!

16. a common problem at exam time

17. wall painting

18. this type of bank account is included in money supply, M1

21. what Adam Smith's factory made

25. what people do with goods

26. this is very important in a market economy

27. early monetary theorist (see inside cover of text)

28. man's name (abbrev.)

29. a teachers' organization (abbrev.)

GROWTH AND PRODUCTIVITY: Why Have They Varied So?

LEARNING OBJECTIVES

After you have studied this chapter in the textbook and study guide, you should be able to

✔ Explain the relationship between total output, total number of hours worked, and productivity

✔ Identify the period in the twentieth century when productivity rose most rapidly, and when it rose most slowly

✔ Summarize Denison's main conclusions regarding:

   1. The reasons for increases in output per person, 1948-73
   2. The reasons for the slowdown of the 1973-81 period

✔ Explain the vicious circle of poverty that can impede the growth of very poor countries

✔ List and explain seven problems that can make it difficult for poorer countries to develop

✔ Explain how ties to the international economy can help countries break out of the vicious circle

✔ Explain some of the secrets of success of the "four tigers" of East Asia

✔ Explain some of the ways in which those four economies are similar, and the ways in which they differ

✔ Explain how foreign borrowing can help to promote economic development, but why it can also cause trouble

MAJOR PURPOSE

The major purpose of this chapter is to study economic growth — that is, the increase in the productive potential of the economy. The chapter deals with two major puzzles — why the U.S. economy has grown so much more rapidly at some periods than others, and why some nations grow so much more rapidly than others.

The key to economic growth is an increase in **productivity**, that is, an increase in output per worker. Economists have been able to identify some of the reasons for changes in productivity—most notably, the increase in the *capital stock* and the improved *education* and *training* of the labor force. But economists do not have a good explanation of why productivity increased so much more slowly after 1973 than during the previous decades.

Some of the most rapidly growing nations in the world are in East Asia. These rapidly growing nations have high rates of saving and investment, and they are strongly export oriented.

HIGHLIGHTS OF CHAPTER

The average productivity of labor is equal to total output (Q) divided by the number of labor hours worked (L). To understand the growth of output, we must look at the increases in labor hours and productivity. Figure 16-1 in the textbook shows these changes since 1800. Over the past century, output has grown at an average rate of a little more than 3% per year. Population has grown more than 1% per year, while labor hours have on average increased at a somewhat slower rate. Productivity has increased at an average annual rate of around 2%.

This increase has not, however, been steady. The improvement in labor productivity was particularly rapid in the quarter century after the Second World War. It was very low—only 0.7% per year—between 1973 and 1981. Since 1981, the productivity performance of the U.S. economy has been reviving.

Observe in Figure 16-1 in the text that productivity has generally improved very rapidly when labor hours were growing slowly, and vice versa. With more people on the job, each works with less capital than would be the case with a lower growth in the labor force. As a result, there is a drag in output per labor hour. When the labor force increases, there are two important effects:

- *total* output increases, since there is an increase in the labor input; and

- output *per labor hour* decreases (or increases more slowly than it otherwise would), since the amount of capital per worker is kept down.

Those who have studied productivity and growth in detail include Edward F. Denison. Denison has estimated the reasons for the increase in output per person employed. The first column of Table 16-1 in the text lists his estimates for the period from 1948 to 1973. The most important

conclusion is that *no single item* accounted for most of the increase. There were a number of sources, each contributing small amounts to the overall increase in output per person. Of the sources identified by Denison, the most important were the increased education of the labor force, the increase in physical capital, greater economies of scale, and an improved allocation of resources. (In passing, observe that Denison's measure—output per person employed—does not correspond precisely to the standard definition of productivity, namely, output per labor *hour*. However the two measures are closely related.)

The second column of Table 16-1 shows Denison's attempt to explain why output per person employed remained stagnant in the period from 1973 to 1981. The most important conclusion here is that Denison's explanations don't in fact explain most of the slowdown. In fact, he explains only a third of the deterioration, leaving a large unexplained residual (1.8%, at the bottom of the last column). The reasons for the poor performance during this period remain something of a mystery, although the increase in the price of oil may have been more important than Denison estimated.

Not only has growth varied considerably from decade to decade; it has also varied considerably from country to country. Some countries have grown very rapidly, while others have grown very slowly.

The very poor nations sometimes seem caught in a *vicious circle of poverty*. When incomes are very low, people have a very difficult time saving. Because almost everything that is being produced is being consumed, the nation does not have many resources to devote to investment in real capital, education, and training. With low capital formation, productivity is stagnant. In addition to low saving and investment (shown in the outer loop of Figure 16-3), a number of other problems may act as drag on output per person and living standards:

- slow improvements in technology,

- small, stagnant markets that make it difficult to capture economies of scale,

- rapid population growth that reduces the amount of capital per person,

- social and cultural barriers to growth,

- a lack of social capital, such as good transportation and communications systems, and

- military conflicts.

The international economy can help countries to break out of the vicious circle by providing

- financial capital to finance real investments,
- technology, and
- markets.

Four of the most rapidly growing economies are in East Asia—South Korea, Taiwan, Hong Kong, and Singapore. These nations have all had very high rates of saving and investment. They have all been strongly export oriented; much of their output has been sold abroad. They have all made extensive use of foreign technology and imported capital equipment. However, the economies have differed in some important respects. The government has been much more directly involved in the economy in Korea than in Singapore or Hong Kong. Large conglomerates dominate the Korean economy, while small and medium sized businesses are the core of the Taiwanese economy.

Borrowing from foreign nations can help to provide the financing for investment and growth. However, if foreign borrowing is not put to good use, it can cause major problems. Borrowers may have difficulty servicing their loans (paying interest and repaying the loans).

IMPORTANT TERMS

Match the first column with the corresponding phrase in the second column.

_____ 1. Average productivity of labor
_____ 2. Technological improvement
_____ 3. Economies of scale
_____ 4. Slower growth
_____ 5. Examples of first world countries
_____ 6. Examples of second world countries
_____ 7. Examples of third world countries
_____ 8. Vicious circle of poverty
_____ 9. Infrastructure
_____ 10. The "four tigers"
_____ 11. Exchange rate

a. The Soviet Union and Bulgaria
b. A characteristic of the U.S. economy after 1973
c. Korea, Hong Kong, Taiwan, and Singapore
d. Q/L
e. The price of one currency in terms of another
f. Low income leads to low saving and investment, which in turn keeps income low
g. An example: the electric power system
h. An increase of all inputs by 100% leads to an increase of more than 100% in output
i. India, Nigeria, Peru, and Indonesia
j. Inventions and better methods of production
k. France, Germany, Japan, and Canada

TRUE-FALSE

T   F   1. If the labor force grows at a rapid rate, this will act as a drag on productivity.

T   F   2. If the labor force grows at a rapid rate, this will act as a drag on the growth of output.

T   F   3. Denison found that most of the slowdown in the growth of output per person after 1973 was due to a single cause, the increase in the price of oil.

T   F   4. If an economy grows at 2% each year, it will double in size in 25 years.

T   F   5. The rapid increase in the international price of oil in 1973-1974 acted as a drag on growth, since it required some industries to retool

T   F   6. Three major reasons for an increase in output per worker are investment in real capital, investment in education and training, and improvements in technology

T   F   7.   Gross domestic product (GDP) is the same as gross national product (GNP) except that GNP includes government purchases of goods and services, but GDP does not.

MULTIPLE CHOICE

1. Growth of the economy causes

   a. the long-run Phillips curve to shift to the right
   b. the long-run Phillips curve to become flatter
   c. the aggregate supply curve to shift to the right
   d. an increasing gap between actual and potential GNP
   e. all of the above

2. Since 1920, real GNP in the United States has grown at approximately what rate per year?

   a. 0.5%
   b. 1%
   c. 3%
   d. 6%
   e. 9%

3. In the past two decades, total labor hours worked have grown at a more rapid rate than the population. The major reason has been:

   a. an increase in the average length of the work week
   b. an increase in the participation of women in the labor force
   c. an increase in the number of people working for the government
   d. a very rapid increase in population
   e. an unusually slow growth in population

4. When the number of labor hours increases very rapidly, the most likely effect is:

   a. a slow increase in productivity
   b. a very rapid increase in productivity
   c. a very slow increase in total output
   d. no change in output, since workers have less capital
   e. a decline in output, since workers have less capital

5. Consider an economy in which output *per capita* grows at 2% per year, while population grows at 1.5% per year. Then growth in real GNP is approximately what percent per year:

   a. 2/1.5 = 1.33
   b. 1.5
   c. 2

   d. 1.5 x 2 = 3
   e. 1.5 + 2 = 3.5

6. One of the topics studied by Denison was the change in the quality of the labor force, as measured by education. Denison concluded that the education of the U.S. labor force has:

   a. improved, and this improvement contributed as much to productivity as the increase in machinery and other physical capital
   b. improved, although this improvement contributed less to productivity than the increase in machinery and other physical capital
   c. deteriorated, since SAT scores have fallen
   d. deteriorated, since literacy levels have declined
   e. deteriorated, at least during the 1970s, since labor productivity deteriorated during that decade

7. Output per person increased much more slowly between 1973 and 1981 than in the previous quarter century. According to Denison, what accounted for more than half of the slowdown:

   a. a decrease in labor hours worked by the average worker
   b. a decrease in rate of investment in physical capital
   c. a decrease in rate of investment in education
   d. a smaller increase in economies of scale, because of stronger foreign competition
   e. none of the above

8. For a country in the process of development, a high saving rate is generally

   a. helpful, because it makes resources available for investment
   b. helpful, because it causes a rapid growth of aggregate demand and thus makes it easier to capture economies of scale
   c. harmful, because it causes a stagnation of aggregate demand
   d. harmful, because it promotes imports of consumer goods
   e. unimportant; there is no observable relationship (either positive or negative) between saving and growth

9. A country is overpopulated whenever

   a. the rate of population is increasing by more than 1% per year
   b. real per capital GNP is falling
   c. there are an average of more than 100 people per square mile
   d. any of (a), (b), or (c) exists
   e. we can't conclude that any of the above necessarily means a country is overpopulated

10. The four rapidly-growing economies of Asia, known as the "four tigers," have all had

    a. export-oriented policies
    b. laissez-faire economies
    c. very large and rapidly growing government sectors
    d. very large corporations that dominate the economy
    e. all of the above

11. Countries which faced crises in servicing their foreign debts during the 1980s

    a. were only oil importers, who were adversely affected by spiraling oil prices
    b. were only oil exporters, because they looked forward to large future export earnings and therefore mistakenly thought they could afford to borrow
    c. were only exporters of agricultural products, who were hurt by the fall in the prices of their exports
    d. were only emerging exporters of manufactures, who faced extremely tough competition in breaking into world markets
    e. included all four types of countries: oil importers, oil exporters, exporters of agricultural products, and exporters of manufactured goods

12. According to Thomas Malthus, the wage rate would be depressed to the subsistence level because of

    a. the power of monopolies
    b. the desire of capitalists to exploit the working class
    c. the natural tendency of population to grow more rapidly than the production of food
    d. the long-run downward trend in investment
    e. pestilence, war, and famine

EXERCISES

1. Fill in the blanks.

   a. Denison found that, during the period from 1948 to 1973, the increase in output per worker could be attributed to the following four sources (in addition to the unexplained residual, due partly to technological improvement):

      1._____

      2._____

      3._____

      4._____

   b. Over this period, a small drag on the growth of output per worker was attributable to

      _____

   c. Denison found that he could not explain most of the slowdown in the period from 1973 to 1981. He may have underestimated the effects of:

      1._____

2. A more rapid rate of increase in population leads to a (more, less) rapid rate of growth of output. It generally acts as a (stimulus to, drag on) productivity, because the average worker has less _____ to work with. However, this effect may be offset, or more than offset, by _____, which act to (increase, decrease) productivity as the size of the economy grows.

ESSAY QUESTIONS

1. Since 1966, labor hours (L) increased at a much faster rate than between 1919 and 1966 (Figure 16-1 in the textbook). How do you explain this rapid increase? Would you expect a rapid increase in the next decade? What do you think explains the *inverse* relationship between the growth in labor

input and the increase in labor productivity? On the basis of these answers, do you have any predictions about what will happen to labor productivity in the next decade? How about the rate of growth of out put? Are you confident regarding your last two answers? Why or why not?

2. Recall the "measure of economic welfare" (MEW) introduced in Chapter 6. If this, rather than GNP, were used to measure economic growth and productivity, how would the historical record in Figure 16-1 in the textbook be affected? How would the costs of economic growth be affected?

How do your answers depend on how leisure is treated in MEW?

3. Suppose that a new industrial policy agency is set up by the U.S. government, to assist selected industries. Suppose you are chosen to run this agency. Would you favor assisting new, high-tech industries, or declining industries, or both? Or perhaps neither of these, but some other group of industries? (If so, explain how you would choose your favored industries.) Explain what problems you might encounter in picking industries for assistance, and the problems which might result from your policies.

ANSWERS

Important terms: 1 d, 2 j, 3 h, 4 b, 5 k, 6 a, 7 i, 8 f, 9 g, 10 c, 11 e

True-False:
1 T (p. 278)
2 F (p. 278)
3 F (p. 280)
4 F (Ch. 15, p. 271)
5 T (p. 281)
6 T (p. 281)
7 F (p. 286)

Multiple Choice:
1 c (p. 277)
2 c (p. 278)
3 b (p. 278)
4 a (p. 278)
5 e (p. 278)
6 a (p. 279)
7 e (p. 280)
8 a (pp. 282-283, 286)
9 e (p. 284)
10 a (p. 288)
11 e (p. 289)
12 c (p. 292, Appendix)

Exercises

1 a. better educated labor force, increase in physical capital, economies of scale, improved allocation of resources.
   b. shorter work week.
   c. higher oil prices.

2. more, drag on, capital, economies of scale, increase.

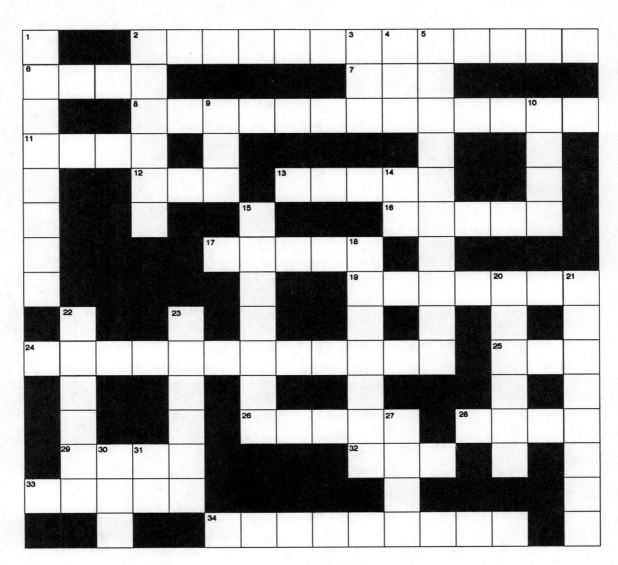

Across

2. what happens when depreciation exceeds gross investment
6. leisure
7. part of the foot
8. has an effect on productivity (2 words)
11. won't he _____ learn?
12. epoch
13. country with rapid economic growth
16. a Nobel prizewinner (see inside cover of text)
17. a major source of innovation (abbrev.)
19. this may suffer, if growth is rapid
24. Q/L
25. pull
26. without this, there would be no production
28. there are many of these in Shakespeare's plays
29. form of capital
32. business organization (abbrev.)
33. bright
34. the most important single contributor to the increase in productivity, according to Denison

Down

1. where bright ideas pay off
2. a Nobel prizewinner (see inside cover of text)
3. they develop the SAT exams (abbrev.)
4. help! (abbrev.)
5. important contributor to growth
9. lots of water
10. important for banks
14. on, in, or near
15. helps workers to produce
18. student of productivity and growth
20. product
21. southern cousin of Russians
22. slowed in 1970s
23. together with demand, this determines price
27. rave
30. a cause of slowdown of 1970s
31. above

Part 5

GREAT MACROECONOMIC ISSUES:
Aggregate Demand

CH19/9367   Accelerator Theory of Invest.   Theor. Quiz back at his office's d

CHM 1407
12/16 1:30-3:30 (PM)

MONETARY POLICY AND FISCAL POLICY: Which is the Key to Aggregate Demand?

LEARNING OBJECTIVES

After you have studied this chapter in the textbook and study guide, you should be able to

✔ Explain the three steps in the Keynesian explanation of how a change in the quantity of money can cause a change in aggregate demand

✔ Explain how problems at two of these three steps might mean that aggregate demand will not change much as a result of a change in the quantity of money

✔ Explain how, at the first step, the quantity of money and people's willingness to hold money determine the rate of interest

✔ Explain what the investment demand curve means, and remember what "price" is measured on the vertical axis

✔ Explain the key propositions of monetarists, and the major points of disagreement between monetarists and Keynesians

✔ Explain how deficit spending may lead to a decrease in investment and/or in net exports

✔ Explain why, in spite of strength of the case for using both policies, the United States has nevertheless relied almost exclusively on monetary policy as a demand-management tool in recent years

MAJOR PURPOSE

One of the important controversies of recent decades has been over the relative importance of monetary and fiscal policies. If the economy is heading into an inflationary boom or into a recession, should we turn to fiscal policy to stabilize the economy? Or to monetary policy? Most economists would now say that a *combination* of monetary and fiscal policies is best. However, there has been a sharp debate between Keynesians — who have often emphasized fiscal policy — and monetarists, who have emphasized that money is the key to aggregate demand. The purpose of this chapter is to review the highlights of this debate, and suggest that it

Chapter 17   Monetary Policy and Fiscal Policy

179

is unwise to rely exclusively on either monetary or fiscal policy.

HIGHLIGHTS OF CHAPTER

This chapter deals with the controversy over the relative importance of monetary and fiscal policies. Although most economists take an intermediate position, two extreme views may be identified. One position—the position of strong Keynesians, particularly during the 1950s and 1960s—is that fiscal policy is very important, while monetary policy has little or no effect. The other extreme position—the strong monetarist view—is just the opposite. An earlier chapter explained the Keynesian view of how fiscal policy affects aggregate expenditures. This chapter rounds out the discussion by explaining:

- the reasons why strong Keynesians have dismissed monetary policy,

- the monetarist view as to why monetary policy is important, and

- the monetarist view as to why fiscal policy does not have much effect on aggregate demand.

This chapter also explains why the historical evidence does not give unqualified support to either extreme view; we are left with a case for using both monetary and fiscal policies.

The Keynesian View of Monetary Policy

In the Keynesian view, there are three links in the chain of events whereby an open market purchase can increase aggregate demand. At the *first link*, an open market purchase can cause a *fall in interest rates*. In Chapter 12, we have already seen why. Specifically, the increase in the Fed's demand for bonds will work to bid up the prices of bonds—that is, to bid down interest rates. With excess reserves, commercial banks will be anxious to make loans; this will create additional downward pressure on interest rates. This chapter explains this first link (between an expansive monetary policy and a fall in interest rates) in more detail.

To see how monetary policy affects interest rates, Keynesian economists look at the demand for and supply of money. By the supply of money, they mean the quantity which exists in the economy. By the demand, they mean the *willingness* of people to hold money. This willingness depends in part on interest rates—the lower are interest rates, the more money people are willing to hold. This is

reflected in the downward slope of the demand curve in Figure 17-2 in the text.

Now, suppose that the economy is initially in equilibrium, and that the Fed then increases the quantity of money. At the existing interest rate, people now have more money than they are willing to hold. They try to reduce their money balances. How do they do so? The answer is: by buying bonds. As people buy bonds, bond prices rise. That is, interest rates fall. Once the interest rate has fallen to its equilibrium, people no longer have more money than they are willing to hold; the demand for bonds levels off. (Note that, overall, people don't actually reduce their money balances. Instead, they bid down the interest rate until they are willing to hold the quantity of money in existence.)

The *second link* represents the *effect that a change in the interest rate has on investment*. Interest represents one of the expenses that businesses face in deciding whether to buy machinery or make other investments. If interest rates fall, the costs of investment will accordingly fall, and businesses will be more eager to make investments. The increase in investment as interest rates fall is illustrated by the *investment demand curve*. For example, consider the investment demand curve in Figure 17-3 on p. 299 of the text. If the interest rate is 8%, businesses want to undertake $100 billion in investment. Then, if the interest rate falls to 6% as a result of an expansive monetary policy, businesses will want to increase investment by $25 billion (*ceteris paribus*). In other words, the policy leads to an increase in investment at this second step.

At the *third step*, an increase in investment has a *multiplied effect on aggregate demand*. The theory of the multiplier was explained in detail in Chapter 9.

Keynesian economists foresee two situations in which monetary policy may not have much effect. First, Keynes himself saw a problem at the first step. He was skeptical that monetary policy could be used as a way out of the depression of the 1930s. Interest rates were already very low, and there was not much prospect that they could be lowered significantly with monetary policy. After all, there is a downward limit on interest rates: They cannot be pushed below zero. In other words, in the special case of the depression when interest rates were already low, Keynes believed that the authorities could not rely on monetary policy. They would have to use fiscal policy to get the economy out of the depression.

Some of his followers had a more general skepticism regarding monetary policy; they doubted its effectiveness even during more normal times. Specifically, they foresaw a problem at the second step. They believed that the investment demand curve might be almost vertical. As a result, they were skeptical that changes in interest rates would lead to a significant change in investment. Even if monetary policy did change interest rates at step 1, there might be very little change in investment at step 2.

(The skepticism of some Keynesians over monetary policy lasted through the 1960s. Now, however, almost all Keynesians see an important role for monetary policy. The recent difficulties in actually using fiscal policy—explained toward the end of the chapter—have increased their interest in monetary policy. There has been a move away from polar views and toward more central views.)

The Monetarist View of Monetary Policy

The monetarist view begins with the equation of exchange: $MV = PQ$, where M is the stock of money, V is the velocity of money, P is the average level of prices, and Q is the quantity of output (that is, real national product). This equation is not a "theory," because it is simply true *by definition*. Specifically, V is defined as PQ/M. However, a theory has been built on this equation. This theory—the **quantity theory**—is the proposition that V is stable. If this is so, then a change in the quantity of M will cause an approximately proportional change in PQ, and monetary policy has a strong and predictable effect on nominal GNP.

Monetarism is built on the quantity theory. Five key propositions of monetarism are:

- The money supply M is the most important determinant of aggregate demand and nominal national product PQ.

- In the *long run*, real GNP tends moves to its full-employment level. Consequently, the only long-run effect of M is on P, not on Q.

- However, in the short run, an increase (decrease) in M can cause *both* P and Q to increase (decrease).

- If M is increased at a slow, stable rate, then aggregate demand will also increase at a slow, stable rate.

- Such a slow, stable increase in aggregate demand is the best way to reduce the magnitude of business cycles and keep inflation down. Therefore, the central bank should follow a monetary *rule*, aiming for a slow, steady increase in M.

The Monetarist View of Fiscal Policy

Monetarists doubt that fiscal policy has a strong and predictable effect on aggregate demand. The major reason for this is because of **crowding out**. Suppose that the government spends more, and finances the resulting deficit by borrowing from the public. Interest rates will rise. As a result, businesses will move upward to the left along the investment demand curve; desired investment will decline. Thus, the government spending will crowd out investment; the net effect on aggregate demand will be smaller than foreseen in the simple discussion of Chapter 10. The strength of the crowding out effect will depend on the slope of the investment demand curve. The flatter it is, the more investment will decrease for any increase in the interest rate. Monetarists generally believe that the investment demand curve is quite flat (in contrast to the almost vertical curve of early Keynesians). As a result, they foresee a strong crowding out effect, with little or no net effect of fiscal policy on aggregate demand.

This crowding out argument is based on the assumption that the government sells bonds *to the public*. In this case, there will be no effect on the money stock; this will be an example of **pure fiscal policy**. If, on the other hand, the Fed buys the additional government bonds, interest rates may be kept down and investment and aggregate demand will increase. But the money stock will rise, and a monetarist will consider money, not government spending, to be the cause of the increase in aggregate demand. Thus, if we want to distinguish between the Keynesian and monetarist viewpoints, we should look at a *pure* fiscal policy—a change in G or in tax rates with no change in M—and compare it with what we might call a *pure* monetary policy: an open market operation and a change in M with no change in fiscal policy. If an expansive fiscal policy is accompanied by an increase in M, there is no disagreement: Aggregate demand will increase. Keynesians will generally attribute the increase to fiscal policy, and monetarists to a change in M.

A second reason that deficit spending may have a weak effect on aggregate demand has attracted considerable attention in recent years. An increase in deficit spending by the government can cause an increase in interest rates, encouraging foreigners to buy U.S. bonds and bidding up the price of the U.S. dollar in terms of foreign currencies. U.S. exports are discouraged, and imports stimulated. In other words, a budgetary deficit can cause a deficit in international trade, with the trade deficit offsetting the stimulative effects of the government's deficit spending.

The events of the past quarter century do not give unqualified support to either the strong monetarist nor to the strong Keynesian view. Strong Keynesians were shaken by the events of the late 1960s, when money, not fiscal policy, appeared to be the major engine driving aggregate demand. During the past 15 years, large changes in the velocity of money have shaken the beliefs of strong monetarists.

Now, there is widespread uncertainty over the relative effectiveness of monetary and fiscal policies. Because we do not know exactly how the economy operates,

it makes sense to diversify — to use some of each policy, rather than putting all our eggs in one basket. But, while the importance of diversification is widely recognized, we have in fact placed almost exclusive reliance on monetary policy as a demand-management tool in recent years. The reason is that fiscal policy is caught in a political impasse. Many people believe that smaller deficits would be desirable, but there is little agreement on how to achieve that goal.

MATCHING COLUMNS

Match the first column with the corresponding phrase in the second column.

d	1.	Investment demand curve
f	2.	More investment
a	3.	Equation of exchange
h	4.	Velocity
c	5.	Quantity theory
g	6.	Crowding out
e	7.	Pure fiscal policy
b	8.	Trade deficit

a. $MV = PQ$
b. Possibly, a result of a budget deficit
c. Proposition that V is stable
d. Relationship between the interest rate and I^*
e. Change in G with no change in rate of growth of M
f. Caused by a lower rate of interest
g. More G leads to higher i, which leads to less I^*
h. PQ / M

TRUE-FALSE

T   F   1.   If interest rates fall, people will be willing to hold a larger quantity of money.

T   F   2.   According to Keynes, interest rates might be low during a depression. He argued that in this case, expansive monetary policy would not be an effective tool for promoting recovery.

T   F   3.   The flatter is the investment demand curve, the more effective is monetary policy as a way of controlling aggregate demand.

T   F   4.   Keynesians generally argue that, while the equation of exchange is correct (MV does equal PQ), it is not the best way to analyse changes in demand and output; the equation $Y = C + I^* + G$ is a better place to begin.

T   F   5.   According to the quantity theory of money, V is stable through time, and PQ therefore changes by about the same percentage as M.

T   F   6.   According to quantity theorists, a change in M will have little or no effect on P in the long run.

T   F   7.   According to quantity theorists, a change in M will have a greater effect on P in the long run than in the short run.

T   F   8.   The stronger is the crowding out effect, the more powerful will be the effect of fiscal policy on aggregate demand.

T   F   9.   The flatter is the investment demand curve, the more effective is fiscal policy as a way of controlling aggregate demand.

T   F   10.   According to monetarists, fiscal policy can have a powerful effect on aggregate demand, provided that changes in government spending are financed by borrowing from the central bank.

MULTIPLE CHOICE

1. According to the Keynesian approach, the effectiveness of monetary policy on aggregate expenditures should be analyzed by looking at three steps. These three steps include each of the following *except* one. That one is:

   a. the effect of monetary policy on the rate of interest
   b. the effect of a change in the interest rate on open market purchases by the Fed
   c. the effect of a change in the interest rate on desired investment
   d. the effect of a change in desired investment on aggregate expenditures

2. Which of the following is most likely to *decrease* when the quantity of money *increases*?

   a. P
   b. Q
   c. $P \times Q$
   d. the interest rate
   e. the quantity of money demanded

3. In the Keynesian approach to monetary policy, if the quantity of money exceeds the quantity demanded, the most likely result is a:

   a. fall in the interest rate
   b. rise in the interest rate
   c. fall in investment
   d. fall in national product
   e. fall in the size of the multiplier

4. Suppose that the amount of money people have exceeds the quantity that they want to hold. Then, according to Keynesian theory, they will try to get rid of excess money balances by:

   a. saving more
   b. buying more goods
   c. buying more services
   d. switching from checking deposits to currency
   e. switching from money into bonds or other financial assets

5. The investment demand curve shows the relationship between:

   a. the rate of interest and the quantity of bonds that people are willing to hold
   b. the rate of interest and the quantity of of money that people want to invest in bonds
   c. the interest rate and desired investment
   d. the interest rate and actual investment
   e. the investment demand curve shows all of the above

6. Keynes believed that an expansive monetary policy might not be very effective as a way to stimulate the economy out of a depression. Monetary policy was most likely to be *ineffective* if:

   a. V were stable
   b. the investment demand curve were flat
   c. the demand curve for money were steep
   d. interest rates were already very high
   e. interest rates were already very low

7. The quantity theory of money is the proposition that:

   a. $MV = PQ$
   b. $MQ = PV$
   c. P is stable
   d. V is stable
   e. according to the quantity theory, all of the above must be true

8. Most Keynesians argue that the equation of exchange, $MV = PQ$

   a. is incorrect, because V does not equal PQ/M
   b. is incorrect, because V is unstable
   c. is incorrect, because M does not equal PQ/V
   d. is incorrect, because M is unstable
   e. is correct, but is not the most enlightening place to begin macroeconomic theory, because V is unstable

9. Keynesians and monetarists are most likely to agree that:

    a. monetary policy is more effective than fiscal policy
    b. fiscal policy is more effective than monetary policy
    c. neither fiscal nor monetary policy can effect Q; the only effect will be on P
    d. the investment demand curve is generally steep
    e. $V = PQ / M$

10. According to the quantity theory of money, a rise in the quantity of money causes an increase in:

    a. the ratio of demand deposits to currency
    b. the ratio of currency to demand deposits
    c. the gold stock
    d. $P \times Q$
    e. Q/P

11. According to the quantity theory of money, a rise in the quantity of money causes:

    a. a rise in P in the long run, and also, possibly, a rise in Q in the short run
    b. a rise in Q in the long run, and also, possibly, a rise in P in the short run
    c. a fall in P in the short run, and a rise in Q in the long run
    d. a rise in both P and Q in both the long run and the short run
    e. a rise in Q in the long run, with no change in P

12. Suppose that the amount of money people have exceeds the quantity that they want to hold. Then, monetarists emphasize that they will try to get rid of excess money balances by:

    a. saving more
    b. buying bonds
    c. buying goods
    d. switching from currency to checking deposits
    e. switching from checking deposits to currency

13. Which of the following views is most likely to be held by a monetarist?

    a. a decrease in the rate of growth of the money stock will cause the level of national product to stay below the full employment level permanently
    b. the money stock should be increased at a steady, constant rate
    c. desired investment is quite unresponsive to changes in the rate of interest
    d. the quantity of money demanded responds strongly to changes in the rate of interest
    e. fiscal policy has a powerful affect on aggregate demand

14. The "crowding out" effect of fiscal policy applies to which of the following ideas?

    a. an increase in G leads to an increase in interest rates, which leads to an increase in I^*
    b. an increase in G leads to a decrease in interest rates, which leads to an increase in I^*
    c. an increase in G leads to an increase in interest rates, which leads to a decline in I^*
    d. an increase in G leads to an increase in I^*, which leads to an increase in interest rates
    e. an increase in G leads to an increase in I^*, which leads to a decrease in interest rates

15. If the investment demand curve is quite flat, then we would expect the effects on aggregate demand of:

    a. monetary policy to be strong while fiscal policy is weak
    b. fiscal policy to be strong while monetary policy is weak
    c. both monetary and fiscal policies to be strong
    d. both monetary and fiscal policies to be weak

16. By "pure" fiscal policies, economists mean:

    a. fiscal policies uninfluenced by special interests
    b. fiscal policies where all changes take place in the non-defense sectors of the government's budget
    c. fiscal policies concentrated in the defense sectors of the government's budget, because these have little effect on the productive capacity of the economy
    d. changes in government spending or tax rates unaccompanied by changes in the rate of growth of the money stock
    e. changes in government spending or tax rates while interest rates are held constant

17. Deficit spending by the U.S. government can lead to U.S. deficits in international trade by the following sequence of events:

   a. budget deficits cause a rise in interest rates, which causes a rise in the price of the dollar in terms of foreign currencies, which causes a rise in imports

   b. budget deficits cause a rise in interest rates, which causes a fall in the price of the dollar in terms of foreign currencies, which causes a rise in imports

   c. budget deficits cause a rise in interest rates, which causes a fall in the price of the dollar in terms of foreign currencies, which causes a fall in imports

   d. budget deficits cause a fall in interest rates, which causes a fall in the price of the dollar in terms of foreign currencies, which causes a rise in imports

   e. budget deficits cause a fall in interest rates, which causes a fall in the price of the dollar in terms of foreign currencies, which causes a fall in imports

18. The recessions of 1980 and 1981-1982 were preceded by

   a. an historically unprecedented decline in the money stock; the Fed was determined to reduce inflation

   b. a slower rate of growth of the money stock; the Fed was determined to reduce inflation

   c. a moderate increase in the rate of growth of the money stock; the Fed was determined to keep the expansion going

   d. a very rapid increase in the rate of growth of the money stock; the Fed was determined to keep the expansion going

   e. a very steady growth in the money stock; the Fed tried to avoid either recession or inflation, but was unsuccessful

19. During the last half of the 1980s

   a. fiscal and monetary policies were both used actively to stabilize the economy

   b. fiscal policy was the primary demand management tool used by the authorities

   c. monetary policy was the primary demand management tool used by the authorities

   d. both fiscal policy and monetary policy were held rigidly constant by political constraints

   e. both fiscal and monetary policies were very restrictive, and the result was a major recession in 1987-1988

20. Fiscal policy was stuck in a "gridlock" in the late 1980s; monetary policy was the only macro-economic "game in town." The reason was:

   a. the Fed's firm commitment to high interest rates meant that the government could not afford to run deficits

   b. the Fed's firm commitment to low interest rates meant that the fiscal policy could not become expansive without the danger of hyperinflation

   c. there were large surpluses; the president's firm committment to new taxes to "soak the rich" meant that the surpluses would become even larger

   d. there were large deficits, and the president was firmly committed to new taxes to "soak the rich"

   e. there were large deficits, and the president was committed to no new taxes

---

EXERCISES

1. According to the Keynesian approach, money can affect aggregate demand as a result of a three-step process. Specifically, an increase in the quantity of money will lead to:

   a. _____; which in turn will cause

   b. _____; which in turn will lead to

   c. _____.

Keynesians foresee no problem at the third step. However, problems might occur at each of the first two steps. Specifically, there might be a problem at the first step, particularly if (interest rates were al-ready very low, interest rates were already high, the rate of inflation were high). There also could be a major problem at the second step, if (the demand for money, the investment demand curve, the consumption function) were steep.

In Keynesian theory, if the amount of money people have exceeds the quantity that they want to hold, they will (buy bonds, buy goods, save more). As a result, (prices will rise, interest rates will fall). Monetarists foresee a different response. If the amount of money people have exceeds the quantity that they want to hold, they will (buy bonds, buy goods, save more). As a result, (aggregate demand will increase, interest rates will fall). In the short run, monetarists believe that this will lead to (higher P, higher Q, both); in the long run, it will cause (higher P, higher Q, both). Monetarism is based on the quantity theory of money. That is, it is based on the view that (M, V, P, Q, all of them) is/are stable.

2. Suppose that the investment demand curve is very steep. This suggests that monetary policy will be (effective, weak). Specifically, suppose the Federal Reserve engages in a very restrictive policy, selling Treasury bills on the open market. As a result, the prices of bills will (fall, rise), and their interest rates or yields will (fall, rise). This will lead to an (increase, decrease) in I^*, with the size of this effect being very (large, small) because of the steepness of the investment demand curve.

3. In Figure 17.1 below, the curves labelled A and B are two alternative ways the investment demand curve may be drawn. Of the two, curve (A, B) is the one in which I^* is most responsive to changes in the rate of interest. According to curve A, when the rate of interest is 10%, I^* will be _____; when the rate of interest is 5%, I^* will be _____. According to curve B, when the rate of interest is 10%, I^* will be _____; when the rate of interest is 5%, I^* will be _____. If the two economies are identical except for the investment demand, then monetary policy will be more powerful in (A, B), and fiscal policy will be more powerful in (A, B).

Figure 17.1

Rate of interest

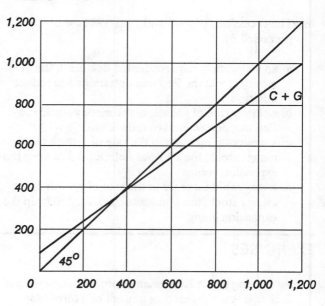

Quantity of investment

Figure 17.2 shows the 45° line and the line indicating consumption expenditures plus government expenditures for goods and services in either economy A or B. (Assume there are no international transactions.) The slope of this line is equal to _____. This means that the multiplier is equal to _____. [If you have trouble with this point, refer back to Chapter 9.] Suppose that the interest rate in economy A is 10%. Draw the aggregate expenditures line ($C + I^* + G$) for economy A. The equilibrium is at a national product of _____. Now suppose that the interest rate decreases to 5%. I^* will (increase, decrease) from _____ to _____ in economy A. Draw in a new aggregate expenditures line. The new equilibrium national product is _____. From your last two answers, confirm the size of the multiplier shown earlier in the paragraph.

Figure 17.2

Aggregate Expenditures

National Product

Now go through the same exercise for economy B. That is, draw in the aggregate expenditures line when the interest rate is equal to 10%, and then when it is equal to 5%. As a result of the fall in the interest rate, investment (increases, decreases) from _____ to _____, and equilibrium national product (increases, decreases) from _____ to _____. By comparing answers, we see that the multiplier is (higher than in A, lower than in A, the same as in A). [Do you see why this is so?] A fall in interest rates from 10% to 5% has (a more powerful, a less powerful, the same) effect on national product in economy B, compared to economy A.

ESSAY QUESTIONS

1. One reason for using both monetary and fiscal policies together is that diversification spreads the benefit or pain. For each of the following policies, explain who the major gainers and losers are, and why.

   a. expansive monetary policy

   b. expansive fiscal policy

   c. restrictive monetary policy

   d. restrictive fiscal policy

2. Suppose one economist told you that the investment demand curve was quite steep, and another told you it was quite flat. Which is more likely to be a monetarist, and which a Keynesian? Explain.

3. "The equation of exchange, $MV = PQ$, is a tautology. Therefore it is useless in helping us understand how the economy works." Evaluate this statement. Also evaluate the following: "The basic Keynesian equation,
   Aggregate expenditures $= C + I^* + G + X_n$,
   is also a tautology. Therefore it is also useless in helping us understand how the economy works."

ANSWERS

Important terms: 1 d, 2 f, 3 a, 4 h, 5 c, 6 g, 7 e, 8 b

True-False:
1 T (p. 298)
2 T (p. 301)
3 T (p. 301)
4 T (Ch. 9 and p. 302)
5 T (p. 302)
6 F (p. 302)
7 T (p. 302)
8 F (p. 304)
9 F (p. 305)
10 T (p. 305)

Multiple Choice:
1 b (p. 297)
2 d (p. 298)
3 a (p. 298)
4 e (p. 298)
5 c (p. 299)
6 e (p. 301)
7 d (p. 302)
8 e (p. 302)
9 e (p. 302)
10 d (p. 302)
11 a (p. 302)
12 c (p. 303)
13 b (p. 303)
14 c (p. 304)
15 a (p. 305)
16 d (p. 305)

Exercises:

1.   a.   a fall in the interest rate,
        b.   a rise in desired investment,
        c.   a multiplied increase in national product,

        interest rates were already very low, the investment demand curve, buy bonds, interest rates will fall, buy goods, aggregate demand will increase, both, higher P, V.

2.   weak, fall, rise, decrease, small.

3.   A, 50, 200, 50, 100, A, B, 0.75, 4, 600, increase, 50, 200, 1,200, increases, 50, 100, increases, 600, 800, the same as in A (because the multiplier depends on the slope of the aggregate expenditures function, which is the same in the two countries), less powerful.

Figure 17.2 Completed:

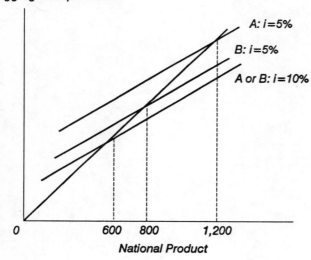

Aggregate Expenditures

A: *i*=5%

B: *i*=5%

A or B: *i*=10%

0   600   800   1,200

National Product

CHAPTER 18

FINE TUNING OR STABLE POLICY SETTINGS?

After you have studied this chapter in the textbook and study guide, you should be able to

✔ Describe the various steps in the active Keynesian approach to aggregate demand management

✔ Explain why lags make it difficult to stabilize aggregate demand through active management

✔ Explain the important role of potential GNP in the active approach

✔ Explain how problems in estimating potential were a major source of difficulty during the 1970s

✔ Explain the case for and the case against a discretionary policy

If your class covers the appendix, you should also be able to

✔ Explain why investment is much more volatile than consumption during the business cycle

✔ Explain why a moderate expansion may be more likely to last than a very rapid expansion

MAJOR PURPOSE

This chapter deals with the one of the major, continuing controversies in macroeconomics: Should aggregate demand policies be adjusted as conditions change, or should the Fed follow a monetary policy rule? On the one side are those in the Keynesian tradition, who argue that aggregate demand should be *actively managed* in pursuit of the goals of high employment and stable prices. On the other side are the monetarists, who generally favor a rule: The Fed should aim for a slow, *steady increase in the money stock*. No matter how well

intentioned the authorities, they do not know enough to stabilize the economy. Discretionary policies do not work in practice. So say the monetarists.

This debate has been dominated by strong advocates of rules on the one hand, and strong opponents on the other. One of the major conclusions of this chapter is that the question before us is not really whether we should chose a rigid, permanent rule that would be followed without regard to "how the chips" fall. There is no way that future policymakers could be bound firmly to such a rule. (Even if it were feasible to enshrine a policy rule in the Constitution, the Constitution could be amended again.) There is, however, a *very* important policy issue which remains—even if rigid, permanent rules are discarded as a logical impossibility. The issue is: Should policies be adjusted frequently in the light of unfolding conditions? Or would we be better off to aim for a stable growth of the money stock and make adjustments only rarely, when very strong evidence for a change accumulates? Unfortunately, the experience of the past quarter century does not provide a clear answer. Sometimes discretionary policies have worked quite well; sometimes they have not. The ambiguous lesson of history is, of course, one of the reasons why the controversy continues.

HIGHLIGHTS OF CHAPTER

Keynes and his followers argued that the government has the responsibility to maintain full employment and reasonably stable prices. Particularly in the early years between 1935 and 1965, Keynesians believed that an untended market economy would suffer from two major problems: Aggregate demand would often be:

- inadequate, and

- unstable.

Authorities should actively intervene to bring aggregate demand up to the full employment level, and then manage it on a continuing basis to offset forces of instability.

This idea was particularly influential during the 1960s, a decade that has sometimes been called the "Age of Keynes." Figure 18-1 in the textbook illustrates the general Keynesian demand-management strategy; Figure 18-2 presents the same idea as it was applied in the early 1960s. There were several major steps in bringing aggregate demand up to the full-employment level:

- First, the path of potential GNP was estimated.

- Next, forecasts were made of where actual GNP would go in the absence of policy changes; in other words, the size of the prospective GNP gap was estimated.

- Finally, fiscal and monetary policies were adjusted with the objective of closing the gap in a reasonably brief period.

Until 1965-1966, this strategy was very successful. The estimated GNP gap closed and prices remained reasonably stable. However, by the late 1960s, inflation was accelerating. This was only partly the result of failures in economic analysis. Even more fundamentally, it was a result of political problems that delayed a change in policies. By the mid 1960s, the Council of Economic Advisers was becoming concerned with the growing inflationary pressures. They recommended to President Johnson that taxes be increased in order to restrain aggregate demand and thus reduce inflationary pressures. President Johnson waited several years before actually recommending a tax increase to Congress; he was reluctant to ask the public to pay higher taxes to finance an unpopular war. This was just one extreme example of the problem of lags.

Critics of active management make five major arguments:

- *Lags* in the operation of policies mean that the government, like the panicky helmsman, may overreact to current events.

- Because of lags, policies developed today must be designed to deal with problems several months in the future. But economists are *only moderately successful in their ability to forecast* either the probable course of the economy in the absence of policy changes, or the effects of policy changes themselves.

- *Prices respond even more slowly* than real output when monetary and fiscal policies are changed. As a consequence, there may be an *inflationary bias* to discretionary policies. Decision makers may choose expansionary policies for the short-run benefits of higher output, and worry later about the inflationary consequences.

- Activists may *overestimate potential GNP*. As a result, they may strive to achieve an unattainable goal, creating strong inflationary pressures in the process. Figure 18-4 in the textbook illustrates this argument in general terms; Figure 18-5 applies it to the 1970s.

- The active management of aggregate demand means government meddling in the economy; rules are more consistent with *economic freedom* than are discretionary policies.

Advocates of rules recognize, of course, that it is important to pick the correct rule—one that is consistent with economic stability. It simply won't do to pick any old rule. Some seemingly plausible rules would be a mistake.

For example, the gold standard rule made the banking system vulnerable to runs; it added to the banking chaos of 1931-1933. However, proponents of rules believe that if the money stock were increased at a slow, steady rate, the economy would be more stable than it has been in the past, when proponents of active demand management were in charge. The proposal for a slow, steady increase in the money stock is based directly on the quantity theory of money—that is, on the view that velocity V is stable. If V is in fact stable, then a stable increase in M will mean a stable increase in nominal income PQ.

Opponents of a monetary rule emphasize three points:

- The government would be foolish to adopt rigid rules that may become outdated as circumstances change in unforeseen ways. Indeed, a truly rigid rule is a *logical impossibility*. Future decision makers cannot be bound inflexibly by the present. The *real issue is one of degree:* Will policies be adjusted in the light of a moderate amount of new information, or will policy changes be postponed until the evidence becomes overwhelming? While advocates of policy rules are correct in pointing out that lags create difficulties for discretionary policies, their proposals would increase lags in a major way. The government would be so committed to a course of action that it would not change policy until conditions became very bad indeed.

- There is no guarantee that stable monetary growth will lead to a stable increase in aggregate demand. In the period since 1975, there have been major, unpredictable changes in velocity. For example, there was an abnormal rise in velocity in 1975 a nd 1978 and a sharp decline in 1982. The slowdown in velocity in 1982 made the recession deeper and led the Fed to increase its target for monetary growth. Earlier, in 1979, the Fed had moved toward the monetarist posi-

tion in order to fight inflation more vigorously. In 1982, the Fed backed away from this position in order to combat the recession. It was persuaded to change its monetary target by a moderate amount of evidence—quite rightly so, said the critics of rules.

- The rule advocated by monetarists—a slow, steady growth in the money stock—may lead to aggregate demand that is too low to buy the increasing volume of goods and services that the economy is capable of producing. In other words, the adoption of a rule aimed at slow growth of demand and stable prices may result in high unemployment and slow growth of real output.

Note the contrast between this last point and the fourth point in the earlier list of the criticisms of fine tuning. There is a significant difference in the approach of the two groups to the problems of inflation and unemployment. Advocates of discretionary policies consider monetarists heartless in their willingness to accept unemployment; monetarists consider some Keynesians to be crude inflationists.

As noted earlier, forecasting is required for the implementation of discretionary policies. Some forecasting, either formal or informal, is also needed by businesses that are planning their investment programs. Economic forecasters often use *econometric models*, modified by the results from surveys and the judgment of the forecaster. The record of forecasters is fair. It is much better than would come from a very simple approach, such as projecting the trends of the previous year or so. However, forecasters have not done a very good job in anticipating recessions. In particular, they substantially underestimated the depth of the severe recessions of 1974 and 1982. This is worrisome to the advocates of active demand management. It is particularly important to anticipate recessions, in order to be able to shift to more expansive policies in a timely manner.

IMPORTANT TERMS

*Match the first column with the corresponding phrase in the
second column.*

_____ 1. Potential GNP
_____ 2. GNP gap
_____ 3. V
_____ 4. Policy rule
_____ 5. Recognition lag
_____ 6. Action lag
_____ 7. Impact lag

a. From time weakness begins until time it is
   recognized
b. If this isn't stable, money rule won't work
c. From time policy is changed until aggregate
   demand responds
d. Aggregate demand policies are aimed at
   eliminating this
e. From time weakness is regognized until policies
   are changed
f. Keep money growth low and stable
g. Target path for those who manage aggregate
   demand

TRUE-FALSE

T   F   1.   Monetarists advocate that the Federal Reserve aim for a slow, steady increase in the quantity of money.

T   F   2.   Those who advocate activist Keynesian demand-management policies are led by the logic of their
               position to make an estimate of potential GNP.

T   F   3.   The case for active, discretionary monetary and fiscal policies would be stronger if economists could
               forecast better.

T   F   4.   The "action lag" is the interval between the time when action is taken, and when the action has its effect
               on aggregate demand.

T   F   5.   The "recognition lag" is the interval between the time when a problem is recognized and the time when
               corrective action is taken.

T   F   6.   The inflation rate is a leading indicator.

T   F   7.   If the rate of increase in productivity unexpectedly falls, potential GNP is likely as a result to be
               overestimated.

T   F   8.   The Council of Economic Advisers overestimated potential GNP by a greater amount in the 1970s than
               in the 1960s.

T   F   9.   If the potential GNP path is overestimated, active demand managers are likely as a consequence to
               follow overly stimulative demand management policies.

T   F   10. Because of the errors in estimating potential GNP during the 1970s, almost all economists now believe
               in a monetary policy rule.

MULTIPLE CHOICE

1. An economist is most likely to favor discretionary aggregate demand policies, rather than a policy rule, if he or she is in which economic tradition?

    a. Keynesian
    b. classical
    c. monetarist
    d. marginalist
    e. libertarian

2. Economists who argue for a policy rule aimed at stabilizing aggregate demand are most likely to favor which rule?

    a. the gold standard
    b. a balanced actual budget
    c. a balanced full-employment budget
    d. a steady growth in the money stock
    e. all the above rules are equally good; the thing that matters is to have *some* rule

3. Milton Friedman is the most famous monetarist. He argues that:

    a. monetary policy should be actively managed to stabilize aggregate demand, but the budget should be kept in balance
    b. the government's budget has no major effect on aggregate demand or on the allocation of resources
    c. both monetary and fiscal policies should be actively managed to stabilize aggregate demand
    d. active monetary and fiscal policies have both been oversold as a way of managing aggregate demand
    e. active monetary policy is the best way to keep full employment without any major risk of inflation

4. Keynes was concerned that:

    a. aggregate demand would be too low, although it would generally be stable
    b. aggregate demand would be unstable, even though it would generally be high enough
    c. aggregate demand was likely to be both too low and unstable
    d. inadequate productive capacity would be the major macroeconomic disease
    e. productive capacity could be kept growing at an adequate rate only if income were redistributed toward those who already had high incomes

5. The discretionary aggregate demand policies followed during the 1960s were aimed primarily at:

    a. increasing the GNP gap
    b. increasing potential GNP
    c. increasing real GNP
    d. increasing prices
    e. reducing prices

6. The discretionary policies of the 1960s involved each of the following steps *except one*. Which is the exception?

    a. estimate potential GNP
    b. forecast the probable course of GNP in the absence of policy changes
    c. forecast the effects of various changes in aggregate demand policies
    d. select the policies aimed at closing the GNP gap in a reasonably brief time
    e. revise the potential GNP path upward, since an even better performance now becomes possible

7. Suppose that the Council of Economic Advisers forecasts a GNP gap of $100 billion for the coming year if no change is made in policies. Then an advocate of:

    a. rules would prescribe a faster growth in the quantity of money
    b. rules would prescribe a faster growth in government spending
    c. active management would prescribe an increase in tax rates, to balance the budget
    d. active management would prescribe an increase in government spending
    e. active management would prescribe an increase in government spending to increase real output, plus a decrease in the money stock to reduce inflation

8. The recognition lag is the lag between the time when

   a. a problem is recognized and the time when corrective action is taken
   b. a problem is recognized and the time when it is corrected
   c. a recession begins and the time when the authorities recognize it has begun
   d. aggregate demand increases and the time when producers recognize that they can raise their prices
   e. aggregate demand increases and producers recognize that they should produce more

9. The time between the beginning of a downturn and the adoption of expansive aggregate demand policies is equal to the:

   a. recognition lag
   b. action lag
   c. recognition lag + the action lag
   d. impact lag
   e. recognition lag + the action lag + the impact lag

10. Monetarists criticize the activist approach to aggregate demand management on the ground that

    a. lags between changes in policy and changes in demand cause policy mistakes
    b. the inflationary effects of an increase in aggregate demand lag after the real output effects; as a result, aggregate demand is stimulated too much and too long in many expansions
    c. aggregate demand managers tend to be too ambitious
    d. all of the above
    e. none of the above

11. The "helmsman's dilemma" illustrates the difficulty of making policy in the presence of:

    a. inflation
    b. deflation
    c. unemployment
    d. low growth
    e. lags

12. Those who advocate policy rules rather than active management argue that active managers tend to:

    a. overestimate potential, and therefore follow inflationary policies
    b. underestimate potential, and therefore follow deflationary policies
    c. underestimate growth, and therefore follow inflationary policies
    d. underestimate the effects of government spending, and therefore rely too much on monetary policy
    e. underestimate the effects of tax changes, and therefore rely too much on monetary policy

13. Sometimes, "everything seems to be going wrong"— that is, output is falling, unemployment rising, and the rate of inflation rising. This is most likely to occur:

    a. early in an expansion
    b. late in an expansion, about 3 or 4 months before the peak
    c. early in a recession
    d. late in a recession, about 3 or 4 months before the trough
    e. at the trough of a recession

14. Potential GNP is most likely to be overestimated when

    a. productivity is improving at an unexpectedly rapid rate
    b. productivity is improving at an unexpectedly slow rate
    c. population is growing
    d. population is stable
    e. population is declining

15. The monetarist case is based on each of the following propositions *except one*. Which is the exception?

    a. the desirable path of aggregate demand is one of steady, moderate growth
    b. the desirable trend of prices is a gradual upward movement, by about 4% per year
    c. the best way to get a steady, moderate increase in aggregate demand is by a steady, moderate increase in the money stock
    d. following a monetary rule increases economic freedom, and probably political freedom, too

16. Opponents of a monetary rule argue that there cannot in fact be a rigid rule because

    a. it would be unconstitutional
    b. the Fed in fact has almost no control over the money stock
    c. money does not affect aggregate demand
    d. money does not affect interest rates
    e. future governments cannot be committed to a rule regardless of the consequences

17. Activists criticize "policy rules" on the ground that

    a. most advocates of policy rules would settle for a rate of growth of aggregate demand that is too low, and a rate of unemployment that is too high

    b. most advocates of policy rules concentrate on fiscal policy, and ignore monetary policy

    c. most advocates of rules concentrate on changes in government spending, and ignore the effects of changes in tax rates

    d. all of the above

    e. none of the above

18. In the face of a large and predictable decrease in V, the best policy for the Federal Reserve is to

    a. increase M

    b. decrease M

    c. increase Q

    d. decrease Q

    e. increase P

19. Suppose that $C = 0.5$ GNP; $I^*_g = 500$; $G = 700$; $X = 300$; and imports are 10% of GNP. Then equilibrium GNP equals

    a. 2,500

    b. 3,000

    c. 3,750

    d. 3,950

    e. 5,200

20. Which of the following is the best leading indicator

    a. increases in the rate of inflation during expansions

    b. decreases in the rate of inflation during recessions

    c. any increases in the rate of inflation during a recession, because this signals a coming expansion

    d. new orders for durable goods

    e. deliveries of durable goods

EXERCISE

1. There are three lags before monetary and fiscal policies affect aggregate demand. First is the _____ lag, next the _____ lag, and then the _____ lag. In addition, there is another lag that occurs after aggregate demand changes. Specifically, the effects of demand on (output, prices) generally lags behind its effect on (output, prices). Critics of active demand management argue that the first set of lags means that policies may destabilize the economy. The second set means that discretionary policies can have an (inflationary, deflationary) bias.

Lags are, however, not the only problem facing the managers of aggregate demand. They also have the difficult task of estimating (the path of potential GNP, the effects of monetary policy on demand, the effects of fiscal policy on demand, all of these). Suppose they overestimate the potential path. This means that, starting from a recession, they are likely to (keep expansive policies too long, abandon expansive policies too soon). The reason is that (the economy will remain below the estimated potential path, they will soon give up trying). As a result, the problem of (inflation, low growth) may become worse.

ESSAY QUESTIONS

1. Suppose that a 4% monetary rule were adopted. Then suppose that the introduction of an electronic transfer system for making payments caused a large increase in the velocity of money. What would happen to the price level? Could this have been avoided if the rule hadn't been adopted? Can you think of a rule that would allow for such contingencies?

2. Presidents have objectives in addition to their economic goals—for example, national defense and getting reelected. How do these other goals strengthen or weaken the case for discretionary policies, rather than a monetary rule?

3. A passage in the chapter highlights section reads as follows: "Advocates of discretionary policies consider monetarists heartless in their willingness to accept unemployment; monetarists consider some Keynesians to be crude inflationists." Explain why these criticisms are made. In the first case, what defense might a monetarist have? (Hint: does it depend on the aggregate supply function?) In the second case, what defense might a Keynesian have? (Hint: does it depend on the relative social costs of unemployment and inflation?)

ANSWERS

Important terms:	**1** g, **2** d, **3** b, **4** f, **5** a, **6** e, **7** c

True-False:
    1 T (p. 313)
    2 T (p. 314)
    3 T (p. 315)
    4 F (316)
    5 F (p. 316)
    6 F (p. 317)
    7 T (p. 320)
    8 T (p. 320)
    9 T (p. 322)
    10 F (p. 325)

Multiple Choice:
    1 a (p. 313)
    2 d (p. 313)
    3 d (p. 314)
    4 c (p. 314)
    5 c (p. 314)
    6 e (pp. 314-315)
    7 d (Ch. 10 and p. 315)
    8 c (p. 316)
    9 c (p. 316)
    10 d (pp. 315-320)
    11 e (p. 317)
    12 a (pp. 318-319)
    13 c (p. 319)
    14 b (p. 320)
    15 b (p. 321)
    16 e (p. 321)
    17 a (p. 322)
    18 a (p. 325)
    19 a (p. 326)
    20 d (p. 328 and throughout chapter)

Exercises

1. recognition, action, impact, prices, output, inflationary, all of these, keep expansive policies too long, the economy will remain below the estimated potential path, inflation.

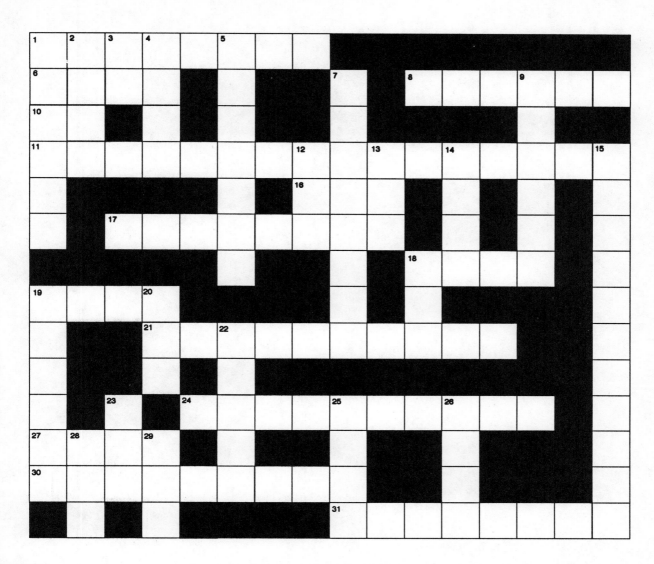

Across

1. someone to whom money is owed
6. holiday season
8. type of lag
10. a chemical element (abbrev.)
11. this is watched by forecasters (2 words)
16. this group has made projections of potential GNP (abbrev.)
17. the _____ of money is the key to aggregate demand, say the proponents of a monetary rule
18. transactions on the _____ market are a key to controlling the quantity of money
19. a healthy economy does this
21. policymakers want to keep this high
24. should we use this, or follow rules?
27. old
30. this level of GNP is sometimes used as a target
31. classical macroeconomics was built on the _____ of exchange

Down

1. demand management policy is aimed at reducing the amplitude of business _____
2. the alternative to active management
3. Keynesian aggregate supply reverses this
4. our condition in the long run, said Keynes
5., 22. peak or trough
7, 25. what monetarists have proposed
9. type of lag
12. here (French)
13. fraction of a week
14. applaud
15. type of lag
18. lengthy lyrical poem
19. eliminating this may be a policy objective (2 "words")
20. spider's home
23. at least six games of tennis
26. researchers should have this
28. U.S. political party (abbrev.)
29. animal's home

CHAPTER 19

FIXED OR FLEXIBLE EXCHANGE RATES?

LEARNING OBJECTIVES

After you have studied this chapter in the textbook and study guide, you should be able to

✔ Identify three sources of demand for a country's currency on the foreign exchange markets, and three sources of supply

✔ Describe four options open to a government when the demand or supply for its currency shifts

✔ Explain why intervention in the exchange market does not provide a permanent solution to disequilibrium in the foreign exchange market

✔ Describe the relationship between the gold stock and the money stock under the gold standard

✔ Describe the mechanism of adjustment under the gold standard, and explain why it is "automatic"

✔ Explain the two major shortcomings of the gold standard

✔ Describe how the "adjustable peg" worked

✔ Explain how problems can arise under the adjustable peg system if people doubt that the present pegged rate will be maintained

✔ Explain the advantages and disadvantages of flexible exchange rates

✔ Explain the ways in which the sharp rise of the dollar between 1981 and 1984 caused problems for the United States

MAJOR PURPOSE

The major purpose of this chapter is to explain the relationship between **international payments** and **macroeconomic policy**. This relationship depends to a considerable extent on the exchange rate system. Under the old **gold standard**, inflows and outflows of gold were a major reason for changes in the money stock, aggregate demand, prices, and unemployment. Changes in aggregate demand which resulted from gold flows were not necessarily best for the domestic economy. A deficit country might go through a painful *deflationary process*, with high unemployment. Under the International Monetary Fund (IMF) system, exchange rates were **pegged**, but a deficit country could escape the need for a painful deflation by devaluing its currency. The present system of **flexible exchange rates** provides countries with a **greater degree of independence** to follow the aggregate demand policies they think best for their domestic economies. However, problems can still be created by the relationship between domestic policies and international transactions. Large U.S. government deficits, combined with monetary restraint, led to high interest rates in the early 1980s, to a rise in the dollar on the international exchanges, and to severe competititve problems for a number of basic U.S. industries such as autos and steel.

HIGHLIGHTS OF CHAPTER

This chapter deals with the issue of whether a government should regulate the country's exchange rate, and, if so, how. The topic is developed by looking at three historical exchange rate arrangements: the **gold standard** of the 19th and early 20th century; the **pegged-but-adjustable** exchange rate system of 1945-71; and the recent sytem of **flexible** or **floating** exchange rates. As a preliminary topic, the chapter explains the foreign exchange market.

The Foreign Exchange Market

International trade differs from domestic trade for two main reasons:

- International trade must overcome barriers such as tariffs

- International trade involves two or more currencies (national monies).

As a result of the second complication, international trade leads to transactions in the *foreign exchange market*, where one national currency is bought in exchange for another.

Exchange rates are determined in the foreign exchange market. The demand for, say, Canadian dollars, arises when people offer foreign currencies in order to buy Canadian dollars. They want the Canadian dollars in order to buy

- Canada's exports of goods, such as automobiles and newsprint;

- Canadian services, such as hotel accommodations for tourists; and

- Canadian assets, such as Canadian government bonds or shares in Canadian nickel mines.

On the other side of the market, the supply of Canadian dollars arises when people offer Canadian dollars in order to buy foreign currencies. Canadians use foreign currencies to buy

- imports of goods;

- imports of services; and

- foreign assets.

An *exchange rate* is the price of one currency in terms of another. An exchange rate may be quoted either way. For example, $1 U.S. = $1.25 Can. is the same as $1 Can. = $0.80 U.S. To verify this, multiply each side of the first equation by four fifths and switch the two sides.

An equilibrium exchange rate is one at which the quantity of currency supplied is equal to the quantity demanded. When demand for a country's currency decreases (the demand curve shifts to the left), the government has four options:

- Buy the surplus the surplus quantity of the home currency at the existing exchange rate, in order to prevent the exchange rate from changing.

- Decrease the supply by direct actions, such as increasing tariffs or limiting the amount of foreign assets that citizens are permitted to acquire.

- Decrease the supply and increase the demand for the country's currency by more restrictive monetary and fiscal policies. By restraining aggregate demand, such policies will keep prices and incomes down, thereby reducing imports and stimulating exports.

- Let the price of the currency fall to its new equilibrium.

The first option is only a temporary expedient. If the shift in demand is permanent, a country will run out of foreign exchange reserves if it relies solely on this option.

The Gold Standard

The gold standard is an example of a fixed exchange rate system—that is, a system which fixes the exchange rates within narrow limits. If, for example, the pound is worth 4.86 times as much as the U.S. dollar, then nobody will pay much more than $4.86 for a pound, or sell it for much less.

Under the gold standard, there was an **automatic adjustment mechanism** ensuring that there would not be large, persistent internatonal imbalances, with one country ending up with all the gold and the others having none. Specifically, a country losing gold had an *automatic* decrease in its money stock for two reasons:

- Gold itself was one form of money; when gold coins left the country, the money was directly reduced.

- Gold was also a bank reserve.

When banks had smaller gold reserves, their ability to make loans was restricted. As we saw in Chapter 11, the ability of banks to make loans helps to determine the money stock.

The decline in the money stock was the first step in the adjustment process. The remaining steps were as follows: As the money supply fell, aggregate demand, incomes, and prices fell in the deficit countries. This made the country's goods more competitive on world markets, and its trade balance therefore improved. This process was aided by an automatic increase in money and inflation in the surplus countries. With prices rising in the surplus countries, it was even easier for the deficit countries to compete. This process—involving changes in the *relative prices* of the goods of the deficit and surplus countries— tended to continue until balance of payments deficits and surpluses were eliminated and gold flows stopped.

Observe that the gold system worked through changes in domestic demand—that is, the third option in the previous section (although the monetary policy worked automatically in the case of the gold standard). However, even though the gold standard worked to eliminate surpluses and deficits, it had two *major* defects:

- The automatic mechanism could be very costly for a country with a payments deficit because the monetary contraction could cause large-scale unemployment. On the other side, inflationary pressures could be generated in the surplus countries. That is, there could be a **conflict** between the policies needed for a stable domestic prosperity and the monetary changes needed to bring about balance-of-payments adjustment.

- The gold standard could lead to **very unstable** conditions, particularly if there was a run on the gold reserves of banks. This point was explained in detail in Chapter 12.

The Adjustable Peg, 1945-1971

Under the adjustable peg system:

- Countries intervened in their foreign exchange markets as necessary, to keep the exchange rate within 1% of an official "par value."

- Countries with temporary balance-of-payments deficits kept their exchange rates stable by selling reserves on the foreign exchange markets. Countries with temporary balance-of-payments surpluses kept their exchange rates stable by buying foreign currencies, thus increasing their foreign exchange reserves.

- Countries facing a long-term, *fundamental* disequilibrium were to change their official par values. The change in exchange rates would affect the prices of their goods on international markets, and help to eliminate international deficits or surpluses.

There were three major problems with the adjustable peg system:

- It was not clear how to distinguish between a "fundamental" disequilibrium and a "temporary" disequilibrium.

- If a government tried to hold its exchange rate close to the official par when *speculators* believed that there was a fundamental disequilibrium, speculators often made large profits at the government's expense. For example, when a country had a large balance-of-payments deficit, speculators would sell its currency in large quantities.

- The government would have to use its reserves of foreign exchange to buy up the excess supply of its currency, in order to maintain the peg. As reserves dwindled, this strategy became less and less tenable, and the government was forced to devalue. Speculators were able to benefit by selling high before the devaluation, and buying low after the devaluation. The government, however, lost: It bought high and sold low.

Pressures on the exchange rate system led to its abandonment in the early 1970s; most major countries allowed their currencies to float on the exchange market.

Flexible Exchange Rates

A flexible exchange rate is allowed to change in response to changes in the demand and supply for foreign currencies. Flexible exchange rates have a number of advantages:

- When pegged exchange rates break down, flexible rates may be the only feasible option. The lack of a good alternative may be the strongest argument for flexible exchange rates.

- They permit fiscal and monetary policies to be directed primarily toward the important goal of stabilizing the domestic economy, rather than toward maintaining the exchange rate.

- A country following stable domestic policies is insulated from foreign inflation (the *virtuous circle*).

The major disadvantages are:

- Changes in exchange rates may disrupt international trade and investment.

- Many of the large fluctuations in exchange rates since 1973 appear to have served no useful purpose; they have not been necessary to eliminate fundamental disequilibria. The rise in the dollar in the early 1980s put severe pressures on U.S. manufacturing firms, who were faced with very severe foreign competition.

- Depreciation of the currency adds to domestic inflation. A country can fall into a *vicious circle* of depreciation-inflation-depreciation-inflation.

Because of these disadvantages, some of the Western European nations set up the European Monetary System, which provides for pegged rates among their currencies. However, there is more flexibility in this sytem than in the earlier system of pegged rates. For example, rates do not have to be kept so close to the official value.

Recent Developments

The U.S. dollar has fluctuated widely since 1973. Between 1976 and 1978, as inflation accelerated in the United States, the dollar fell sharply on the exchange markets. Fearing that the country was falling into a vicious circle, the administration moved toward more restrained domestic policies.

Between 1980 and the beginning of 1985, the dollar moved much higher on the exchange markets. Large foreign purchases of U.S. assets were the major reason. The high price of the dollar made U.S. goods more expensive to foreigners, and made foreign goods cheaper to Americans buying with dollars. As a result, U.S. industry had difficulty exporting, and faced severe competition from imports into the domestic market.

One reason for foreign purchase of U.S. assets was the high level of U.S. interest rates, which in turn were partly attributable to large U.S. government deficits. Recall the discussion in Chapter 17 of how the government's deficits caused a rise in the exchange value of the dollar and a trade deficit.

IMPORTANT TERMS

Match the first column with the corresponding phrase in the second column.

_____ 1. Foreign exchange
_____ 2. Exchange rate
_____ 3. Par value
_____ 4. Fundamental disequilibrium
_____ 5. Foreign exchange reserves
_____ 6. Devaluation
_____ 7. Depreciation
_____ 8. Speculate
_____ 9. Dirty float

a. Reduction in the par value of a currency
b. Fall in the market price of a currency
c. Buy something in anticipation of a price rise
d. Occurs when governments intervene to influence price of currency
e. Money of another country
f. Officially-chosen exchange rate
g. Price of one currency in terms of another
h. Government's holdings of foreign currency
i. Reason for devaluation

TRUE-FALSE

T F 1. When the Japanese buy Saudi Arabian oil, this creates a supply of yen

T F 2. If the United States cuts its tariffs, this will lead to an increase in imports and an increase in the supply of dollars on the world market

T F 3. Under the gold standard, the adjustment mechanism worked primarily through changes in aggregate demand, not through changes in exchange rates

T F 4. Under the gold standard, a country was expected to change its par value in the event of a fundamental disequilibrium

T F 5. With a pegged exchange rate, sales of reserves are a good way to deal with international deficits, in both the short run and the long

T F 6. Under the pegged system of the IMF, a country was expected to change its par value in the event of a fundamental disequilibrium

T F 7. The gold standard was *automatic*; it would work without government intervention. This means that it was an example of a clean float.

T F 8. Under a pegged exchange rate system, when foreign exchange speculators make profits, governments generally lose

T F 9. By "self-fulfilling expectations," economists mean any speculation undertaken at the recommendation of government authorities.

T F 10. With a flexible exchange rate, central banks have more freedom to combat recessions than they do under the gold standard

MULTIPLE CHOICE

1. Which of the following is a source of *demand* for the U.S. dollar on the foreign exchange markets?

   a. purchases of foreign currencies by the Federal Reserve
   b. U.S. demand for foreign goods
   c. U.S. demand for foreign services
   d. U.S. investment in foreign countries
   e. foreign demand for U.S. exports

2. Which of the following leads to a decline in the demand for British pounds on the foreign exchange markets?

   a. a decrease in British purchases of German chemicals
   b. an increase in the number of U.S. tourists in Britain
   c. a switch by U.S. consumers from British to Japanese cars
   d. an increase in U.S. purchases of British cars
   e. an increase in British sales of textiles to the United States

3. Under the old gold standard, an inflow of gold into the United States worked to:

   a. automatically increase the U.S. money stock
   b. increase the U.S. money stock, but only if the Fed engaged in open market purchases of government securities
   c. automatically decrease the U.S. money stock
   d. decrease the U.S. money stock, but only if the Fed sold government securities on the open market at the same time
   e. automatically increase the U.S. government's deficit

4. Under the old gold standard system, an inflow of gold into the United States caused what sequence of events?

   a. an increase in the U.S. money stock, an increase in the U.S. price level, and an increase in U.S. exports
   b. an increase in the U.S. money stock, an increase in the U.S. price level, and an increase in U.S. imports
   c. an increase in the U.S. money stock, an increase in the U.S. price level, and an increase in spending by foreign visitors to the United States
   d. an increase in the U.S. money stock, an increase

in the U.S. price level, and a decrease in spending by U.S. visitors to foreign countries
   e. an increase in the U.S. money stock, an increase in the budget deficits of the U.S. government, and an increase in U.S. exports of goods

5. Under the old gold standard, a country faced a *conflict* between the policies needed for domestic stability and those needed for international adjustment when:

   a. it was losing gold and was in a recession
   b. it was gaining gold and was in a recession
   c. its prices were rising and its tariffs were also rising
   d. its unemployment rate was high
   e. its inflation rate was high

6. Under the original IMF system (prior to 1971), the par value of a currency was:

   a. the value of the currency whenever central banks kept bond prices stable
   b. the value of the currency whenever central banks followed a monetary rule
   c. the official price of the currency, usually specified in terms of the U.S. dollar
   d. the value of the currency when policies were up to par, and inflation was low
   e. the value of the currency when policies were up to par, and both inflation and unemployment were low

7. From time to time, speculation a major problem under the adjustable peg system of the early IMF. The major cause of severe speculation was

   a. the wildly fluctuating price of government securities
   b. the wildly fluctuating price of gold
   c. the wild upward and downward movements in the price of oil
   d. speculators would win if the par value were changed, but would not lose much if the par value were held
   e. speculators would win if the IMF made loans to a country to help it maintain the par value of its currency

8. Suppose that a British machine costs £400,000, while the exchange rate is £1 = $2.00. Then the price of that machine, in dollars, is:

   a. $800,000
   b. $600,000
   c. $400,000
   d. $200,000
   e. $100,000

9. Under the IMF system of adjustable pegs, one problem was that of "self-fulfilling expectations." This meant that:

   a. when countries expected to have surpluses, they in fact had them
   b. when countries expected to have deficits, they in fact had them
   c. when officials expected to avoid a devaluation, they usually succeeded, because of the power of positive thinking
   d. when speculators thought that a currency might be devalued, they sold it, increasing the probability that it would in fact have to be devalued
   e. when speculators thought that a currency might be devalued, they bought it, increasing the probability that it would in fact have to be devalued

10. Under the IMF system of adjustable pegs, some countries followed "stop-go" aggregate demand policies. A major reason for this was:

   a. the short-run Phillips curve sloped upward to the right with a pegged exchange rate; this meant that authorities had to switch policies often
   b. the short-run Phillips curve sloped upward to the right with a pegged exchange rate; this meant that authorities had to follow a monetary rule
   c. the short-run Phillips curve sloped upward to the right with a pegged exchange rate; this meant that authorities had to rely on monetary policy rather than fiscal policy
   d. the short-run Phillips curve sloped upward to the right with a pegged exchange rate; this meant that authorities had to rely on fiscal policy rather than monetary policy
   e. a country might restrict aggregate demand when it was losing foreign exchange reserves, and switch to expansive ("go") policies when the balance of payments improved

11. A "dirty float" is called "dirty" because:

   a. it is unfair to foreign countries
   b. it is unfair to exporters
   c. it is unfair to importers
   d. it is not "clean;" that is, the central bank intervenes in exchange markets to influence exchange rates
   e. it is not "clean;" that is, the central bank departs from the rule of aiming for a steady growth in the money stock

12. Under a flexible exchange rate system, which of the following would be a "vicious circle" for the United States?

   a. U.S. inflation causes an appreciation of the dollar on the exchange markets, which causes higher U.S. inflation, which causes more appreciation of the dollar
   b. U.S. inflation causes a depreciation of the dollar on the exchange markets, which causes higher U.S. inflation, which causes more depreciation of the dollar
   c. higher U.S. interest rates lead to a depreciation of the dollar, which causes even higher interest rates
   d. lower U.S. interest rates lead to an appreciation of the dollar, which causes even lower interest rates
   e. lower U.S. interest rates lead to an appreciation of the dollar, which causes U.S. interest rates to rebound sharply

13. Suppose that the price of the U.S. dollar rises on the foreign exchange markets. This will:

   a. encourage U.S. exports, and slow down inflation in the United States
   b. discourage U.S. exports, and make inflation worse in the United States
   c. discourage U.S. exports, and slow down inflation in the United States
   d. encourage U.S. exports, and make inflation worse in the United States
   e. encourage U.S. exports, and ease the U.S. problem of unemployment

14. Suppose that an exchange rate between the United States and Britain is initially in equilibrium, at £1 = $2.00. Now, suppose that domestic prices in the United States double while domestic prices in Britain remain constant. Then, according to the purchasing-power parity theory, the new equilibrium exchange rate will be:

   a. £1 = $1.00
   b. between 1 = $1.00 and £1 = $2.00, but we can't say exactly where
   c. still at £1 = $2.00
   d. between £1 = $2.00 and £1 = $4.00, but we can't say exactly where
   e. £1 = $4.00

15. Which of the following discourage exports of U.S. goods, and encourage imports of foreign goods into the United States:

   a. U.S. inflation and a depreciation of the dollar
   b. foreign inflation and a depreciation of the dollar
   c. U.S. inflation and an appreciation of the dollar
   d. foreign inflation and an appreciation of the dollar
   e. a depreciation of the dollar, and an appreciation of foreign currencies

16. Between 1981 and 1985, when the U.S. dollar was rising strongly on the international exchanges:

   a. foreigners were acquiring U.S. assets, and the U.S. was running a trade surplus
   b. Americans were acquiring foreign assets, and the U.S. was running a trade surplus
   c. foreigners were acquiring U.S. assets, and the U.S. was running a trade deficit
   d. Americans were acquiring foreign assets, and the U.S. was running a trade deficit
   e. changes in exchange rates encouraged more foreigners to visit the United States

17. U.S. macroeconomic policies contributed to the sharp rise in the exchange value of the U.S. dollar between 1980 and 1984. Specifically:

   a. expansive monetary and fiscal policies made U.S. inflation higher, and this strengthened the dollar
   b. the combination of government deficits and monetary restraint resulted in high interest rates, which encouraged foreigners to buy U.S. assets
   c. the combination of government surpluses and monetary restraint resulted in high interest rates, which encouraged foreigners to buy U.S. assets
   d. the combination of government surpluses and monetary restraint resulted in low interest rates, which encouraged investment in the United States
   e. the combination of government deficits and monetary restraint resulted in low interest rates, which encouraged investment in the United States

18. In the European Monetary System (EMS), exchange rates among the Western European currencies are:

   a. permanently fixed, because the gold standard was restored for transactions within Europe
   b. permanently fixed by a new international bank that coordinates monetary policies among the European member nations
   c. pegged-but-adjustable, with wider bands than under the old IMF system
   d. pegged-but-adjustable, with narrower bands than under the old IMF system
   e. freely flexible

Note: the following two questions are based on the appendix

19. In the balance of payments of the United States, exports of U.S. goods to Japan are entered as a:

   a. positive item
   b. negative item
   c. long-term capital account item
   d. short-term capital account item
   e. change in reserve

20. In the balance of payments accounts of the United States, an increase in U.S. official reserve holdings of German marks is entered as:

   a. a positive item
   b. a negative item
   c. a current account item
   d. a statistical discrepancy
   e. direct investment

EXERCISES

1. The data in Table 19.1 describe the demand and supply of pounds in the foreign exchange market. Plot the demand and supply curves in Figure 19.1, and label the demand curve D1.

Table 19.1

Exchange rate ($ per £)	Quantity demanded (millions of £)	Quantity supplied (millions of £)
$1.25	100	40
$1.50	90	50
$1.75	80	60
$2.00	70	70
$2.25	60	80
$2.50	50	90
$2.75	40	100
$3.00	30	110
$3.25	20	120

a. The equilibrium exchange rate is $ _____ per pound, or _____ per dollar. The equilibrium quantity of pounds sold is _____ million, in exchange for $ _____ million.

b. Suppose now that the demand for pounds decreases by £20 million at each exchange rate. Plot the new demand curve, and label it D2. The new equilibrium exchange rate is $ _____ per pound. The equilibrium quantity of pounds sold is now £_____ million, in exchange for

Figure 19.1

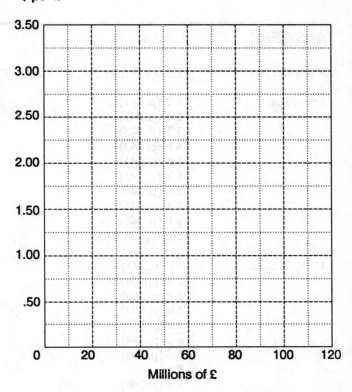

$ _____ million. If the British government wanted to hold the exchange rate at its *previous* equilibrium (in part a), it would have to (buy, sell) £_____ million on the foreign exchange markets; that is, it would have to (buy, sell) $ _____ million.

ESSAY QUESTIONS

1. Suppose that, under the adjustable peg, the British government announced that it was going to devalue the pound by 10% in one week. How would this affect the demand and/or supply of pounds today? What would happen to the British government's holdings of dollar reserves? Would there be much risk in speculating today in the market for pounds? Why or why not? Would the government in fact be able to wait for a week before devaluing? Why or why not?

2. In early 1969, there was a public controversy between the German central bank (which wanted to raise the par value of the DM) and the German government (which didn't). What effect do you think this had on exchange markets? Why do you think the central bank took the position that it did? Why do you think the government took the position that it did?

3. Explain how a country might fall into a "vicious circle." Now suppose that the world has only two countries, and they are approximately the same size. If one country is in a "vicious circle," will the other country also be in a "vicious circle" too, or will it be in a "virtuous circle?" Why?

4. Many people believe that there is a relationship between the two large U.S. deficits of the early 1980s—the U.S. government deficits, and the U.S. deficit in international trade. How might one cause the other?

ANSWERS

Important terms:	1 e, 2 g, 3 f, 4 i, 5 h, 6 a, 7 b, 8 c, 9 d

True-False:	1 T (p. 341)
	2 T (p. 341)
	3 T (p. 343)
	4 F (p. 343)
	5 F (p. 344)
	6 T (p. 345)
	7 F (p. 346)
	8 T (p. 346)
	9 F (p. 346)
	10 T (p. 347)

Multiple Choice:	1 e (p. 341)
	2 c (pp. 341-342)
	3 a (p. 343)
	4 b (p. 343)
	5 a (p. 343)
	6 c (p. 344)
	7 d (p. 345)
	8 a
	9 d (p. 346)
	10 e (p. 346)
	11 d (p. 346)
	12 b (p. 347)
	13 c (p. 348)
	14 e (p. 348)
	15 c (p. 350)
	16 c (p. 350)
	17 b (p. 350)
	18 c (p. 352)
	19 a (p. 355, appendix)
	20 b (p. 356, appendix)

Exercises

1 a. $2.00, £0.50, £70 m, $140 m.
   b. $1.75, £60 m, $105 m, buy, £20 m., sell, $40 m.

Figure 19.1 completed:

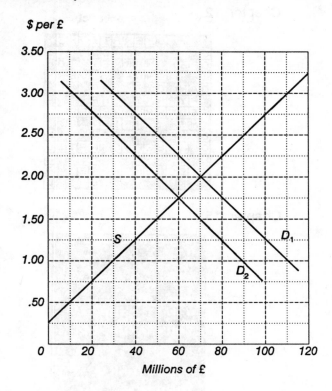

Chapter 1

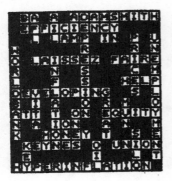

Chapter 12

Chapter 3

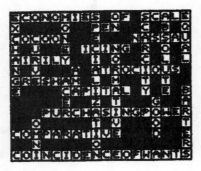

Chapter 15

Chapter 8

Chapter 16

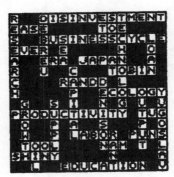

Chapter 10

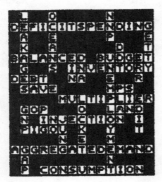

Chapter 18

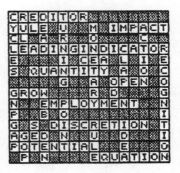

1. c.
2. a.
3. c
4. d
5. d
6. b
7. b
8. c
9.
10.